# The Spycatcher's Encyclopedia of Espionage

## PETER WRIGHT

William Heinemann Aust

First published 1991 by
William Heinemann Australia
22 Salmon Street, Port Melbourne, Victoria 3207
Reprinted 1991

Typeset in Palatino by Bookset, Melbourne
Printed in Finland by Werner Söderström Osakeyhtiö

National Library of Australia
   cataloguing-in-publication data:

Wright, Peter, 1916– .
   The Spycatcher's encyclopedia of espionage.

   ISBN 0 85561 449 8.
   ISBN 0 85561 435 8 (pbk.).

   1. Espionage – Encyclopedias. 2. Spies. I. Title.
   II. Title: Encyclopedia of espionage.

327.1203

# The Spycatcher's Encyclopedia of Espionage

## DELETED

Peter Wright was a key figure in British intelligence for nearly a quarter of a century. In 1955 he joined MI5 as the organisation's first scientific officer. He devoted himself in the early years to technological inventions for use in the espionage trade, demonstrating a brilliant flair for the art of counter-intelligence. He later became, for nearly two decades, the central figure in Britain's efforts to detect and expose Soviet infiltration of the Security Service.

Peter Wright's account of his time in the service, *Spycatcher*, became the centre of the greatest controversy in publishing history. Margaret Thatcher and the British government fought desperately to prevent the book from being published and the subsequent trial created unprecedented public interest across the world.

To my father who taught me to think and persevere and whose early fostering of my scientific interests made my career possible

To my mother whose persistence made my life possible

To my wife and children without whose support this book would not have been possible

To Malcolm Turnbull whose brilliance in the courtroom made all things possible

# A

**A Branch** When I joined MI5 as their first Scientific Officer, they were not sure where to put me, so they put me in A Branch. It was the section which handled resources.

I say 'was' because of course I am talking about how things were in the 1960s. There may be no A Branch now, or it may be doing something quite different. Indeed, the whole of MI5 may have been sold to the Arabs. I cannot say, because it is all an Official Secret.

However, in my day, A Branch was where you went if your operation called for a green barrage balloon or a one-legged Chinese washerwoman with an understanding of explosives. You knew that A Branch could always oblige. It was run by an overgrown schoolboy called Malcolm Cumming, who was not very bright, but who knew a great many people who were. A Branch had four divisions:

*A1* was the gadgets department run by Leslie Jagger, providing bugging equipment, skeleton keys and lock-picking tools, jemmies, getaway cars, etc. It operated from the cellars under the MI5 headquarters in Leconfield House, known as The Dungeons. For some practical details, see *Picking locks*. Leslie Jagger also offered some excellent lines in quick-drying plaster and paint, which came in handy if you accidentally fell through somebody's ceiling when you were installing some wiring, as once happened to me; see *Tidying up*.

*A2* was the gadget people. This is where they put me, in a small cupboard next to a man called Hugh Winterborn, who was as inventive and imaginative as **Cumming** was dull. We made a good team; see *Bugging the CPGB*.

*A3* was the liaison with Police Special Branch. As MI5 was not supposed to exist, it could not arrest anyone. When it came to the time for an arrest, therefore, the Special Branch were called in to do the handcuffing and fix up the press. They loved the TV cameras; see *Lonsdale, Gordon*.

*A4* was the Watchers, whose job it was to undertake surveillance of foreign embassies, etc., to identify the people coming and going there and, on occasions, to follow espionage suspects to find out where they were going and what they did when they got there. They were very good at it. For more about them; see *Watchers*.

**Abwehr** This was the name of the German army intelligence organisation in the Second World War. For what happened to it after the war; see *Gehlen, General Reinhard*.

**Accidents, motor vehicle** How should an agent behave when in collision with an enemy agent? The rule is to act naturally: to do whatever a normal person would do in the same situation.

An example of correct procedure was provided one wet day when a KGB car, driving very fast down The Mall towards Buckingham Palace, skidded on a slippery patch and went into a slide. The car carrying our Watchers was close behind it when it hit the same patch, skidded and crashed into the back of the KGB car.

Both drivers acted correctly. Like any other drivers in the same situation, they got out of their respective cars and quietly exchanged false names and addresses.

**Apostles, The** The Apostles were an upper-class left-wing intellectual group in Cambridge University in the 1930s.

It was not a new group – it went back for nearly a hundred years – and its members had always been chosen for outstanding intelligence. Its senior members included the economist John Maynard Keynes and the social historian G.M. Trevelyan. However, in the thirties it became the focus for a group of upper crust socialists.

There were many such groups in British universities at the time, socialism having become very fashionable. The sons of the Establishment joined these groups partly to cock snooks at their Conservative parents, partly as a penance for being rich and privileged, but at least partly as a genuine protest against a society which had produced and tolerated the Depression. Sights like that of the Hunger Marchers from Jarrow, who marched through the streets of Cambridge on their way to London, had brought home to some of them the realities of working class life, realities which they had previously managed to ignore.

It was a relatively simple move from this sort of armchair socialism (talking about the need for socialist reform in Britain) to talk about world revolution (as preached by the followers of Trotsky) or enthusiasm for Soviet communism (as preached in the Comintern, the main international front organisation of Stalin's Russia). Thus there were in the 1930s many people in British universities who were ripe for recruitment as Russian agents.

These were agents of a new type: intelligent, highly educated, cultured members of the ruling Establishment. They were generally recruited with the idea that they would be 'working for peace'. At least, that was the phrase Guy Burgess used. In practice, this meant helping to protect the new order in Russia from its many enemies abroad, and in particular the common enemy, the Fascists.

The first major confrontation between Communists and Fascists was the Spanish Civil War, where the Republican government was supported by the Communist-led International Brigade and Franco's Fascists were supported by the Germans. Several Apostles joined the International Brigade. Others, like Kim Philby, obeyed Russian orders and pretended to support the Fascists, laying the foundations for a life of deception and treachery.

The Comintern's anti-fascist story wore a little thin following the Molotov-Ribbentrop pact in 1939 when Soviet Russia and Nazi Germany carved up Poland between them; but when Hitler attacked Russia two years later, dragging Russia into the war on our side, the recruits found themselves able both to serve their Russian masters and be patriotic Britons most of the time.

It was in the period 1941–5 that many of them rose to positions of trust within the Civil Service and, in particular, the security services. They were thus in place and ready when called upon to fill a much more treacherous role in the largely bloodless battles of the Cold War.

For a list of the Cambridge traitors; see *Cambridge*. For a particularly important group of them; see *Ring of Five*.

**Archbishops, bugging of**  Some people claim that you should not bug archbishops, because they are men of peace. However, Greek Orthodox archbishops are different. This helps to explain what we did in Cyprus.

During the centuries when Greece was part of the Ottoman Empire, the Orthodox Church was not just a bulwark of Christianity against Islam. It also provided a focus for the survival of the Greek culture and language against the Turkish culture and language. The Orthodox Church was in a real sense a resistance organisation.

When the time came for the Greek War of Independence in 1821, the priests and bishops were the natural leaders of the struggle, and when Greece won its independence, they provided the natural leaders for the new nation. They had a long tradition of being social, political and military leaders as well as religious ones.

It was not therefore surprising that Archbishop Makarios, the head of the Greek Orthodox Church in Cyprus, was the leader of the campaign to kick the British out and achieve *Enosis*, the unification of Cyprus with Greece. In theory, he was only involved in the political side of the campaign, but he never had much time for all that stuff about turning the other cheek, and he showed no distress when the campaign developed into a guerrilla war. Forty thousand British troops were being steadily worn down by a few hundred Greek Cypriots led by a man who called himself General Grivas.

We knew we would never get Makarios to talk sense

until we had captured Grivas and disarmed his guerrillas. The problem was to locate Grivas' hideout. He was operating in an area where almost everybody was friendly to him, so it was not easy. However, we were certain that he was in communication with Archbishop Makarios. Knowing this, we decided to tap the Archbishop's phone.

This was difficult, because almost all the local telephone operators and technicians were on his side, and even if we had got the administration to give us a warrant, the first person to hear about it would have been Makarios himself. So we had to put a secure tap on the line between his house and the exchange, and do it without being noticed by the people at the exchange.

It was a very dangerous operation, because the line to the exchange ran down the side of a road which was constantly patrolled by his bodyguards. We did it at night. We knew that if they saw someone up one of their telephone poles they would shoot first and ask questions later.

The work at the top of the pole was done by MI6's best technical man, John Wyke, while I stood at the bottom acting as Bugger's Mate, putting tools and equipment in a basket which he hauled up.

We had scouts out on the road who gave us a few moments warning when patrols came along, but this was not long enough to get under cover. We just had to freeze and hope that we would not be noticed.

With all the interruptions, the job took two hours. John got right up to the top of the pole and bored a hole down the middle of it, big enough to hold a small transmitter, powered from the telephone circuit. The leads were threaded though a small hole which came out of the side of the pole just above one of the cross trees, and then ran along the top of the cross tree to the telephone wires. The whole thing was brilliantly done. Of course, if you climbed up the pole you could see the wires, but they were virtually invisible from below.

It worked very well. We picked up the signals in a house we rented a mile of so away, and would have got some useful intelligence if we had kept it up. We had only just got it going, however, when the Colonial Office patched up a deal with Makarios and his boys. The outcome was a bad settlement which resulted in endless trouble between the Greek and the Turkish Cypriots, trouble that continues to this day.

I still think about the much better solution we might have reached if we had settled the guerrilla war first. It never pays to bargain with people who reckon they have won. The only worse thing is trying to bargain with people who have nothing more to lose.

**Argentine meat, price of**  We were very upset when the Board of Trade, the Civil Service department which looks after all commercial matters, sent a request to MI5 to bug the room where an Argentinian trade delegation were staying. The Board of Trade said they wanted to know the lowest price the Argentinians would accept for their meat.

We refused, saying that we had not joined the Security Service to do this sort of thing. I think we were right to refuse. Security agents should not be expected to concern themselves with the price of fish or meat.

I am not sure that they should be expected to marry, either. Guy Burgess probably felt rather put upon when the Russians told him to marry Clarissa Churchill, one of Winston's nieces.

Anthony Blunt told me the story during one of my many debriefing sessions with him. He found the whole episode hilariously funny, but to Burgess it must have been pretty serious. It says something about his commitment to the Party that he made a solid effort to do what they told him to do, although even if he had been the marrying kind he would have put Clarissa a very long way down the list of eligibles.

Despite this, he obeyed the call of the Party, and got far enough with Clarissa to cause her chief admirer at the time, James Pope-Hennessy, to go after him with a gun. Burgess knew that being a Russian spy would be danger-ous, but this was not what he'd had in mind, and he begged to be excused. The Russians relented, so instead of becoming Mrs Guy Burgess, Clarissa married Sir Anthony Eden and became Lady Avon.

Years later, in 1951, Eden was visiting New York, and who should be seconded to look after him and Clarissa but Guy Burgess. Sir Anthony wrote afterwards thanking Guy for being so solicitous.

**ARL** Admiralty Research Laboratory. This was my first employer. For things I did there, see *Magnetic Mines*, *Degaussing the* Prince of Wales, and *Millimetric Radar*.

**Armstrong, Sir Robert** This very unfortunate man was the British Cabinet Secretary, who was sent out by Mrs Thatcher to give evidence against me in the Spycatcher trial in the New South Wales Supreme Court; see *Spycatcher trial, The*.

It was all a bit of a shock to him. He was expected to behave like an ordinary person. He asked the judge to let him go up to the court in the lift reserved for the judges and other special people, but the judge told him to go up in the ordinary lift with the rest of us.

Next, he was expected to tell the truth. This was a problem: he could not tell the truth, as it was an Official Secret; see *Secrets, Official*. So he told some Official Lies instead.

All might still have gone well, except that after he left London some of the Official Lies were changed without telling him, so he was caught and had to apologise to the court.

When he got back home he was made into a Lord. This was very unfair. Mrs Thatcher was really responsible, so she should have been made into a Lord.

**ASIO** ASIO is the Australian Security Intelligence Organisation. My first connection with it was in 1959. A new Russian embassy was being built in Canberra, and ASIO decided to seize this opportunity to install the latest breed of bugs. Its Director, Brigadier Sir Charles Spry, who was never one to turn up an excuse to visit London, selected himself as the person to come to us for advice.

I was called in to give the advice. It was clearly an ideal

location for a Satyr-type operation (see *Satyr*). The advantage of Satyr was that it needed no wires or batteries and radiated only when it was told to. The snag was that it only worked reliably over a distance of a few hundred metres, so it was no good unless there was a place close to the target in which its parabolic aerials could be set up without arousing suspicion. This was the case in Canberra.

The mikes were installed in the window frames of the KGB Resident's room. Technically, the scheme went very well: the system worked perfectly. The ASIO monitors were able to hear everything that went on in the room – the Resident puffing and blowing and the scratch of his pen. But he never uttered a word.

There was only one possible explanation: that the whole operation had been blown from the start. But it was known only to a handful of people. On our staff, the list was very short – my assistant, who had made the installation, Malcolm Cumming as head of A Branch and Sir Roger Hollis as Director General of MI5. At the Australian end it was Spry and a very small number of key ASIO people. At least one of these was a member of the original staff hand picked by Hollis when he had gone out to Australia in 1948 to help them set up ASIO.

All of this proved nothing, of course. But it was one of many similar fiascos – operations which were technically successful but got nowhere: Dew Worm was another. Each time it happened, I made a list of all the people who were in the know, and one name appeared on every list: Sir Roger Hollis. For the outcome of this, see *Hollis, Sir Roger*.

I became involved with ASIO again over the Charles Ellis case; see *Ellis, Charles*. Ellis was an Australian who worked for nearly thirty years for MI6, and then returned to Australia and took up a consultancy with ASIS, the Australian Secret Intelligence Service.

ASIS is the Australian equivalent of MI6. However, whereas MI6 is a non-existent *organisation*, ASIS is a non-existent *department* of ASIO, an organisation which exists openly. (It can be phoned ISD on 613 654 8985 any time of the day and night provided it is a weekday between 9 am and 5 pm, Australian Eastern Standard Time.)

Brigadier Spry entered into the spirit of non-existence well when he denied later that Ellis had ever been recruited by ASIO. He clearly felt it unnecessary to add that Ellis had been recruited by ASIO's non-existent department, ASIS.

Investigating Ellis led me to look at the Petrov case, which was the high spot of ASIO's achievement. Petrov was an MGB man, but his job was not to spy on the Australians; his job was to spy on the other Russians in the embassy. In July 1953 his boss, Lavrenti Beria, had been arrested for treason in Moscow, and word went out that all Beria's men were to be recalled. Petrov found this prospect unattractive, and decided to defect. His problem was that he really had no information to sell, as he was not involved in the intelligence gathering side of the business. He stitched together a bundle of scurrilous trivia, however, and approached ASIO with an offer to defect.

He needn't have bothered with the trivia. The Australian Prime Minister, Robert Menzies, was delighted with the idea of receiving a defector, and would not have minded if his portfolio of secrets had been copies of the *Sporting Globe*. The defector was needed as part of an election strategy, and it worked better than he could have hoped. Starting from a hopeless position, Menzies won the election on the slogan 'Don't give the Reds a second chance'.

In the years that followed, ASIO achieved very little of any note. They scored one much publicised success when their telephone taps and bugs in the Russian embassy enabled them to overhear conversations between Valery Ivanov, the Third Secretary at the embassy, and David Combe, a former Federal Secretary of the Australian Labor Party who had become a Canberra lobbyist. Combe was overheard regaling Ivanov with a grandiose account of his power to develop Australian trade with Russia. This was seen as deeply threatening, and Ivanov was expelled, while the unfortunate Combe was denied access to his former colleagues who were by then ministers in the new Hawke government. His credentials as a lobbyist were ruined, but it was never made clear quite what he could have delivered, or why it would have been dangerous to Australian security if he had done so.

ASIO's other headline-grabbing exploit occurred when their non-existent department, ASIS, messed up a training operation for some new recruits. The recruits arrived at the Sheraton Hotel in Melbourne dressed up as terrorists complete with masks and guns, held up the manager and guests and started breaking down doors, much to everybody's distress. Someone summoned the police, who moved in smartly and arrested the lot.

The moral is, of course, that if you are running a non-existent organisation and want to attack a tourist hotel as part of an exercise, you should pretend that you are an organisation which exists, like the IRA or the PLO. Otherwise you may find it hard afterwards to persuade people that you do not exist. Also, you should warn the management first, and it is not a bad idea to tell the police, too. Otherwise somebody may get hurt, or at least you may get described as a bunch of stumblebums, which is how the *Sydney Morning Herald* described ASIS the next day.

The reporter's criticism was really not fair. MI6 made a similar mistake; see *Details, small, importance of.*

**ASIS** Australian Secret Intelligence Service (roughly equivalent to MI6); see *ASIO.*

**AWRE** Even in the deepest economic crisis, there is always some organisation at which the government is throwing money without asking what they do with it. In Britain in the 1950s, it was the Atomic Weapons Research Establishment, AWRE, at Harwell. Meanwhile, we at MI5 had no money at all.

When we had a scheme which needed funding, therefore, we got the AWRE people to fund it; see *Money.*

# B

**Beaconing** This is the name given to a procedure for making it difficult to find out where a wireless signal is coming from. It involves the setting up of several wireless transmitters tuned to exactly the same frequency and transmitting exactly the same message at the same time. This makes it difficult to pinpoint the source because the signal appears to be coming from all directions at once.

The scheme was used successfully during the Second World War to interfere with navigation systems for aircraft. Aircraft which were navigating by signals from wireless beacons could be sent the wrong way by transmissions from false beacons operating on the same frequencies. We called it 'bending the beams'. Once we sent the German bombers so far off course that they bombed Dublin. This was tough on the Irish, but they were being pretty beastly to us at the time, so we weren't too upset.

At MI5, the same principle was involved in a scheme for making it difficult for the Russians to pinpoint the Watchers by listening to their wireless messages. So long as the Watchers were broadcasting straight back to base, all the Russians needed was a directional antenna and they could find out where they were. This was very bad, because the Russians then knew who we were watching or following.

The scheme was theoretically very simple. London was to be covered with a forest of 100-foot wireless masts, and every message from one of the Watchers would be instantly re-broadcast from all the transmitters so that the

Russians would not know where it had started from.

A small-scale trial version was built and actually worked. It was technically very difficult to maintain all the transmitters on exactly the same frequency, but I am sure that we would have solved all the problems if someone had put up a million pounds for it. However, Whitehall would never have let us have that much money, so the forest of aerials was never planted; see *Money*.

**BfV**  This is the *Bundesamt für Verfassungsschutz*, the Federal Office for the Protection of the Constitution, the West German equivalent of MI5.

The Federal Republic of Germany had massive domestic security problems throughout its existence. At first, it was hard to see whether the greater threats came from the so-called Gehlen Organisation, with its roots in the Nazi past (see *Gehlen, General Reinhard*) or from East Germany, to which the BfV's first director either defected or was kidnapped; see *John, Otto*. Later, the BfV devoted most of its time to countering terrorism, both home grown (e.g. the Baader-Meinhof gang, the 'Red Army Faction') and imported (e.g. the Palestinian assault on Israeli participants at the Munich Olympic Games).

We never had much to do with the BfV. Whatever you thought about Otto John, the BfV was so riddled with Communist agents that it was best to assume that the whole organisation was as straight as a corkscrew.

**Blackmail, avoidance of**  The chairman of a large British company was travelling to Moscow to sell a petrochemical works to the Russians. He was well known as a womaniser, and we were worried that he would be compromised by the KGB and then blackmailed.

I briefed him on the dangers, advising him to reject any unexpected approaches from attractive women, and in particular to watch out for photographers wanting to take pictures of him in compromising situations. I then asked him to phone me immediately on his return.

A week later I had a call from him at Heathrow airport. I asked whether he had been compromised. 'Yes and no,' he replied. 'Come straight in,' I said. 'Don't speak to anybody until you have seen me.'

When he arrived I came quickly to the point: did he sleep with any unknown women in Moscow? 'Yes,' he said. 'There was this beautiful woman who came to my hotel room. She said she would like to have a drink with me, and she was much too attractive to send away. Then, after a few drinks, she invited me to come to bed with her. How could I say no? But I fooled the photographers. I went into the bathroom, where I had a pillow case all ready, with holes cut out for the eyes. I put it over my head, and never took it off until after she had gone.'

**Bletchley** A railway town in Buckinghamshire. It built carriages for the London and North Western Railway Company for many years, and was of no merit or interest until it – or, to be more precise, Bletchley Park – became the home of the cryptographic unit which cracked the German Enigma code in the Second World War; see *Enigma*. The unit later formed the nucleus of the organisation known as the Government Communications Head Quarters, GCHQ (q.v.), quartered in the large geriatric centre of Cheltenham Spa.

**Blunt, Anthony** We don't need to call this man *Sir* Anthony Blunt any more, thank God, because the Queen took away his knighthood in 1979. But all the time that I was interrogating him, which I did at roughly monthly intervals for six years, he was still Sir Anthony. Of course, I didn't call him Sir Anthony when we were just chatting. But if I rang him up or wrote to him, or mentioned him in an official document, he still had to be given his title even though he was a self-confessed spy. It was part of the deal.

My friend and colleague Arthur Martin had suspected Anthony Blunt ever since he was interrogated following the defection of Burgess and Maclean in 1951, but the evidence had been, as it so often was, circumstantial: too many things went wrong when he was around. The doubt was resolved in July 1963 when an American, Michael Whitney Straight, revealed to the FBI that he had been recruited as an agent by Blunt when he was in Cambridge, and promised to repeat the story in court if necessary.

Blunt was offered two choices: to be prosecuted, or to be given immunity from prosecution in return for a promise of full disclosure of his activities and associates. He accepted the immunity. Arthur Martin conducted the first interrogation sessions, but the job devolved on me after Arthur was sacked following the Mitchell investigation; see *Mitchell, Graham*.

I felt that Blunt would be most likely to talk freely if he felt physically secure and comfortable, and where better than in his own beautiful office at the Courtauld Institute? At first, I tried to keep written notes of our discussions, but it is not easy to generate a relaxed casual atmosphere when you are scribbling away all the time, so after a short time we arranged to mike the room. We bored through the wall behind a Poussin. It is probably the most valuable and certainly the finest painting ever to be used to conceal a microphone.

You get to know people very well interrogating them, especially if the interrogation is as civilised as mine was of Blunt. So I reckon I know what made him tick.

Blunt didn't think of himself as a spy or as a traitor to England. He believed that he had a job to do which was too important to neglect. According to him, it was like this: originally, in the 1930s, the job had been to save the world from fascism. To do this, he had to support Russia, the bastion of anti-fascism. Between 1941 and 1945 this had been fine, as Russia was Britain's ally. Then, as the fascist threat had receded and the world moved into the Cold War, he had continued to support Russia, though Russia was now seen as an enemy by the Western powers. Thus, his attitudes had been consistent; it was we who had turned our coats. Given time, he said, everybody would see the light and he would be vindicated.

It was strange to hear these ideas coming from the lips of a man like him: elegant, highly intelligent and articulate, the epitome of culture and civilisation. He showed grief at having abused the trust of so many of his fellow men, of having betrayed others and even sent a few to their deaths, but it was just grief, not remorse. He was not repenting of a past error; he was just sad that doing what he saw as the right thing had inevitably produced these tragic side effects.

When it came to giving information about other people, however, Blunt was less forthcoming. Although he had promised full and frank disclosure, it was evident from the start that he would only talk fully and frankly about what we already new, plus a few trivia.

Despite this, I still think that the decision to offer him immunity was the right one. For a discussion of the argument, see *Traitors, how to deal with*.

**BND** These initials stand for *Bundesnachrichtendienst*, the Federal News Agency, which is the name of the West German equivalent of MI6. It was started in 1956, largely to find gainful employment for a man called Otto Gehlen and his 'spooky Nazi outfit at Pullach', as the so-called 'Gehlen Organisation' was dubbed by US General Arthur Trudeau; see *Gehlen, General Reinhard*.

After Gehlen retired, the worst of the old Nazis were cleaned out and the operation became a useful aid for Western intelligence, but we always had to be careful because, like the BfV, it was riddled with Communist moles, who were not much better than the Nazis.

**Boffin** Boffin was a term used in Britain in the Second World War for a scientist, and in particular an eccentric, mild-mannered individual who worked out all sorts of diabolical ways of conducting a war. The maker of the bouncing-bomb, Barnes Wallis, was everybody's idea of a boffin, especially as he was portrayed by Michael Redgrave in the film, *The Dam Busters*.

There were also people called erks. The boilersuited ground crews who serviced the RAF planes were called erks, but there were also erks in white coats who helped the boffins with the practical work, building and testing new devices the boffins dreamed up. Nowadays, we would

Airc-naftsman.

call them lab technicians, and treat them as a lower form of life than the research scientists. In my day, the strength of British science lay in the very close relationship between erks and boffins, so that most boffins had (and all of them appreciated) the skills of the erk, and every erk felt (and most of them were) competent to contribute ideas to the boffin.

At the beginning of the Second World War, Britain was able to call on hundreds of ham wireless people for important jobs in the war. Ham wireless operators provided the first generation of radar operators, and those of us who had built our own wireless sets became erks and boffins, contributing to the design of electronic devices. We were also good at taking captured devices apart and finding out how they worked (or why they didn't).

This was one thing we had over the Germans. Hitler had banned ham wirelesses. So although their top scientists were brilliant, they did not have as many people with the unique combination of practical experience and creativity which characterised our boffins and erks. For a funny example of the effect of this; see *Tidy mind, dangers of a.*

I became a boffin by a strange route. I was studying agricultural science when the war came, but I had been messing about with wirelesses for almost as long as I could remember. When I was about five years old, my father brought home an experimental crystal set from Marconi's, where he was a research scientist. They were testing the idea of using wireless as a medium of home entertainment, which at that time was an outlandish idea, and my father wanted to see whether I would find it entertaining. The next day, I put on the earphones at a pre-arranged time, and heard my father speaking from his laboratory at Marconi's, reciting *Mary had a little lamb* to me. He went on to recite some of Harry Graham's *Ruthless Rhymes for Heartless Homes*. At the time, I was probably the youngest listener-in (as we called them) in the world.

That was 1922. From then on throughout my childhood, there were always wireless sets being taken to pieces and assembled in our house. And a procession of well-known physicists came visiting. One was J.J. Thompson, whose work on the conductivity of gases led to his discovery of the electron which in turn made the Cavendish Laboratory at Cambridge into the world centre of research in fundamental physics. Another visitor was Sir Arthur Eddington, the Professor of Astronomy at Cambridge University, who had not only made considerable contributions to the theory of relativity, but was also a genius at communicating the splendours of science to ordinary people. Not many boys had their first attempts at electronic circuitry admired and criticised by such a distinguished panel of assessors.

But it was still a bumpy road. By 1931 my father had risen to the top of the Marconi wireless research section and invented (amongst other things) a practical facsimile system for wireless transmission (see *Wright, G.M.*), but this did not save him from being one of the first to be retrenched when the Depression hit the firm. Thus it became evident to me when I was quite young that being a research physicist was not a safe job.

In any case, I was also very keen on animals, so when my father lost his job and I had to leave school, I went to work on a farm. It was not really a job at all, just an opportunity to do a lot of work. I got my keep but no wages. It was, however, a very important few years for me.

Firstly, I became really fit. I had been born with rickets and had my legs in and out of irons for many years, but the farmwork completed the process of recovery and left me fit.

Secondly, my 'boss', Margaret Leigh, helped me to overcome my stutter. She was a writer, and she made me read her manuscripts aloud as therapy. Her first book was called *Highland Homespun*, and was all about the farm in Scotland where I first worked for her. Then we moved to Cornwall, and she wrote *Harvest of the Moor* about that. I appear in both books as a hardworking and efficient agricultural labourer. Perhaps I should have stuck to it. The books were published in 1937 and sold very well.

The third good thing about working for Margaret Leigh was that, although I was not paid, I was able to earn some money on the side dealing in livestock. I became quite skilled at buying and selling animals, and particularly at picking the ones which were going cheap at auction because the right buyers for them happened not to be there. I would buy them, and then contact the appropriate people to resell them at a small profit.

By 1937 I had saved enough to have a try at university, and got a place at St Peter's Hall, Oxford, to read agriculture. The next year I married Lois, who is with me as I write today. (She thought she was going to be a farmer's wife. What has actually happened is that I am a farmer's husband, as Lois runs our stud farm, Duloe Arabians. She is running thirty-five horses as well as me at the moment, so she is kept busy.)

But to return to Oxford in the late 1930s. Although agricultural science was my academic field, when the war broke out I wanted to get into electronic warfare. My practical background in wireless meant that I had no difficulty in winning a place in the Admiralty Research Laboratory as a physicist.

My first job was not as a boffin or even an erk but as an errand boy. I was sent out to acquire three miles of special square-section aluminium wire over the weekend. For more about this, see *Magnetic mines*. After that I worked in degaussing, another application of magnetism; see *Degaussing the* Prince of Wales. I transferred to radar, working on ways of tracking the snorkels of submerged submarines with very short wavelength radar. This was real boffinry; see *Millimetric radar*.

So it came about that I joined MI5 as a boffin. Not as eccentric or as mild mannered as the bouncing bomb man, but still a boffin. This set me apart from the rest of the MI5 people. Some of them joined for the glamour and excitement, and others for the opportunity it supplied for acts of patriotism or treachery. I had always loved security intelligence work, but I was invited to join MI5 because Sir Frederick Brundrett, the Chief Scientist at the Ministry of

Defence, told them they needed a boffin.

If they had been able to get a peer or a knight they would have done so. The only thing MI5 liked more than a knight was a peer, and they employed a lot of them as consultants, paying them fat fees for their services. But none of these scientifically qualified peers and knights wanted to work for MI5, day in, day out. They preferred to earn their fees for having an expensive lunch with the top people. Then they'd bugger off again.

It was only people like me who were prepared to work full time for MI5, so in the end they accepted Sir Frederick Brundrett's suggestion and took me on. But they still kept the consultants. God knows what advice they got for their money, because I was handling all scientific questions and I never saw a report or proposal coming in from any of the consultants. All I saw was the cheques going out, made out to various peers and knights with FRS after their names. *(Fellow of the Royal Society.)*

I would have liked to have been an FRS, and when I compare the originality of my work for MI5 with the kind of work that earns a fellowship, I know I could have made it. Even so, my great strength was my experience of practical laboratory and workshop investigations. It helped me solve many problems where other people had failed (see, for example, *Thing, The*) and in devising my own innovations (see, for example, *Stockade, Engulf* and *Rafter*). And that is what I enjoyed most.

Being paid a week's wages to have a gourmet lunch with someone sounds rather attractive, but it probably gets boring after a time.

**BOSS** or the Bureau of State Security. This is the former name of the South African security service; see *NIS, National Intelligence Service*.

**Bride** This was the original name of an operation to decipher some Russian traffic (our word for wireless messages) which were intercepted during the war. (The operation was also known by other names, e.g. Venona, but in this book it will be called Bride.)

The story started when an American cryptographer

called Meredith Gardner was looking over the transcripts of these messages, and saw what he believed were some repeating patterns, suggesting that the same 'one-time' cipher pad had been used for more than one message. He realised that if this was true, there was a possibility of breaking the cipher.

The evidence on which he was going was incredibly thin; so thin, in fact, that many people went on denying that the patterns were really there – right up to the moment when the first phrase was deciphered.

I am sorry if the next few paragraphs are not easy to follow. If you get bogged down, skip it. But to some people it may be the most interesting topic in the whole book, so I am going to press on.

The way the pads work is described in *One-time pads*, and if you haven't read that, read it now.

If the pads are used only once, as they should be, there is no way to attack the cipher. But the Russians had used them more than once. What had apparently happened was that they were faced with a sudden need for more cipher pads at a moment when their resources were fully stretched fighting Hitler, so they decided to make several copies of each pad. They then distributed them in such a way that the same pad was never used twice within any one channel. The assumption was that no *one* person would see, for example, the trade channel to Buenos Aires *and* the diplomatic channel to Washington, or notice any similarity if they did.

They were reckoning without Meredith Gardner.

An illustration may give some idea of his problem. Let us suppose that we knew that the third group of numbers in many Russian messages was the name of the place it was coming from. Next, let us say that, in the Russian code book, the code number for Washington was 1000 and Buenos Aires was 2000. If they were enciphered using the same pad, the two numbers would still be exactly 1000 apart. For example, if the third random number on the cipher pad was 3792, the third word in the Washington message would be 4792 and the Buenos Aires one would be 5792.

If you found a match like this among the tens of thousands of messages you were checking, you might have found a pair which were based on the same cipher pad. It was never certain on the first match, but at least it was worth testing. So you then started to attack the message itself. You thought of a word which was likely to be in one of the messages and be spelled out in full, like the surname of a politician who was in the news that day. Using the Russian numerical codes for the letters (e.g. A = 01, B = 02) you turned it into a string of 2-digit numbers.

You would then work through the document, moving this string of numbers along two digits at a time. Each position gave a possible value for the equivalent random numbers on the pad. You then deciphered the other document using these same numbers, and checked whether the result made sense. If it didn't, you moved the string along and started again.

There were tens of millions of ways for it to be wrong and only one way for it to be right. With today's computers, testing millions or even billions of permutations and combinations is easy: you feed the data in and go home to bed. In the morning, it gives you a list of the promising pairings. But Meredith Gardner had to do most of the work manually.

Anyway, he triumphed over all the odds. The first phrase to drop out was in English, spelled out in full, and was the title of a current book on strategy: 'Defense does not win wars'. This has to be one of the great moments in the history of cryptography and counter-espionage.

And that is how there came to be this great pile of Russian traffic waiting to be sorted by source pad and then broken.

The problem with Bride was to find collateral. Collateral is the name given to words or phrases that you expected would occur in a document. For more about this, see *Collateral*. It is very difficult to break a cipher unless you know what words to expect; you can only solve the problem if you already know the answer.

The cipher-breakers assumed that, somewhere in each day's traffic, the main items of news in that area would be included. Thus, when a major story broke, they would expect it to be in the despatches to Moscow soon afterwards, and could 'drag' the texts for evidence of the names of the principal characters, as described above.

All this had happened a long time before I joined the service. It was important because one of the things they had come up with was the code names of a large number of their agents in various countries, including over two hundred of them in the upper echelons of society and government in the United Kingdom.

When I found out about this, I was appalled. At that stage, only about a dozen of these Russian agents had been revealed. This meant that there were still over two hundred people in senior positions in the Civil Service and so on, all Russian agents and none of them unmasked.

It struck me that it was pretty silly to be spending a lot of money on defence when there were so many people in positions of trust who would betray anything we did to the main enemy of the day, the Soviet Union. So I decided that I would make it my job to get rid of the whole lot.

As many of them were senior members of the Establishment, this was not easy. In fact, I was obstructed at every turn, and in the end they won: they got rid of me.

**Bugging a car**   It is more difficult than you might think to bug a car. You can plant a wireless beacon in it which will enable you to follow it, but that won't last long. Ordinary beacons were generally found in the first routine sweep, which the Russians did every day.

So you have to get a more sophisticated beacon, one which can be turned on and off from a distance (see *Transponder*). But then you have to know when to turn it on and off, and the only way to find out whether conditions are right to turn it on is to turn it on. In short, you still have a problem.

IT MUST BE NOTED, THOUGH, THAT THE SOVIETS CLASSED AS AN 'AGENT' ANYONE IN A POSITION OF INFLUENCE, WHOM THEY 'HAD CONTA... ie. NOT NECESSARILY ESPIONAGE AGENT.

There are not many places in a car to hide a transmitter and still have its signal detectable over any distance. The metal body of the car acts as a Faraday shield, screening any radiations trying to get in or out, as anyone knows who has tried to work a portable wireless in a car. The aerial must be outside the screening effect, and it therefore has to be very carefully camouflaged. We found that you had to get hold of the car for a couple of hours and take it to your own garage to install the bug properly, and the Russians didn't like people taking their cars even for a couple of hours.

Another thing which didn't work was following their cars from the moment they left the embassy. They almost always noticed us, and although it was fun chasing them they generally gave us the slip. The getaway car always has the advantage over the pursuit car in city traffic, because it is the getaway car which picks the route.

Instead of tracking them by wireless, we stationed Watchers to pick them up as they crossed the Thames bridges. By then it was generally clear where they were headed, and hence much easier to follow them without being noticed.

**Bugging the CPGB** With most people we had to get a fresh warrant whenever we wanted to tap their phones or open their mail. However, in a few cases of the most offensive people we could get a bulk warrant, allowing us to bug them all the time without saying why. One of these was the CPGB (Communist Party of Great Britain).

I was not involved much with the CPGB at first. Domestic surveillance was F Branch business, and we at A Branch became involved only when they wanted to supplement the permanent facilities with some temporary ones; when, for example, they were having a meeting in some public hall.

We got our information about such events through three channels:

1. the permanent phone taps —PHONE IN USE
2. SF (see *SF*) —VIA PHONE MICROPHONE.
3. our agents in the Party

There was also a period during which we had one of the rooms in their King Street headquarters bugged with a concealed microphone/transmitter (see below) and we checked over all their incoming mail; see *General Post Office*. So we were kept well informed.

The telephone taps were of limited use. The comrades knew their phones were tapped and were careful not to use them for important messages. But they used them for things like booking halls for public meetings, so except for the very secret meetings we always had plenty of advance warning, giving us time to get the halls bugged.

One actual example shows how it worked. First, our monitoring people heard them over the phone booking a meeting hall in the East End, and passed this information to F Branch, which dealt with domestic surveillance. F Branch worked out what was likely to be discussed, and had to decide whether to ignore it, to make sure one of our agents would be there or to bug the hall and record the whole proceedings. They decided that it was important enough to warrant bugging the hall, so they contacted us.

We had several options ourselves. The first problem was getting access to the hall. In some cases the owners of the halls were friends, and would help us bug it. However, this applied mainly to the better-class meeting halls in the West End, not to the kind of hall the comrades met in. The next possibility was to talk to Special Branch or even the ordinary police and see whether we could work out some plausible excuse for getting into the hall legally. Generally there wasn't, and we would fall back on the last option, which was to break in.

We also had to decide how to bug the hall. The main options were a wired microphone or a microphone/transmitter, with a cavity microphone (see *Satyr*) as a third option if we thought they would make a serious attempt to check the hall for bugs.

Wherever possible we went for wired microphones. In one case we installed them under the floorboards of the platform, and got a BBC-quality recording. It was so good that we were able to use extracts from it in training exercises, when we wanted to demonstrate what a Communist Party meeting was like.

Our second source of information on the CPGB was SF (see *SF*). SF had been installed in the CPGB phones ever since 1942, but Anthony Blunt, who was working on the Director General's staff at the time, blew it to the Russians the same day. His idea was just to warn them to be careful what they said over the phone to the CPGB. However, the Russians went further, and blew it to the CPGB. They didn't tell them how it worked, or how it could be removed, but they did tell them it was there. They told them to be careful what they said when they were near a phone, whether it was in use or not. As a result the amount of chatter suddenly went down. They either talked in whispers or not at all. They even had a tea cosy which they put over the phone if they wanted to talk.

This change of behaviour meant that MI5 must have known there and then that the operation had been blown. Had they investigated immediately Blunt would almost certainly have been caught. He told me later that he was furious with the Russians for telling the CPGB as much as they did, as it endangered his position. There were so few people who knew about SF that it would not have taken too much of an investigation to show that he had to be responsible. But there was no investigation, and he went on spying for them.

Our third source of information was from agents within the Party. Some of them were plants – people we recruited whose job it was to infiltrate the Party – but most of them were just garrulous comrades. Agent M8, Tom Driberg, was one of these. If he had a juicy bit of gossip, he just had to share it with you ... and with anyone else who was interested enough to listen; see *Driberg, Tom*.

The comrades held many of their really important meetings in secret places away from their King Street office, but the time came when they wanted a secure conference room at King Street for some discussions they were having with various union leaders. F Branch heard from one of our agents within the party that a new conference room was being established in a basement room without a phone.

We walked up and down King Street past the building, hoping for inspiration, and noticed a very small opening in the wall at pavement level, with a door in it. It had been a coal chute, and calculations on the plans showed that it led into the conference area.

Getting wires to it would have been very difficult, but there was a telephone pit nearby, so we decided to install a probe microphone through the keyhole of the door, feeding the signal into a transmitter which would transmit as far as the telephone pit. There we would have a wireless receiver feeding the signal into an ordinary telephone pair, which would take it to the transcription room on the Seventh Floor of MI5 headquarters at Leconfield House.

This still left the problem of concealing the transmitter and its batteries. We decided to fit a false door in front of the real door, made to look exactly like the real one. It would be a bit closer to the face of the wall than the real door, but being small and low down and well-recessed, we thought that it would not be noticed.

One of the Watchers went down the street one night, playing drunk, snapping passers by with a flash camera. When he came opposite to the door, he tripped over, and as he fell snapped a good head-on picture of the door from ankle level.

Leslie Jagger's people made up a false door from the photograph, and matched the paint by sending a fleck of it to our friendly paint maker, who identified the exact batch number it was from.

We had to fix the false door very quickly and without leaving any sawdust or brick dust, so there was no question of boring into the existing door or the wall. Instead, it was held in place by spring clips. This left only the problem of installing it.

It was another job calling for some acting. One evening, groups of Watchers, with their wives, converged on King

Street and happened to run into one another outside CPGB headquarters. While the people milled around making a noise, my partner Hugh Winterborn dropped to his knees, pulled the false door complete with microphone and batteries from under his coat, delicately fed the probe into the keyhole and slipped the door into place over it. The whole operation took around forty seconds.

For the next six months we had an astonishing insight into the whole operation of the CPGB. But it couldn't last. One day the caretaker, who had a flat at the top of the building, must have been playing with a new short wave wireless, because it seems that he picked up the transmission. The first we knew of it was the sound of people searching the room for the offending microphone. Hugh Winterborn immediately raced to King Street and removed it. So they never found it, but we never tried putting it back.

Bugging the CPGB in the 1950s was a real eye-opener. A lot of people thought at the time that they had given up all their ideas about World Revolution, but they hadn't. They really believed that the Communist millennium was around the corner, and all it needed from them was a little kick to speed it on its way.

I remember one meeting they had to discuss the next targets for industrial sabotage. Jack Jones and Hugh Scanlon were there representing the TUC (Trade Union Congress), and there were a lot of union leaders and two Russian trade union people. The Russians had just attended a similar meeting in Germany, and they reported that it had decided to attack the German motor industry. The meeting solemnly voted to do the same in Britain – destroy the British motor industry with a campaign of strikes.

As it happens, somebody leaked the news of the German meeting to the press, and there was a big article about it in *The Times*. As a result, they decided to delay the British campaign to give people time to forget. But they still went ahead with it as soon as the fuss died down, not only organising strikes but having people in management who made sure that the workers had something to go on strike about. They very nearly succeeded in killing the whole industry. ?

**Burgess, Guy**  Some people seem to think that it is easy to pick an agent or a traitor, as if they were different from ordinary people. I have investigated hundreds of spies and agents in my time, and I couldn't see anything significantly different about them. They just seemed to be like any ordinary group of people.

One or two, however, were exceptional; not because they looked and behaved like spies, but quite the opposite: they looked and behaved like the kind of people who couldn't possibly be spies. Of these, one of the best examples was Guy Burgess.

At one level, Guy Burgess was the caricature aesthete and man-about-town; 'one of them', as we used to say in those days, always dashing off to be measured for a new pair of silk pyjamas. But as an Old Etonian with friends in every branch of the Establishment, he was the kind of person who, according to the wisdom prevailing at MI5, was simply not a candidate for suspicion as a Communist agent; see *Class*.

The next thing was that he drank too much. He used to have rooms at the Rothschild house in Bentinck Street, which he shared with his friend Anthony Blunt, and Victor Rothschild's wife Tess used to find the two of them dumped on the doormat by cabbies, incapable of going anywhere and least of all upstairs. She had to help them into bed, a curious occupation for a well brought up young lady.

It does not take any special intelligence to know that you do not entrust State secrets to people like that. They are just too prone to blackmail and careless talk, even if they are loyal subjects of the Queen. However, both Burgess and Blunt had got positions of considerable trust, Blunt in MI5 and Burgess in the Diplomatic Service and had worked there for years without arousing suspicions.

Arthur Martin took a different view, not sharing the

view that Old Etonians were above suspicion and saying that people like Burgess were too unreliable to be given positions of trust, even if there was no direct proof of active treachery. He was not listened to.

Burgess was eventually dismissed from the Diplomatic Service, but it was still not because he was under suspicion as a Russian agent. His outrageous behaviour had become notorious, but instead of being dismissed, he had been posted to the embassy in Washington in October 1950. Here, so far from mending his ways, his behaviour became increasingly bizarre. There was an accumulation of trivial problems, like abusing diplomatic immunity to avoid speeding tickets and outrageous choice of homosexual partners. (When asked for comment on his getting a ticket for driving at 80 mph, he said that the accusation was false, since he had been doing over 100 mph.) He became such an embarrassment to the Ambassador, Sir Oliver Franks, that in May 1951 he was recalled to London and dismissed; but he was dismissed for administrative incompetence, not because they believed that he was a traitor, whatever they said after the event.

Burgess defected on the spur of the moment, when he heard that they had become suspicious of Donald Maclean. (For more about how he discovered this, see *Maclean, Donald*.) Maclean went missing after having had dinner with a certain Roger Styles. He was reported to have gone off with Styles in a car. Investigation showed that 'Roger Styles' was Guy Burgess, and on enquiry it was soon found that he, too, had disappeared.

The investigation led to a London car hire firm which had supplied Burgess with an Austin A70, and a description of the car was circulated. A few hours later it was found on the docks at Southampton, and the two were assumed to have fled the country.

At this stage, there was one of those strange doubling-ups which should only happen in plays written for very small casts. The person chosen to head the MI5 team which broke into Burgess's flat to search for incriminating papers was none other than his old friend, Anthony Blunt. It was the more odd because Blunt had left MI5 to become the Director of the Courtauld Institute, a department of the University of London devoted to the study of art.

This prompts two questions: first, why break in at all? Why not get a warrant and have a proper police search? Secondly, if you want to find an outsider to do a burglary job, why pick the Director of the Courtauld Institute?

There were simple answers to both questions.

MI5 had to move fast, and on evidence which even then looked hazy and circumstantial, with a lot of hearsay and guesses. Getting a warrant was at best a slow business, and there was a serious risk that the application would be refused. Far better to mount a quick, deniable operation.

But why Blunt? The operation was so ticklish that it was being personally handled by the Deputy Director General of MI5, Guy Liddell. But Liddell was a personal friend of Guy Burgess. This put him in an invidious position. When he received news of the disappearance, he was appalled not only at the thought of the damage it could do to MI5 but also because it could prejudice his own position.

The best solution seemed to him to be an approach to the only person he could really trust with such a delicate mission, Anthony Blunt. Blunt had worked as his assistant for several years through the war, and was, he felt, proven loyal and trustworthy. Furthermore, Liddell knew that Blunt, too, was a friend of Burgess's, and was likely to share his concern that the whole affair should be handled as discreetly as possible. It seemed the perfect choice.

It is not every day that the Director of the Courtauld Institute is asked to go out on a burgling expedition by a senior civil servant, but that is what happened that day. And, as Blunt explained to me years later during my long interrogation of him, he realised that he was being given a heaven-sent opportunity to keep his own name out of the muck, and said yes.

So it was that the burgling party got into Guy Burgess's flat with Anthony Blunt's personal duplicate key, and the burglars brought all the loot to Blunt. He divided it neatly into two piles, 'ours' and 'theirs'. On the 'ours' pile went any documents which might point at himself, Philby or the fifth member of the Ring of Five, and details of their current activities. On the 'theirs' pile went all the rest, including just enough new and incriminating material to ensure that no one would suspect that the material had already been sanitised.

This was the pile that landed on the desk of my friend, Arthur Martin. He had been working on the Operation Bride material, and knew what it meant: that there were two hundred senior British civil servants acting as agents for the Russians, whose operations must sooner or later be revealed. He had wondered what it would be like to see direct evidence of treachery in high places, rather than the cryptic references to it in fragments of deciphered Russian traffic, which was all that ever came out of Bride. Even so, the evidence, when it hit his desk appalled him. He told me later that, if he had had any doubt about it before, he was from then on never able to regard anyone, however well connected and apparently respectable, as above suspicion.

The impact on MI5 was rather different. Instead of immediately reforming the vetting and internal security procedures to make sure that the same thing didn't happen again, all they did was close ranks. It was as if the real culprits were not Burgess and Maclean but the people who were unmasking them; as if the real problem was not how to limit the damage done by Burgess and Maclean to the security of Britain, but how to limit the damage done to the credibility of MI5. They immediately concocted a story designed to minimise their own failures.

So it was that Arthur Martin was shot across to America to allay their fears. (Nominally, the explanation was delivered by Sir Percy Sillitoe as Director General, but Sillitoe was recognised as being ill equipped for so tricky a mission, and Arthur was sent to make sure the case was properly put.) In the event, Arthur's big problem was not to explain the spies themselves – the CIA had had their own moles, and knew the difficulty of keeping them out – but to explain why MI5 were being less than frank about it, trying to cover up their incompetence. The Americans saw straight through the MI5 cover story, and this is what *really* damaged MI5.

To the last, there were still people who, not having seen all the evidence, believed that Burgess and Maclean could have been kidnapped or murdered. But five years later they turned up at a press conference in Moscow, and no one could have any doubts any more.

Meanwhile Burgess proved almost as embarrassing to the Russians as he had to poor old Sir Oliver Franks. Unlike Kim Philby, he was not the kind of person who fitted the part as a Hero of Socialism. He remained an outrageous English aristocrat. They fixed him up with a flat and a boyfriend, but there were not too many people who mourned when he died in Moscow in 1963.

# C

**Cairncross, John** I remember an item in *Private Eye* a few years back. It was one of those photos with speech balloons added, and showed the Pope talking to a beaming black prelate. The Pope was saying, 'Would you chaps mind taking the blame for Calvary?' I was reminded of this when I saw a television show recently about John Cairncross.

It seems that Her Majesty's Government had decided to use Cairncross in much the same way, making him take the rap as the Fifth Man in the Ring of Five. They had to find a candidate, as the evidence for the existence of the Fifth Man was overwhelming. In rejecting my nominee, Sir Roger Hollis, they had created a bigger question mark than the one they had disposed of. So they looked around for a replacement, and picked on John Cairncross.

There are many very good reasons why Cairncross is not the answer, some of them too complicated to go into. However, the easy ones are enough. The main one is that his career does not fit the knowledge we have of the Fifth Man. By contrast, Donald Maclean not only fitted, he was actually identified by the fit of fine details. In short, we knew a lot about the person we were looking for, and Cairncross was not it.

If any further argument is needed, it comes from the way Cairncross originally came under suspicion. Documents carrying his handwriting were found in the papers under the bed in Burgess's flat after his defection, which were handed to Arthur Martin for analysis. But the bits which reached Arthur Martin had been gone over by Anthony Blunt, who had removed anything which could have implicated himself, Philby or the Fifth Man. Either Blunt did not recognise the handwriting (which he would have done in the case of the Fifth Man) or he recognised it and decided that its owner was of little importance and would therefore make a good sacrificial lamb. Either way, Cairncross is in the clear.

At the subsequent interrogation by Arthur Martin, Cairncross was able to wriggle out of it – or, at least, to show that there was no point in trying to take him to court, as the case simply wouldn't stick. So we had to watch helplessly while he left the country.

However, in 1964 Sir Anthony Blunt named him as one of his own recruits, and when re-interrogated shortly afterwards by Arthur Martin, he confessed.

**Cambridge**   I am not sure what it was about Cambridge University that made it such a hotbed of treachery in the 1930s, but the evidence speaks for itself. Here is a list of some of the spies we knew about:

*Astbury, Peter*  Revealed by Anthony Blunt and Leo Long.

*Blunt, Anthony*  Revealed by Michael Whitney Straight and confessed, 1964; see the main entries *Blunt, Anthony* and *Traitors*.

*Burgess, Guy*  Suspected by Arthur Martin and others, but finally revealed himself by defection; see the main entry *Burgess, Guy*.

*Burn, Michael*  Recruited by Guy Burgess, confessed to me.

*Cairncross, John*  Confessed 1964 to Arthur Martin; see the main entry *Cairncross, John*.

*Cohen, Sir Andrew*  Confirmed by Phoebe Pool, colleague of Sir Anthony Blunt.

*Costello, Paddy*  He became a diplomat, a job in which he provided the Krogers with passports; see *Lonsdale, Gordon*. He was later Professor of Russian at Manchester

University. We discovered that he was having clandestine meetings with Russian Intelligence Officers, and were about to move in on him when he suddenly died. We interrogated his wife but got nowhere.

*Klugman, James* Leading intellectual of the Communist Party of Great Britain. Recruited Cairncross.

*Long, Leo* Recruited by and revealed by Sir Anthony Blunt.

*Maclean, Donald* Identified as 'Homer' in Bride material, and defected; see the main entry *Maclean, Donald.*

*Norman, Herbert* A Canadian diplomat, he committed suicide when recalled from Cairo for questioning. Subsequently Blunt revealed to me that he had recruited him.

*Philby, Kim* Suspected, confessed, defected; see the main entry *Philby, Kim.*

*Proctor, Sir Dennis* Admitted being an agent for Guy Burgess

*Simon, Brian* Son of Lord Simon. Recruited by Anthony Blunt.

*Smolka alias Smollett, Peter* In partnership with Philby in a magazine venture in the 1930s; named by Russian defector Anatoli Golitsin.

*Straight, Michael Whitney* American. Recruited by Sir Anthony Blunt, and revealed by him to the CIA.

*Watson, Alister* Interrogated for six weeks and admitted he knew four top Russian IOs, but never admitted he was a spy. Blunt said he was.

*Wylie, Tom* Recruited by Guy Burgess, who regarded him highly. Revealed by Sir Anthony Blunt.

Much of the information came from Anthony Blunt, and the strange thing was that all the people he mentioned were either already on our lists or were dead. I tried to believe that this meant that we had been pretty successful in ferreting them all out. In fact, it meant nothing of the sort: he was still just playing with us. He only gave us information which would be of no use to us.

**Centimetric radar** One of the great challenges of the Second

World War was the building of radar units operating on very short wavelengths. You may wonder why. If not, don't read any more of this entry.

Radar depends on the fact that waves are disturbed when they hit an obstruction. The reflection and refraction of light waves is the most obvious example, but you can see the process happening by looking at water waves, which are reflected off the sides of containers and interfere with one another. Even ocean waves show similar patterns, which can be seen in aerial photographs: they are reflected and refracted by rocks and shorelines.

If you look at these patterns, you will notice that a small object, like a post stuck in the sea, or a nail stuck in a ripple tank, makes no difference to the main pattern. This is an example of a general rule: waves do not get disturbed by objects which are smaller than their own wavelength. This is why we will never be able to 'see' atoms or any but the largest macro-molecules with a normal optical microscope: they are smaller than the wavelength of the light we see things by. Beams of electrons have a smaller wavelength and are used in electron microscopes to 'see' objects too small for optical microscopes.

Radar works by transmitting a radio wave and measuring how long it takes for its reflection (echo) to come back. The longer it takes, the further away is the object off which it is being reflected.

In the radar sets we had in the Second World War, these very short time intervals were measured on an oscilloscope. For example, suppose that Figure A is of an oscilloscope working at 5000 Hz, which means that the image is a straight line formed by a spot of light moving across the screen five thousand times a second. If such an oscilloscope were arranged so that a radar pulse was transmitted every time the spot was at the left-hand end of the screen, the time between the pulse and the echo can be measured off. If the echo appears in the middle of the screen, as in Figure B, it means that the pulse has taken ten thousandths of a second to reach the object and come back.

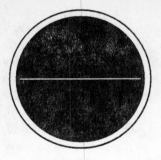 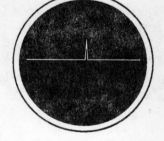

Figure A                                    Figure B

In ten thousandths of a second, a radio wave will have gone 30 km, so the object reflecting it must be 15 km away.

So much for the distance. In order to find direction, the transmitting aerial was rotated to scan the horizon, and the oscilloscope trace was made to rotated round its left-hand end in time at the same rate. The pattern of blips on the screen was then a map of the all the objects in the surrounding region which reflected radio waves.

Such a display showed the two crucial elements in the name of radar: radio direction and ranging.

However, these short wavelengths, which today are commonplace, were at first difficult to generate. In particular, it was very difficult to produce a large, steady output of ultra-short radio waves. Initially, the Germans were much better at it than us, but then the invention of the magnetron put us ahead.

Until the invention of the transistor, the main source of high frequency waves was thermionic valves. In these valves, electrons were emitted by a hot cathode (the *therm-*part of the name indicates heat) and travelled down the length of the valve to the anode.

The frequency of the output depended on the number of electrons which shot down the valve every second, and this depended on the potential difference (PD) between the cathode and the anode. But this was strictly limited. Beyond a certain level, the current would simply arc across from the cathode to the anode, burning out the valve.

In order to produce the very high frequencies required for very high frequency (VHF) and ultra high frequency (UHF) wireless and radar transmissions, much higher PDs were needed, PDs which would burn out an ordinary thermionic valve. The answer was the magnetron, in which there was a magnetic field running perpendicular to the path of the electrons. This caused the electrons to spiral. The anode was a great ring of copper round the cathode, with a series of slots in it, aligned to the spiralling paths of the electrons. This meant that there could be a far larger number of separate paths between the anode and the cathode than in an ordinary valve, allowing a much greater flow of electrons to occur without arcing.

The next problem was to tune the magnetron to produce particular frequencies. This problem was solved in a particularly clever way.

As we have seen, the anode of a magnetron contained a series of slots, each one receiving a proportion of the electrons. These slots acted as resonators, and could be 'strapped' (joined together with bits of copper wire) to produce an output with roughly the required characteristics.

It was then realised that these straps, whose main purpose was simply to link the slots in a prescribed way, would also produce electric fields, and that these could themselves moderate the flow of electrons. Furthermore, the amount they affected the flow depended on the exact shape of the strap. Thus the magnetrons could be fine-tuned by bending the straps slightly. For an intriguing outcome of this, see *Tidy mind, dangers of a*.

The magnetron was the power source for all the very short wavelength devices available to Britain and the Allies during the war, most notably the radar device known as $H_2S$. The story of how an electronic device got a chemical name is one of the sillier stories of the war. It seems that Churchill's head boffin, Prof. Lindemann, was visiting the Telecommunications Research Establishment, and was asking why the development of the device had been delayed. Nobody dared tell him that it was because he, Lindemann, had belittled the project on an earlier visit, and they were all offering lame excuses, to each of which Lindemann muttered 'It stinks, it stinks'. After he had gone, somebody said 'If he reckons it stinks, let's call it $H_2S$'. The name stuck.

Having helped to win the war, the magnetron then found an even more vital role, being a central component in the microwave oven.

**Chatter** An awful lot of intelligence is got by listening to signals you cannot understand. My father and I tracked the Home Fleet's movement up the English Channel in the late thirties, just by tuning to their wavelengths. We could not tell what they were saying, but we could find their positions; see *RDF*.

It therefore did not surprise me when we found out through Operation Rafter that, twenty years later, the Russians were listening to the British and American Polaris submarines coming up the English Channel. Just by listening to the call signs, they were able to find out which submarine was where, how long they went out for, and so forth. They were also listening to the American B52s.

Strangely, it was a surprise to the Americans. In fact, when we told them that the Russians were doing this, it shook them rigid, and after that they paid much greater attention to the need for radio silence.

We applied the same principles to our monitoring of the transmissions between Moscow and their agents here. Even if we could not read the cipher, we often got a lot of information simply from the frequency, timing and length of the messages; see *Rafter*.

**Chest of drawers** When searching a chest of drawers, always start at the bottom. That way, you can pull each drawer out and rest it on the one below. This not only gives the drawers support as you search them, but saves time because you don't have to push them back in. You can just leave them all sticking out and let the owners tidy them up.

**Children** How much should an intelligence officer tell his children about his job?

According to the Official Secrets Act, the answer is

'nothing', and this is not bad advice. But it is not easy advice. Children are always being asked 'And what does your daddy do?' and they cannot very well answer 'I don't know'. So you start off with a cover story for them. I told my children that I was a scientist working for the government, which was true as far as it went.

But there are other difficulties. What do you do when your child says 'What did you do at the office today?' It is bad enough when the honest answer is 'The Times crossword' (which was almost always part of the honest answer, but rarely the whole of it); but it is far worse if the honest answer is 'Something very exciting which I would really like to tell you all about and which you would be fascinated to hear'. But you have to say 'Nothing special, dear'.

I found this very frustrating. Sharing experiences with ones children was one of the great pleasures of parenthood, and one of the ways children learned; but for us who were involved in security intelligence, it was a pleasure that had to be foregone.

This was not just because MI5 was supposed not to exist. There were two common sense reasons why I didn't tell my children about my job. The first one was that secrets are not safe with children, and the second was that children are not safe with secrets.

When I say that secrets were not safe with children, I do not mean that they did not understand what 'secret' meant, or that they could not be trusted. They were no more garrulous or unreliable than adults. But they were less likely to recognise that a secret was being taken from them. It was easy for me, because I knew exactly what information the KGB were after and how they were likely to try to get it. I was all the time piecing big stories together from tiny scraps, and knew what kind of scraps to look for. I could also recognise an intelligence-gathering operation when I saw one. But a child couldn't be expected to recognise that the casual, friendly questions of a stranger on a bus were in fact part of such an operation.

When I say that children were not safe with secrets, I mean just that. If they were known to have information, they became targets for the interrogators. Indeed, a degree of danger could not be avoided, because if they were identified as the children of an intelligence officer, they were in danger of being kidnapped.

In fact, this danger is not confined to children. When my daughter Tessa was learning Russian at Manchester University, I had to warn her that she could never go to Russia to try it out, because there was too much risk that she would be identified as my daughter and grabbed by the KGB.

By that age, of course, she knew that I was working for the Security Service. Children will accept what you tell them up to a point, but sooner of later they realise that they are not getting the full story, and it is more dangerous to try to fob them off than it is to tell them the truth. But you still don't tell them about any current operations.

For a story about the moment of truth for my daughter Jenny, see *Lonsdale, Gordon.*

**CIA**  The Central Intelligence Agency is the US equivalent of MI6, but it is a legally constituted organisation, with its name in big letters on its very impressive headquarters at Langley, Virginia. Those who say that MI6 might as well be legal point to the CIA as an example of how it can work. But this argument can be used both ways: the humiliating public enquiry into the CIA before a Senate Select Committee (the Church Committee) could not have happened in Britain, since MI5 and MI6 are not accountable to Parliament.

The CIA is the successor to the OSS (Office of Strategic Services) which was formed in the Second World War to look after wartime intelligence. Military intelligence had previously been left to the military, but they failed to give any warning of the attack on Pearl Harbor, and the US government realised that intelligence was too important to be left to them. The formation of the OSS was the result. Its best activities were not in the Pacific but in the European theatre, where Allen Dulles led its very effective work with resistance groups in occupied Europe, including the anti-Nazi movement in Germany itself.

After the war the OSS was disbanded, but it was so sorely missed that within a year it was reconstituted under the name CIG (Central Intelligence Group), which a year later (1947) became the CIA. In 1952 Allen Dulles became its head.

Its early days were not happy. Like MI6, on which it was based, it tended to get involved in other people's politics, but this was not always trouble free. It had an early success in Italy, where it ensured that the Communists did not win the 1947 election, and in Iran, where it helped MI6 to overthrow the nationalist government of Mohammed Mossadeq and restore the Shah; but there was a bad mix up further down the gulf when it found itself backing the Saudis against the MI6-backed Omanis in the Buraimi Oasis affair, a minor military confrontation which the MI6 team won.

Meanwhile another organisation, the OPC (Office of Policy Co-ordination) had been set up in 1948 to organise more major subversions. Its biggest operation was organising a revolution in Albania, but this was a total failure, partly (but only partly) because it was blown by Kim Philby. It was then absorbed into the CIA as its Directorate for Plans.

The absorption was nearly disastrous. It was from intelligence collected by the OPC veterans in the Directorate for Plans that Allen Dulles became convinced that the Cubans were ready to rise against Fidel Castro if only the Americans gave the signal. The result was the Bay of Pigs operation, when Cuban exiles were landed in Cuba with massive American support. The promised popular uprising failed to materialise and the whole operation turned into a military and public relations disaster. The remaining veterans of the OPC, and Allen Dulles, were forced to resign.

The Company (as it calls itself) survived, however, to

become involved in even more extraordinary operations during the Vietnam War. It set up the Office of Special Assistance in Saigon, which ran, amongst other things, a bogus commercial airline, Air America, and was deeply involved in drug trafficking. At home, it infiltrated the anti-war movement, despite having a charter forbidding its involvement in domestic operations. At the same time it became obsessed with a leftward shift in South American politics, organising the overthrow of the Chilean government of President Salvador Allende, the first Marxist to gain power in a popular election, and his replacement with the more amenable Augusto Pinochet.

These various immoral, unauthorised and illegal operations came out in the Church Committee, a senate investigation. This was very bad luck. The investigation was originally not into the CIA's actions at all, but into an entirely separate sequence of dirty deeds known as the Watergate affair. Richard Nixon's presidential staff were caught bugging the Democratic Party's Washington headquarters in the Watergate Building. (Bugging is not as easy as some people think, and should be left to experts.)

Anyway, during the Church Committee enquiry, the CIA got linked in, and next thing they were being asked all sorts of difficult questions. Many disclosures had arisen from the release of the so-called Pentagon Papers, a set of confidential memos which were leaked to members of the anti-war movement. The CIA's status as a normal Government body meant that it had little protection against demands for it to testify. Still worse, it had difficulty resisting demands for the release of documents under Freedom of Information legislation, something we never had to put up with. The result was that for the next two years the whole organisation was totally demoralised and ineffective.

It says something for its resilience that it rose again from the dead to champion anti-Communist forces in Afghanistan, Nicaragua and San Salvador, to name just three of the largest and most visible operations. In addition, of course, it has conducted minor operations in virtually every country of the world.

To me, the astonishing thing about the CIA was always the manpower and resources available to them. The cafeteria in their Langley headquarters seated a thousand, but was hopelessly inadequate for the 18,000 people who worked there. What is more, the CIA was a piddling little organisation alongside the National Security Agency; see NSA.

**Cipher**  The word cipher started life as the Arabic *al cifr*, a key element in Arabic mathematics. At the time, people in Western Europe did all their mathematics with Roman numerals. If you have ever tried multiplying CCCLVII by XCIV you will know that they were in deep trouble. So, when they saw the Arabs using their strange symbols to come up with quick answers to questions which took hours to solve with Roman numerals, they first thought it was black magic, and then that they were using some secret code.

They realised that the key to the code was a symbol which had no equivalent in Roman numerals, and which the Arabs could not explain, saying that it meant nothing. The Arabs called this symbol *al cifr*; so they transliterated this word as cipher, and used it to mean secret code. It has had this meaning ever since.

As it happens, *cifr* really did mean nothing, i.e. nought, an empty wire on an abacus. This was the key feature of Arabic mathematics which European mathematics lacked. The Europeans had words for 'none' and 'nothing' in the general senses, but not one which could be used as a counting number.

When Leonardo Fibonacci introduced Arabic mathematics into Europe at the beginning of the thirteenth century, he realised that this was the true secret of the new system, and that they needed a name for it. By then, cipher had become well established as a word for code, so another word was derived from *cifr* to denote the empty wire on the abacus: zero.

The word ciphering is occasionally found in old texts meaning arithmetic, and we talk of a person who is a nonentity as a cipher.

The simplest secret writing systems involve nothing more than the replacement of one letter by another. Since each letter is always represented in the same way in such systems, you have only to count the frequency of the letters in the coded text and can be pretty sure that the most common one will be E, since this is the most common letter in our alphabet. Thus these systems are very easy to break. It is best to use the word code for these one-to-one systems, and to restrict the word cipher to systems involving much more complicated transformations; see *Codes*.

The first essential is that the encoding pattern has to vary, so that the same letter in the original does not always give the same letter in the cipher. There are a number of ways of doing this, and theoretically one can devise a code which will contain no patterns at all.

One-time pads are an example of this: these show a pattern of replacement to be followed, but one which is totally arbitrary and non-repetitive, as is explained in the entry *One-time pads*.

However, pads are laborious, and the need to encipher and decipher long messages led to the invention of the first generation of cipher machines.

Cipher machines are essentially random number generators. However, the numbers are not truly random, but are a sequence generated by the machine and governed by the way it has been set up. If you have two identical machines set up in exactly the same way, both will generate the same 'random' sequence, so that a message encoded on one machine can be decoded by another working on the same settings.

The random numbers are used in the same way as the numbers on one-time pads. For an explanation, see *One-time pads*.

Modern cipher machines work electronically, but the cipher machines of the early Cold War period were mechanical, generating the numbers by means of wheels, which could be considered as a set of meshing cogs with a variable number of moveable teeth. Thus a very large number of different sequences of movements could be generated by changing the number and position of the teeth. However, if the people at the other end knew what setting you had used, they could set their machine to reverse the pattern of yours, so that it would take your cipher and print it out *en clair*.

Despite our success with the German cipher machine Enigma, the received wisdom was that machine ciphers were unbreakable. This included the Hagelin machines used by most of the embassies.

I was reluctant to admit that this was so, and believed that, if we could *hear* the machine being set, we could work out what settings were being used. The machines made a fearful clatter, and as every wheel was slightly different, I believed that each would produce a slightly different brand of clatter. This would tell us which wheel was being set. Further analysis of the sound of the setting being made would tell us what movements of cogs were being made. For the successful outcome of this theory, see *Engulf*.

Computers revolutionised the whole business of ciphering and deciphering. 'Dragging' (that is, testing a cipher for a sequence showing a given pattern) ceased to be a slow, laborious manual exercise and became a job for the computer, which would go away and check millions of combinations without getting bored or falling asleep.

This did not help with one-time pads unless they had been wrongly used, (see *Bride*). If used correctly, a one-time pad will show no patterns at all and is totally unbreakable, the problem being that it is slow. But computers did help with deciphering any mechanical cipher. The number of possible settings of a mechanical cipher machine is very large but in no sense infinite. Computers make it feasible to test a huge number of possible combinations within a practical time limit.

Thus the arrival of powerful, reliable computers made

all the mechanical cipher machines obsolete. Today, the ciphers are generated by computer.

Could there ever be a totally unbreakable cipher? Logically, the answer has to be 'no'. If a message can be enciphered in London and deciphered in Moscow, the rules of the cipher must be agreed in advance at both ends. Even if it is based on a string of random numbers, the same string of random numbers has to be used at both ends, which in a real sense makes the string non-random.

However, another logical truth is that you have to invent a cipher before anyone can start trying to break it, so the breaker is always a lap behind. Also, the computer has made it possible to use complex ciphers which would have been impossibly laborious in the days of manual or mechanical enciphering. As a result, by 1975 the ciphers were winning, and since then most diplomatic and military traffic has been in ciphers which remain unbroken.

**Claridges** This London hotel was a favourite among distinguished foreign visitors. For convenience, it had all rooms permanently bugged. This sensible arrangement saved us at MI5 a great deal of trouble going to and fro.

Originally, coverage was achieved by having SF on all the phones; see *SF*. Note that tapping phones was legal, but you had to get a warrant, whereas SF was illegal, so the question of a warrant didn't arise. However, it was not much use, since all the people who mattered knew all about SF, including how to disable it.

When the Soviet leader Nikita Kruschev stayed there in 1956, we took the opportunity to try out a more sophisticated variant of SF, which only became active when irradiated with microwaves. It worked splendidly, but Kruschev obviously knew that the rooms were bound to be bugged, and we heard nothing except endless talk with his valet. He may have looked to us as if he slept in his suits, but he thought of himself as Beau Brummel the Second.

**Class** It is hard for anyone who does not know the upper echelons of the British Civil Service to understand the meaning of 'class' in MI5. It was so entrenched that it did not need to be mentioned. But there were crucial differences between the sexes in the way it affected expectations.

Upper-crust females were assumed to be rather silly, and were found in the Registry at MI5 – we called them the Registry Queens. If you'd never witnessed a pack of debutantes in full cry, the Registry at 5 pm could be quite instructive.

This did not happen because of any entry requirement. We didn't say 'Must have Roedean accent and talk about Mummy'. It was just that the jobs were never advertised, they were simply offered to girls the personnel people knew, and the personnel people tended to know this sort of girl. They reckoned that doing it this way made sure none of the wrong sort got in, like Communists.

None of these girls needed a job. They were all just filling in time before getting married and becoming Lady So-and-So, and MI5 sounded a more amusing way to fill in the time than rolling bandages for the Red Cross. And they were right there. Cynics said that girls rarely lasted more than nine months in the Registry.

The trouble was, of course, that if the Communists wanted to infiltrate the Registry, it was dead easy for them. All they had to do was to find a comrade with the right accent, give her a list of people to watch for on the social circuit, and tell her the right things to say when she met them. Very soon she would be offered a job in the Registry.

Communists didn't often get in, or at least we don't think they did. On the few occasions when we discovered a suspicious character in the Registry, she had got in without any real vetting at all, just because she looked and sounded the part.

By contrast, the women who had the most responsible jobs in the Service tended to be a rung or two down socially. This was perhaps because their jobs tended to require specific skills and to be awarded on merit. Anybody could be an Intelligence Officer, but everybody could not be a transcriber or a research officer.

Our senior women wore sensible shoes and spoke in

strong, measured tones. They were also the group about whose loyalty I had the least doubt.

Unlike the Upper-crust females, who were restricted to the Registry, the Upper-crust males occupied most of the best jobs. The odd thing was that people like me and my friend Arthur Martin got in, not that there were so few of us. All the cards were stacked against us.

Firstly, as with the girls, almost all recruitment was by recommendation and invitation, and people tended to invite people like themselves. Unless you knew someone there was no way you could get in.

Arthur Martin got in in wartime, when the rules were a bit different and a few people had got in on merit. Later, I got in because they needed someone with specific skills and Sir Frederick Brundrett said that I had them; see *Boffin*. But neither of us would have been taken on as ordinary officers in peacetime. We were a rung or two off the pace.

This style of recruitment made penetration of the Service by the Communists quite easy. The Apostles at Cambridge University and similar groups elsewhere provided a constant stream of recruits with all the right accents and connections, and once one was in, others would follow.

Secondly, the people at the top all suffered from the extraordinary belief that the upper classes were trustworthy in matters of security and the lower classes were not. In fact, if you put your average blue-blood alongside your average cockney, I know which one I'd like to have guarding my front door. Nevertheless, the received wisdom was that their own sort was loyal and that everybody else was potentially disloyal.

If any leak was discovered, their first thought was always to accuse the Watchers. The Watchers were not Upper-crust at all. They were just ordinary chaps doing a job which was most of the time very dull, but which required a lot of skill and intelligence, as well as patience and a phenomenal memory. You have to be very patriotic indeed to do a job like that. By contrast, the boy scout world of the security officer was immensely appealing, attracting all sorts.

I would have liked to discuss these class questions with Arthur Martin, but it was not possible. One of the inviolable rules of the British class system, obeyed at all levels, is that it is not discussed between people on different levels, and Arthur was a rung or two lower than me. Despite that, Michael Whitney Straight, the Cambridge-educated American who denounced Anthony Blunt, said of Arthur 'In contrast to the FBI agents, Martin was sophisticated and urbane.' I liked that.

**Cleaners**   Office cleaners are often agents, but not always so. The Russian embassy in London had their own cleaners, but we provided the cleaners for the Czech and Hungarian embassies.

**Co-operation, international**   There have always been places in the world where spies of all denominations gathered to exchange information. Tangiers, Casablanca, Geneva and Berlin have all at various times been the espionage capitals of the world. But no place has done it as well as Delphi.

Delphi was strictly neutral. Set in the mountains of Phocis, the Switzerland of classical Greece, the Oracle worked in one of two ways: First, agents going to Delphi to consult the Oracle were quite likely to meet agents from enemy States on similar missions, and settle all outstanding problems over a cup of wine in the hotel.

Failing this, however, the Oracle herself could help. By judicious questioning of those who consulted her, the Oracle came to know the secret strengths, weaknesses, hopes and fears of all the people of the Greek world. She was thus able to decide whether a given problem could be resolved peacefully and, if not, to decide who would win the resultant war.

As a device for the redistribution of intelligence, the Oracle of Delphi has never been matched.

Whether she was believed or not was a different question. All the good advice in the world will not help if it is ignored. This was a problem we ran into all too often. We put in accurate reports, only to have them rejected in favour of poorly researched ones which happened to say what our Lords and Masters wanted to hear.

The Oracle of Delphi is best known, however, for another skill she possessed, that of ambiguity. In this respect she was the founder of a great tradition of obscurantism, double-talk and double-think whose heirs are the servants of governments and international organisations of all colours.

For example, Croesus, King of Lydia, asked her what would happen if he attacked Cambyses, King of Persia. The Oracle replied that he would destroy a mighty empire. Which, of course, he did: his own.

This leads us to ask the great unsolved riddle of the Oracle of Delphi: was the ambiguity to cover herself against being proved wrong, or to enable her to tell her clients what they wanted to hear without actually lying? The wise agent does both. I failed to do either, speaking the truth even when it was unpalatable. This meant that I ended up in exile in Tasmania, while the traitors of the period are still there, covered with honours.

**Codes**   There is an important difference between a code and a cipher.

A cipher is a secret way of writing something so that it cannot be understood by the enemy. A code is a way of representing a message by replacing all its letters or words with some pre-arranged substitutes. The Morse code, for example, uses patterns of dots and dashes to represent the letters and digits. The message is incomprehensible if you do not know the code, but it is not a secret code.

Modern military codebooks contain long lists of numbers which are used to represent frequently used words, and even sentences, as well as the names of places and people. There are also codes for single letters which can be used to spell out words which are not in the codebook. Finally, codes meaning 'spell' and 'endspell' are used to indicate the start and finish of sequences in which the words are spelled out in full.

Obviously the encoding of a message using this kind of replacement code makes it impossible for someone without the codebook to read it straight off. However, to an expert, cracking this sort of substitution code is a straightforward matter, rather like opening a bottle without a bottle opener is to a committed drinker. It may take a bit of time, but it can always be done.

The design of any code is related to the way it will be used. Thus semaphore is a code designed to be read visually at a distance; Morse is a simple on-off code, able to be transmitted very easily as a series of electrical impulses of differing lengths. The electronic Ascii code is an internationally agreed set of 256 numbers representing the roman alphabet, the Arabic numerals and a number of punctuation marks.

The advantage of encoding the message as numbers is that they can be transmitted and manipulated in a way that letters cannot. This is easy to see in the case of manual ciphers; see *One-time pads*, where the manipulation was by addition and subtraction. But the early cipher machines were doing much the same thing, the only difference being that the new 'random' number sequence was produced mechanically rather than being written on a pad.

**Collateral**   This is the term used by code breakers for passages of uncoded text which are known to correspond to passages of code, and which can therefore be of immense value in breaking the code. *OR RE-CODED FROM ANOTHER SYSTEM* *OR "CRIB"* *OF "THIS" SYSTEM.*

Perhaps the best example in history is the breaking of the Royal Egyptian code through an operation involving the Rosetta Stone. The Rosetta Stone contained versions of the same message in Greek, *en clair* Egyptian and the hieroglyphic code. By analysis of proper names, approximate phonetic values were assigned to the characters, resulting not only in decoding the script but also establishing the foundations for understanding the language itself.

In the case of the German Enigma cipher machines, collateral was commonly provided by the formulae with which the methodical Germans insisted on starting and finishing their messages, the German equivalent of 'Thank you for yours of the 14th inst'. In the case of Operation Bride, we had a greater difficulty, and had to seek collateral in the news stories which were likely to be referred to in the transmissions of the day; see *Bride*.

**Comintern** Many of the great Soviet agents of the 1930s are said to be agents of the Comintern. *Comintern* was an acronym for the Third or Communist International, founded by Lenin in 1919 largely to stop anyone resurrecting the Second International, a body of which he disapproved for being reformist rather than revolutionary.

The Comintern was thus initially the vehicle for World Revolution. However, on the death of Lenin a tactical dispute arose between Trotsky, who was keen to continue the campaign for World Revolution, and Joseph Stalin, who believed that it would be best to establish communism securely in Russia before taking on the world. Stalin won, and Trotsky was expelled from the Communist Party, driven into exile and finally assassinated by Stalin's agents.

Far from withering, however, the Comintern continued to strengthen its international membership through the 1930s, and to meddle in the affairs of many countries, but it failed to organise any very impressive revolutions. The reality was that it had become an international intelligence agency for Stalin, providing Russia with a vast network of true believers who, in the name of idealistic international communism, acted simply as Russian spies.

Almost all pretence at internationalism ended with Stalin's purges of 1938, when the cream of the Comintern agents were summoned to Moscow and executed, Stalin having come to the conclusion that they had become too powerful and independent. Finally, the organisation was disbanded by Stalin in 1943, largely as a gesture of good-will to his new allies in the West.

Needless to say, the Comintern network did not cease, but was merely taken over by other agencies, notably the KGB and GRU. Furthermore, it was this network estab-lished by the Comintern agents which provided the nucleus of the resistance movement in occupied Europe during the Second World War.

**Communication with a foreign power**  If we wanted to take a foreign agent to court, the best crime to get them on was generally 'communication with a foreign power'.

In the Bossard case (see *Music, as code messages*), we were able to show (a) that Bossard had copies of some special recordings of Russian folk songs, and (b) that these particular versions were played only over certain Russian stations which were identified as Russian intelligence service transmitters. The court regarded that as enough to convict him.

In the Lonsdale case (q.v.), we were able to produce the signal plans (that is, the times at which he was to listen to his wireless) which we had found in his possession. We were then able to put a GCHQ man in the witness box, who said that the signal plans were for some broadcasts which came from Moscow, that their source had been independently checked by direction finding, and that he could say from his personal experience that they were Russian intelligence service broadcasts. Again, we got a conviction.

We did not have to say what the broadcasts were about, or to produce evidence that he had ever listened to them. The handing over of the signal plans (or, in Bossard's case, the records) was itself regarded as evidence of communication. The court did not require us to prove that they had ever turned on their wirelesses and listened to the broadcasts.

This type of evidence (that is, evidence of communication, without any proof of what was communicated and whether it was damaging) is much more impressive to a court than evidence that important information has been handed over, but without evidence of how it was transmitted.

This was our big problem with Anthony Blunt. The evidence of his guilt was great enough before Michael Whitney Straight denounced him, and then became overwhelming; but in terms of the rules of evidence it was largely hearsay, circumstance and assertion. Blunt was careful enough never to be caught with any tangible evidence of communication.

**Computers**   It is hard for agents of today to imagine counter-espionage without computers, or to realise that this was what it was like only fifty years ago. The German World War Two machine-based military code, Enigma, was broken without computers as we know them.

Forty years ago there were a very few primitive contraptions, but they were huge things, rooms full of wires and thermionic valves. They were constantly breaking down, and when they were running they had less power than one of today's toy PCs. And there were very few of them. MI5 didn't have one, and we had to take our problems to someone who had. The Atomic Weapons Research Establishment at Harwell had one, and so did the CIA, and I used to get time at nights on these.

By 1960 we had the first solid state (transistorised) machines, which gave far greater reliability, but they were still huge and, by today's standards, slow and laborious. People had to punch the program instructions and data on cards, and the machine would read them, riffling through the cards at a rate of about ten per second. It looked very dramatic, but represented a Baud rate of around 1000 bytes per second, a tenth the speed of the slowest desktop computer today. Punched tape could be read faster, but had other drawbacks. The pins which punched the holes would get worn, and produce a terrible disease called furry holes, which meant re-punching the whole tape.

If everything went right, the computer would sit there thinking all night, periodically printing out strings of figures or spewing out a length of tape. There were no video screens. It was all cards and punched tape going in and print-outs plus more cards and tape coming out.

It was the Space Race of the sixties which really got things moving. The boffins had to develop powerful small computers to install in the satellites, and transistor technology surged ahead. This gave us the first mini-computers. They were mini when compared with the so-called mainframes, but they still had processing units at least as big as a domestic fridge. And if you wanted a complicated job done, you still had to go to a mainframe.

Computers started looking like they do now when we started getting VDUs, visual display units. Instead of shuffling punched cards and reels of punched tape, computer operation meant peering into a monitor. The first VDUs were just dumb terminals, but they soon invented intelligent terminals (terminals with a bit of processing capacity) and the next moment these developed into the first micro-computers.

I left MI5 just as the micros were coming in. The Registry – the filing system with its millions of files on people and organisations and events – had by then been put on a mainframe, and all sorts of enquiries had become more simple, particularly ones which required searching through thousands of documents looking for matches. The computer would just go on and on doing it without getting bored or tired, whereas the most careful human scanner was bound to make mistakes.

Computers also increased the amount of information available to us. As well as the two million-odd personal files we held in our own registry, we had access to the National Insurance computer in Newcastle, with details on virtually everybody in Britain. Of course, a lot of the information was personal and confidential, so we did not tell people about it unless they needed to know.

And that is how things stood when I left the Service. It looked as if we were going to turn into data processing clerks – no more fast cars and climbing over rooftops at night. No more fun.

However, in the end good security work means asking the right questions as much as it means getting the right answers. They haven't yet built a computer which will crack jokes or even laugh at a good joke, still less to groan if it has heard it before or thinks it is silly. We laughed a lot, and I think that this goes with the kind of mind you need in the security services. Until computers can compete with people in terms of imagination and sense of humour, the old-fashioned human will still have a place.

**Concrete**    I once got a call from the CIA. They said 'Peter, how do you bore through concrete *silently*?' The answer is that it is bloody difficult. You can bore through brick silently using a stainless steel tube which you turn slowly, but to get through concrete you have to use a diamond bit, and this makes a hell of a noise.

The best way is to have some cover noise, and the ideal cover is the noise of builders at work drilling through concrete. We used to send the Russians a note saying 'sorry' because we were going to be making a noise on our side of the party wall, and then we'd make it, boring through their wall.

The fact that it is possible to drill through a wall does not mean that it is always legal to do so. This is one of many important legal points that should be explained to agents as part of their training. You are not allowed to bore through a wall unless you own both sides of it *or* have the permission of the people who own the other side. Boring a hole through a wall into somebody else's house without their permission is trespass.

Late one night, when we were boring into the Hungarian embassy, we made such a noise that it woke them up, and they complained to the police. We explained that we were doing some work for the owners of a flat, and were working late at night because we didn't want to disturb anybody. ( ! )

It was fortunate that we had not quite got through the wall when they complained. If they had found the end of our drill, we might have been in real trouble, as nobody has yet worked out a really innocent explanation for why they were boring through an embassy wall with a diamond drill in the middle of the night.

# D

**D Branch** was the section of MI5 which handled counter-espionage. This was the part which contributed the front line troops in the battle against the Russians. It was therefore the main target for those who wished to make sure that we never got anywhere.

I had personal experience of this soon after I joined D Branch as head of D3. At that time, it had a very effective structure, devised by Arthur Martin, head of D1:

*D1* was investigations – the specific cases

*D2* was operational – it ran the agents and double agents

*D3* was called 'Order of Battle', and dealt with strategies and tactics – defining what we were trying to achieve and devising ways of achieving it.

Whenever D Branch started getting anywhere, it always had its key staff moved somewhere else. The people who did this could not have been more effective in destroying our efficiency if they had been paid to do so by the KGB. In my case the deed was done by Malcolm Cumming, who had become head of D Branch shortly before I joined it.

It all happened in May 1964. I had gone to America to persuade the Americans to help us with our Movements analysis program. I told them how we had collected a great deal of data about people coming and going in the Russian embassy, and needed help processing it. The Americans had been very impressed with the idea, and went a lot further than I had dared hope, not only offering unlimited computer time, but promising to send over a twenty-man team to check out all the angles. The key people for them to meet at our end were Arthur Martin and a man called H. A. Dumas, who had been co-ordinating the collection of data.

I returned full of enthusiasm and hope, only to find that, in my absence, Cumming had transferred Dumas elsewhere and got Arthur Martin suspended for insubordination when he had protested against this move. The KGB were doubtless very relieved, but it is hard to see who else gained. Not long after this, Cumming procured the sacking of Arthur Martin. More relief for the comrades. Indeed, anyone who had never met Cumming might wonder why I didn't suspect *him* of being a mole. Rest assured, you only had to meet him to see why the KGB would not have been interested.

So D Branch staggered on, but it was fatally flawed. In particular, it had no section specifically to deal with Russian penetration of MI5 itself, a task which naturally belonged there. I could have gone on doing it as part of D3's operations, but I realised that it was essential to make a fresh start with new faces in charge. Arthur Martin, who had been worried about it long before I became aware of the problem, was gone, and in any case both he and I were perceived as obsessed, despite the fact that so many of our earlier allegations had been proved correct.

Finally, in 1968, D Branch was totally re-organised as K Branch. The change of name was necessary to keep the records tidy and identify the activities of the new structure from those of the old one. The restructure was more or less as I had proposed: much of the operational structure devised for D Branch by Arthur Martin was restored, but there was one key innovation, K7, a division whose sole job was to deal with all allegations of penetration of the service. I handed over all my files to the first head of K7, Duncum Wagh, happy in the knowledge that the job had gone to a good man.

Amongst the files I handed over were those giving the evidence which had caused me to be worried about the previous Director General of MI5, Sir Roger Hollis. A year later, I was pleased to hear that, having looked at all the evidence, they found that I was right to have been worried. They recommended that the investigation of Sir Roger Hollis be re-opened.

**Degaussing the Prince of Wales**    The Germans very nearly won the Second World War in the first few weeks, thanks to their invention of the magnetic mine; see *Magnetic mines*. In the long run, the way we overcame the threat of magnetic mines was by degaussing.

Degaussing means demagnetising, the gauss being an old unit of magnetic flux. (Today, we measure magnetic flux in webers.) There are many ways in which a 'permanent' magnet can be demagnetised, including heating and hammering, but the peaceful way of doing it is by putting it in an AC electric field. Just as placing an iron block in a DC field can tidy up the magnetic domains in the block, turning it into a magnet, so placing it in an AC field will stir up the alignments of the domains, destroying the magnetism.

In order to make a ship safe against a magnetic mine, however, it was not sufficient to demagnetise it. Any unmagnetised block of metal would attract the magnets in the mine. To stop this happening, it was necessary to find which way the German mines were polarised, and then polarise our ships the other way. Thus the ship would repel the mine's trigger as it passed overhead, and not set the mine off.

We found that the German mines were polarised North down, so we actually had to turn the ships into permanent magnets polarised with the South pole down. We did this by running cables round the ship and feeding a strong DC current into them. This turned the whole ship into a magnet strong enough to repel the magnetic triggers on the mines. For some dramatic results, see *Dunkirk*.

Wherever possible, the degaussing was done in harbours, where there was a supply of electricity. However, until we got it going properly, ships were arriving unprotected, and had to be degaussed at sea. As some of them did not have sufficient generating plant on board, we had a flotilla of submarines standing by, whose generators were connected in parallel to produce the heavy current needed for the job.

If you have experimented with magnets, you will know how a magnetised pin will stand up on the end of a magnet, since the magnet attracts one end of the pin and repels the other. The same thing happened on a ship we were degaussing, except that everything was on a larger scale, and the pin which suddenly stood on end was a six-foot crowbar. It reared up as the current came on, hit a sailor on the head and knocked him out.

A very special problem arose while I was with the degaussing unit. We got the message that they were having difficulty degaussing the new battleship, the *Prince of Wales*. What was worse, it had been selected to carry Winston Churchill to a mid-ocean meeting with Franklin D. Roosevelt, so it was rather important to make it safe.

We soon discovered the source of the problem. Unlike her sister ships, which had been built in North-South aligned slipways in John Brown's yard on the Clyde, the *Prince of Wales* had been built on an East-West aligned slipway in the Harland and Woolf yard in Belfast. As a result, the natural magnetic field ran across the ship instead of along it.

This natural polarity is caused by fact that some components in any ship, particularly the rivets which are driven in red hot and cool in their final positions in the ship, will tend to be polarised by the earth's magnetic field.

In big ships like battleships, with their thousands of tons of heavy armour plate, it was almost impossible to eliminate the natural polarity. So long as the polarity was along the ship, bow-to-stern, it was not too worrying, as it was as if the mine was moving along the lines of force. Changes in the field strength would be small and gentle. By contrast, if the natural polarity was across the ship, port to starboard, it was as if the mine was moving across the lines of force and hence being subjected to a violently changing magnetic field.

This was precisely the kind of situation which would set off the mine.

If we were not able to produce a stronger field in the up-down direction than this transverse field, the ship would not be protected.

We worked out a solution. Instead of attempting to produce powerful permanent magnetism, we wrapped the coil round the ship and connected it to a large DC generator, which from then on ran all the time. The effect was to make possibly the biggest solenoid in the world, and the whole ship became a huge electromagnet.

So it was that the *Prince of Wales* became a safe platform for the conference which led to the signing of the Atlantic Charter in August 1941; but it could do nothing to protect the ship against the Japanese bombers which sent it to the bottom off the Malayan coast six months later.

**Details, small, importance of** In many aspects of security, small details are crucially important.

For example, a new batch of MI6 recruits was being trained with a simulation exercise. They had been told to go to a flat in Mayfair, where they would find a man whom they were to cross question about some information he was known to have. The interrogation was to be done as realistically as possible.

The recruits duly bashed down the door of the flat, found the man, and started the interrogation. They stripped him starkers and said they would do frightful things to him if he didn't tell them all. And he talked, and he told them all. He turned out to be a jewel thief, and he produced from a hiding place a bag of uncut diamonds.

This is not quite what had been expected, and it was only at this point that the recruits realised they had miscounted the floors and were in the wrong flat.

It was extremely embarrassing. As MI6 did not exist, the recruits did not exist, so the raid could not have taken place and the thief could not have been captured. They phoned us and asked us to help them clear up the mess. We gave him back his diamonds and advised him to pack his bags and get to the other side of the Channel as quick as he could.

The Australian ASIS people made a similar mistake when they messed up a training raid on a room in the Sheraton Hotel in Melbourne, but they were naughty. They beat people up, which they ought not to have done; see *ASIO*.

**Dew Worm**   This was the name of an operation I did with the RCMP, the Royal Canadian Mounted Police, to bug the Russian embassy in Ottawa.

It was a difficult one. The embassy stood by itself in the middle of its site. We could not get close enough to mount a Satyr-type operation, and there was no party wall to bore through as we had in many of the embassies in London, so all the usual ways of doing it presented problems.

By happy chance, however, the existing embassy had been burnt down, and they were about to rebuild. This helped because it is easier to install bugs in a new building as it is being built than to plant them in an existing one. It gives you some extra options, one of which is to install wired microphones. I was a great believer in wired microphones, because if you can get them in they are incredibly difficult to detect.

In this case, we thought we could run the wires up the cavity in the walls – the air gap in the middle of the walls of houses to stop moisture seeping in. This building had a massive inside wall, built of fourteen-inch concrete blocks, then the cavity, two inches wide, and then an outer skin of stone, just four inches thick. This meant fourteen inches of concrete in the way of the sweepers' detection equipment if they tried to detect the wires from the inside. I put a call in to MI6 asking whether they had ever come across Russians sweeping the outsides of their buildings, and the answer was no.

The first problem was to get the wires into the building. As it was at that stage just a hole in the ground, we had an opportunity which is not often available: to build our wires into the fabric of the building. We dug a trench below foundation level, positioning the cables under the footings of the walls.

As the building went up, the Mounties went in each night to draw the cables up through the cavity in the newly completed sections of the wall. They didn't ride in on their horses in their red coats, of course. A plain-clothes Mountie looks and behaves just like a burglar.

We had got the plans of the building from the town planning people, and the layout showed quite clearly which rooms were likely to be secure areas and hence worth listening to. We directed the cables to these.

We decided to place the microphones in the windows. These had aluminium frames, which would shield the mikes against detection during normal sweeping procedures, and as they were wired microphones they would have virtually no radiations to detect. When the windows were delivered to the site, we measured the frames, and were able to work out which window was going where. We were thus able to fit the right ones with microphones before they were installed in the building.

We were very lucky with the design of the windows. They were made with U-section extrudings, and installed in such a way that each one had pieces of this extrusion running from head to foot at each side. These side members abutted hard up against the window-sill at the foot, but showed a narrow gap at the head, sufficient to allow air, and hence sound waves, to get into the hollow of the extrusion. This was where we placed the mikes. The surrounding metal made it absolutely impossible to find them with even the most sensitive detector. I have still to find a safer place for a mike.

The last and trickiest task was to couple up the ends of our cables and the leads to the microphones. Although they were within inches of one another, both were concealed, one in the window-frame and the other in the masonry. Our technician scaled the scaffolding one night, disinterred the ends of the wires, joined them up, and made good the damage to the fabric of the building.

At long last the building was finished and the Russians moved in. We sat down to listen to their secrets. The sound came though loud and clear, but it was of nothing but typewriters and typists' chatter. Investigation soon showed that the Russians had, at great inconvenience to themselves, re-organised the layout of the building so that the secure areas were located elsewhere.

What caused them to do this? They had not discovered our microphones, appearing to know which rooms they were in but not the fine detail of where they were hidden. This was exactly the amount of information we had given to the Directorate of MI5. Later, we gave them a more complete report, and within days of our telling them where the mikes were, they were ripped out. This is one of the many coincidences which finally persuaded me that something was rotten at the very centre of MI5.

**DGSE**   These are the initials of the *Direction Général de Sécurité Extérieur*; the French equivalent of MI6.

The first such organisation in France was the Deuxième Bureau, a name which spattered the spy thrillers of the twenties and thirties. Unfortunately, with the fall of France in 1940, the Deuxième Bureau stayed in France, becoming the intelligence network of the Vichy government of Pierre Laval and Marshal Pétain, which collaborated with the victorious Germans.

Meanwhile General de Gaulle had set up his self-styled 'Free French' government in London, and had his own organisation, BCRAM. With the Allied victory in 1945, the Deuxième Bureau passed into history, and the BCRAM formed the basis of the post-war service.

One of the biggest problems of any security service is to decide who the enemy is, and this was well illustrated by the post-war history of the French service. It ran into immediate problems of allegiance because the French Resistance, the Maquis, had tended to be politically left wing and deeply suspicious of the Americans, whereas the Free

French tended to be anti-communist and pro-American.
The patterns of allegiance were further complicated by the
Algerian war, when the division between the political left
and right cut straight across the division between those
who supported the French *colons* (campaigning to keep
Algeria French) and those who accepted that the Algerian
nationalists had to win in the end.

As a result, the security services were in fairly constant
disarray, though in the end they rallied round their old
leader, Charles de Gaulle, to defeat the efforts of the *colons*
and some dissident army officers and support the with-
drawal from Algeria.

By then the service had been renamed the SDECE, and
this name stuck until the arrival of President Mitterrand,
who re-organised it under its present name, DGSE.

I never had much to do with them, for which I was
grateful. A service which cannot decide who is the enemy
at home is unlikely to see clearly who the enemy is overseas. Their most spectacular action of recent years was
in blowing up the Greenpeace ship, *Rainbow Warrior*, in
Auckland harbour, an operation which didn't seem to me
to serve any useful purpose.

**Disinformation**   Disinformation is false information. But the
term is applied particularly to a special class of falsehood,
one which is specifically designed to look like a secret
truth. To achieve this result, you hide it in the most secret
place you can think of where you believe that your enemy
will look. It is no good hiding it too well or too badly.

Many politicians scorn disinformation, saying that
nobody would put any faith in such an unreliable medium
of communication; but they are wrong. It is true that it
depends on your enemy being sufficiently wide awake to
be probing your secret channels and not sufficiently wide
awake to identify disinformation when they see it; but it
fixed the Prime Minister, Sir Anthony Eden.

The affair happened at the time of the Suez crisis, in
1956. We were reading the Egyptian cipher at the time (see
*Engulf*) and intercepted a message saying that the Russians had planes standing by to bomb the British and

French invasion forces if they did not withdraw from the Canal Zone.

We sent the message straight round to Eden. This, more than anything else, persuaded him to pull the troops out. He was afraid of starting a world war, which he hadn't bargained for.

It seems overwhelmingly likely, however, that the whole story was disinformation. Shortly after we started Operation Engulf, the Russians sent a team of sweepers into the Egyptian embassy, and we listened with anguish as they went about their job, the anguish rising to a peak as they unscrewed the base of the phone and peered in.

Now, Sir Anthony Blunt had long before told the Russians all about SF, Special Facility, our device for turning telephones into bugs. So, there was a Russian sweeper, looking straight at the tell-tale washer which he must have immediately noticed and recognised as the sign of SF. But he left it there and screwed the base back on. We ought to have realised that they had guessed that we were using the SF to listen to the movement of the wheels in the machine and hence reading off the cipher, and decided to leave it in place as a channel for disinformation.

This illustrates a very important lesson which every agent should repeat daily at dawn: *if I can do it, so can they*. If you invent the ultimate coding process, you should immediately assume that the enemy have got it too and turn your attention to cracking it. Similarly, if you invent a way of bugging them, you should immediately assume that they know you are doing it and are doing it to you. Finally, whenever you think you have been so clever that you have stolen a march on the world, remember that it is at such moments that you are likely to open a ten-year-old copy of *Mechanix Illustrated* and find your 'invention' described in detail by somebody in Red Bud, Illinois.

For another probable example of disinformation, see *Penkovsky, Colonel Oleg.*

**D-notice** D-notices are like puncture repair outfits for leaky security systems. They work like this:

Suppose that you are the government and you have a

skeleton in your cupboard which somebody is about to
leak to the newspapers. You call in all the top newspaper
people and say 'We have got this secret, but we think you
are so important that you ought to know about it. However, before we tell you, we must ask you to promise that it
won't appear in your paper.'

The newspaper people are very pleased to be reminded
how important they are, and promise not to tell. When
they get back to their offices, the leaked version is on their
desks, but they have promised to keep it out of their
papers, so the story is suppressed.

D-notices were originally invented for censoring the
newspapers in Britain during the Second World War without actually censoring them. After the war, the governments still found plenty of things they wanted to hide, so
D-notices are still around.

**Dossier, The**   When I left the Service, it was quite evident that
there was still a lot of unfinished business to be attended
to, so I wrote an account of it all for Mrs Thatcher, a lady
whom I thought at the time to be just what the country
needed. I called it *The Dossier*.

It said that there were a lot of matters which needed
attention. Of around 230 code names of agents which were
known to us (see *Bride*), we had only identified around
thirty with their owners. This left over two hundred moles
and agents in high places in Britain, plus God knows how
many of their recruits. In particular, there was a fifth agent
who had worked with Philby, Burgess, Maclean and Blunt,
a person high up in MI5.

The Dossier didn't work. Instead of investigating MI5,
Mrs Thatcher gave it to MI5 for their opinion, and they
gave themselves a clean bill of health.

This was how *Spycatcher* came to be written. Few people
who had studied the evidence disputed that there was a
fifth man – they just said I was wrong in thinking it was
Hollis. However, they didn't say who it was. Anyone with
an ounce of concern for the realm would have been trying
to answer that question rather than discrediting the person
who was asking it.

Recently, they seem to have realised that this crucial question ought to be scotched, so they picked on a person called John Cairncross to be the Fifth Man, and made a facile TV documentary about it. The documentary consisted largely of a man walking round and round a TV studio setting with pictures of agents on the walls. Quite why he couldn't stand still was never made clear. At one stage, he started talking about a fire, and they made the lights in the studio flicker like a fire. It was all very melodramatic, but not very convincing. The main problem was that their choice of candidate for the Fifth Man, John Cairncross, had been one of the first we had looked at and rejected as not fitting the facts; see *Cairncross, John*.

**Double agent**   A double agent is a person who is working for both sides. In particular, it refers to a person who pretends to work for one side but is really working for the other.

Of course, he may only be pretending to work for the other, and really be working for the first lot all the time. Or all this may be a pretence, and you find he is really working for someone else altogether, like Mossad.

There are two problems with running double agents: the first is that you can never be really sure who they are working for, or (more importantly) who they will be working for tomorrow if the pay is right; the second problem is that running double agents can take an awful lot of time for very small return.

Both of these problems were apparent when I joined the service. A great proportion of our effort was devoted to getting and running Russian double agents, and I reckoned that it was a waste of time. Apart from anything else, they were all blown.

For example, we had turned two Russian agents, and were running them in place, in other words, telling them to go on pretending to work for the Russians. The Russians gave them suitcases for safe keeping, and told them to put them in their lofts and in due course a mysterious someone would come and collect them.

Well, this was very tempting if you took it for real. If we were able to follow these 'strangers' when they came for the suitcases, they might lead us to the any number of other illegals – agents who were not accredited as diplomats, that is. So we pulled all the Watchers out of London, and sent them to watch those houses for mysterious strangers. Weeks later no strangers had showed up and the whole operation was abandoned.

Actually, it was pretty obvious what they had done. We should have seen it from the contents of the suitcases. They contained a couple of wireless sets of a type which were used early in the war for agents to communicate with one another. Since the war spies had never used wireless to communicate with one another, as it was far too dangerous. So the whole thing was a leg-pull. They wanted the Watchers out of London and thought this scheme up to get them out.

Adding it all up, the net result of recruiting those two double agents was at best nothing, and at worst a lot of damaging waste of time – to say nothing of the mischief the Russians got up to when the Watchers were out of town.

**Driberg, Tom**   Tom Driberg was one of the more colourful Labour members of the House of Commons in the years after the war. For us, however, what was more important was that he was one of our agents in the Communist Party of Great Britain. He was recruited by Maxwell Knight, who specialised in infiltrating the CPGB, and was given the code name M8. At least, that was Maxwell Knight's story.

Maxwell Knight used to hand in reports of what Tom was telling him, just as if he was a real agent. It was all convincing enough for Tom to be blown by Blunt, and thrown out of the Party for a time. However, he was also a Czech agent, under the code name 'Crocodile'. They were paying him a lot of money to work for them. We knew that from the defectors who came over to us after the 1956 troubles in Hungary.

As a result of this, I took over running him from Maxwell Knight. The first thing I asked him about was the Czechs. One of the defectors, a man called Frolik, had given us a list of the Czech Intelligence Officers who had run Crocodile, so I got a whole lot of pictures of Czech IOs and laid them out on the table. I asked Tom which ones he recognised. He picked exactly the ones Frolik had said, but claimed that they had commissioned him to write articles for them about the politics of the Labour party, for publication in a Czech magazine.

How did all this fit together? First, he was undoubtedly telling us things about the CPGB which they did not want us to know, so he was certainly betraying the comrades. Second, there was no doubt at all that, although he was Chairman of the Labour Party and a Member of Parliament and a distinguished man of the left, the cheeky bugger was selling articles on the vulnerabilities of Labour Party leaders to the Czechs. There is also no doubt that his story about them being published in a magazine was rubbish; we had irrefutable evidence that they were going straight to Czech intelligence. So it was easy to make Tom Driberg out as a nasty multiple traitor.

However, he may have genuinely believed that he was a popular columnist in a Czech equivalent of the *New Statesman*, and he seems to have been quite unaware that even if the articles were being published, this was not quite the right thing for the Chairman of the Party to be doing. Similarly, if the comrades had asked him about his connection with Maxwell Knight, he would probably have said 'Maxwell is just a friendly fellow who rings up from time to time asking me how things are going, and it is generally the morning after a CPGB meeting, so we chat a bit about it'. And he might even have believed it.

The fact is that by that time nobody took Tom very seriously.

**DST** This organisation, whose full name is *Direction de la Surveillance du Territoire* is the French equivalent of MI5. I found them very cultured people with a fine taste for food and wine, and so long as you never told them anything important, all was well. It is not that they are riddled with moles – their record in this respect was better than that of MI5. But I never acquired a taste for Frogs.

**Dunkirk** People sometimes wonder why, early in June 1940, the Germans stopped short of overrunning Dunkirk, allowing the greater part of the British Expeditionary Force to escape back to England. Operation Dynamo, as it was called, rescued over 300,000 troops.

The usual explanation is that, having achieved victory thus far by mobility and surprise, they were reluctant to risk it all by becoming involved in a static infantry battle where the numerical superiority of the British, French and Belgian forces might prove decisive.

Maybe this is so, but another reason is that they saw no need to move in closer, as they believed that the British troops were doomed anyway. The shallow waters off Dunkirk were the perfect place for a blockade by magnetic mines, and their planes and E-Boats had sown what looked like an impenetrable minefield. They believed that every sizeable ship which approached the shore would trigger a mine and be destroyed. The survivors would then surrender, and Britain would be forced to sue for peace.

They were unaware that we had in the preceding few weeks perfected our degaussing techniques. By the time the evacuation become necessary, every boat big enough to trigger a mine had been degaussed. The entire operation went off without a single ship being lost to a magnetic mine; see *Degaussing the* Prince of Wales.

**Dust, hairs and dashes** Everybody knows how clearly the slightest disturbance shows up on a dusty surface, and anyone who has tried will know that once you have disturbed a dusty surface it is very difficult to put the dust back.

This makes dust a very good way of checking whether something has been touched or moved. You can use a very light dusting of powdered chalk, coloured to match the material it is on. The effect is to produce immediately a virtually invisible coating of dust, indistinguishable from the one which would settle naturally in a couple of days.

Similarly, if you find you have disturbed some dust, the only way to cover your tracks is to wipe the whole area clean and apply a new coat of dust.

Hairs can be used in much the same way. If you want to know whether a book has been opened, you trap a hair between two pages, and it will be disturbed by any attempt to open the book. What is more, there is no real defence against this: it is very unlikely that you will notice the hair, and, if you do, very difficult to put it back exactly as it was, as people can adopt ways of inserting the hair which are as characteristic as their signature.

Indeed, signatures are another area where a bit of thought can save a lot of trouble. The best protection against forgery is to add some simple element which will appear to be accidental – a small dash or dot – which will not be reproduced by the forger unless he is aware of its significance. My signature has been forged many times, and I could tell you how to pick the forgeries in a moment. As it happens, I won't. That is a secret between me and just a very few people who need to know.

# E

**E Branch**  When I went to Cyprus, it was on E Branch business; see *Archbishops, bugging of.* E Branch was the section of MI5 which operated in the colonies.

It was quite a busy department. They had to keep an eye on the various nationalist and anti-colonialist movements in all the remaining colonies, of which there were still quite a number. Apart from India, which had become independent in 1948, the British Empire was still largely intact.

My first big job for E Branch was to bug the private discussion rooms at Lancaster House. Lancaster House was where the Constitutional Conferences took place between the Colonial Office and the people to whom power was being handed over. However, whenever a really difficult question was being discussed, the emergent gentlemen left the main conference room to have private discussions. The Colonial Office needed to know what they were saying in there, because otherwise they couldn't negotiate properly, not knowing what the bottom line was. So they got us to bug all the rooms.

The rooms were alike, and decorated much the same way, so the temptation was to find the best place for the mike and mike every room in the same way. The trouble with this procedure was that if they found one mike, they would be sure to check the same place in all the other rooms, so we would lose the lot. If we had been doing a temporary job, just for the one conference, we would have had to risk it, but we were asked to install permanent wiring into Lancaster House, as it was used for a lot of important conferences, so it was worthwhile to work out a different position for each mike. What is more, we fitted them all up with high grade microphones, binaural ones, so that you could tell from the direction who was talking. It was very good.

It seems to have worked. The Colonial Office reached satisfactory agreements with almost everybody, and by the time I left the service ten years later, there were virtually no colonies left for E Branch to worry about. None except the Falkland Islands, Gibraltar and Hong Kong, that is.

**Ellis, Charles**   Charles Ellis, known as Dickie, was an Australian who had joined MI6 in the 1920s. He was very good at languages, and at first worked among the White Russian émigré community in Paris, where he got involved with a certain Vladimir von Petrov. The nature of the involvement remains a mystery. According to MI6, Ellis recruited von Petrov to run against the Russians and Germans. But according to Abwehr records, von Petrov was one of their men and had recruited Ellis to run against us, while the GRU defector Krivitski had named von Petrov as one of their best men.

The trouble was that all of these stories could be true. The best cover for any double agent is to claim to be running the person who is running him. But there was enough doubt about it for a memo on the subject to be sent to MI6 by MI5. The report went to the head of the MI6 counter-intelligence department, who scribbled on it 'Who is this man Ellis? NFA' (meaning No Further Action). This was an odd comment, since the name and description exactly fitted the person in the next room but one; not so odd, perhaps, given that the head of MI6 counter-intelligence was Kim Philby.

Some time later Philby himself came under suspicion and left the Service, and Ellis too retired from MI6 and took a trip back to Australia, where he became a consultant for ASIS.

Ellis had not been in Australia long when he was told

about the impending defection of Vladimir Petrov; see *ASIO*. He immediately flew back to London, where he was known to have been in touch with Philby. A few days later, Petrov became aware of unusual activity at the embassy which suggested that his plans to defect had been blown, and defected immediately, some days earlier than had been planned.

Such was the evidence immediately available to me when I took over D3. It was all circumstantial. But I thought it was strong enough to force me to re-open the case.

At one stage, I thought that the coincidence of the pre-war brush with a Vladimir von Petrov and a post-war one with a Vladimir Petrov was too good to be true, but it seems it was a genuine co-incidence: the two men had nothing in common except their names.

After a long investigation we finally persuaded Ellis that the evidence of his having given information to the Abwehr was too strong to be denied, and he confessed, saying that he had been hard up and did it for the money, his last contact being in December 1939, three months after the outbreak of war. But he continued to deny that he had ever worked for the Russians. This seemed to me strange: he was denying action which could have stemmed from an honest, if misguided, ideology, while confessing to selling out for money to a country with whom we were at war.

News of his confession made me no friends at all at MI6. In fact, if there were two affairs which caused trouble between the two organisations, it was the unmasking of two traitors, Philby and Ellis. It was like a Greek tragedy in which the king gets angry with the messenger who brings the bad news. They were quite right when they said that the things I was finding out were depressing, but it is an odd security service which deals with its moles by keeping quiet about them.

**En clair** This French tag means 'in plain language', as opposed to 'in cipher'. It is used as an adjective 'the *en clair* text' and as an adverb 'The message was transmitted *en* *clair'*. Note that a plain language message would still be called *en clair* if transmitted in Morse.

**Engulf**  This is the name of an operation devised by me, to read machine-generated cipher. For the general principles of cipher machines, see *Cipher* and *Enigma*.

It seemed to me that there was one moment in the day of these machines when they were vulnerable, and this was the moment when the machines were being set to the new day's 'core position'. The operation of the system depended on having identical machines at transmitting and receiving ends, both set the same way, and for security they changed the settings each day to a 'core position' which had been determined in advance.

I believed that if we could hear the people setting up the wheels in the morning, we would be able to work out what they were doing. Then, if we could also hear the machine whirring and clacking away, we would be able to identify the positions of the wheels and hence read off the cipher.

This was 1956, and what came to be know as the Suez Affair was brewing. The Egyptian President, Gamal Abdel Nasser, was being very obstreperous, and the Foreign Office wanted to know what he was really up to. The Egyptians used a Hagelin machine, so this was chosen as the machine to try my technique on.

I first tested my theory by borrowing a Hagelin from GCHQ and setting up a model of what I proposed to do. If you get a microphone and attach it to an oscilloscope the oscilloscope will show a 'picture' of the sound the microphone is picking up. The 'picture' is actually a graph of the current coming out of the microphone, but it is exactly proportional to the sound going in, showing how the amplitude (the amount of current) varies over time. Today, sounds can be analysed even more precisely using digital recording and computer analysis, but the visual analysis proved to be remarkably accurate and powerful.

Every sound-making device makes characteristic sounds, with differing transients and overtones, and this goes for noises as much as for music, so the oscilloscope 'picture' identifies a source of sound just as a fingerprint identifies a person. I hoped that each wheel of the Hagelin would be so different that the 'picture' of the noise of adjusting it would not only enable us to say which wheel was being adjusted, but also what adjustment was being made.

The tests worked. I tried several types of microphone, including the latest Satyr and SF devices. I had an oscilloscope running while I messed about with the wheels, and set up a camera to film the oscilloscope. Then the film was sent down to the experts at GCHQ to see whether they could tell what I had been doing.

They could. At least, Hugh Denham, who was looking after things at their end, said that they could interpret enough to crack the cipher, which was all that we needed. Just as the number of permutations goes up exponentially as you increase the number of stages in an enciphering process, so it shrinks rapidly if you remove them. Provided we could read *some* of the wheels, the cipher could be read, as they could test for all the combinations for the remaining wheels, going on until they came up with one which yielded a sensible text. Operation Engulf got the green light.

They had found that the SF mike gave better results than Satyr, so we faulted the Egyptians' phones and waited for them to report it. In the event, we did better with the SF than we had dared hope. I had gone in dressed up as a Post Office engineer, and one of the clerks asked me to lengthen the cable on the phone so that it would reach to his desk – right by the Hagelin.

We recorded the sounds of the machines, and soon became adept at converting the faint clicks and whirrs into movements of the wheels. Operation Engulf was the first of a whole series of similar operations all over the world to read machine cipher from Hagelin-type machines.

For an odd outcome of Operation Engulf, see *Disinformation*. –

**Enigma** Of all the achievements of British intelligence, the greatest was the breaking of the German Enigma machine cipher in World War Two. It had been widely believed that machine ciphers were unbreakable. For a general description of how these machines worked, see *Cipher*.

The Enigma machine was by far the most sophisticated cipher machine in the world at the time. It had been invented in 1929 by Arthur Scherbius, and was immediately adopted by the German military authorities for all their secret communications.

The Enigma machine was essentially an electric typewriter, with a normal typewriter keyboard. You keyed in your message as a string of letters. It then produced a different string of letters, showing no apparent relationship to the original. The output not only used all letters with equal frequency, but also showed equal frequency of all letters in representing any given letter in the original. The substitution thus appeared to be totally random.

The enciphered message was then transmitted as Morse. At the far end, the Morse was decoded into letters, the letters keyboarded and the *en clair* message revealed itself.

The first steps in breaking the cipher were a matter of extraordinary luck for British intelligence following some very smart work by the Poles. They had managed to get hold of the wheels out of one of the Enigma machines, and were working on using this to break the cipher when, on 1 September 1939, the Germans invaded their country. The Poles realised that the wheels could be of immense value to the allied cause, and they were duly conveyed to London.

Diagram A below does not show what the wheels were actually like, but may help to explain how they worked, and hence what was involved in breaking the cipher.

Each wheel had a series of studs on one side connected to pins on the other, and the ends of the pins made electrical contact with the studs on the next wheel. Thus any pulse of electricity which entered at the left hand end passed down the chain and emerged on one of the wires at the right hand end.

However, each pulse triggered a relay which caused the right hand wheel to move round by one notch. Furthermore, every time the right hand wheel completed a cycle, it triggered a one-notch movement of the middle wheel, and this in turn triggered a similar movement of the left hand wheel.

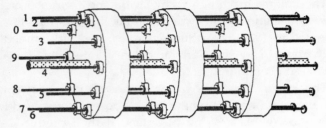

Diagram A

If the wheels had been wired straight through, so that each stud was connected to the pin closest to it, the machine would have shown patterns which would have been obvious to any cipher-breaker; but the wiring through the wheels was not regular. Diagram B shows just one possible configuration.

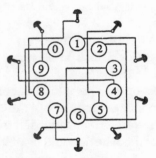

Diagram B

Thus any one of the studs on these ten-stud wheels might be connected to any one of the pins, giving 362,880 settings of each wheel. The three together would still not represent an infinite number of combinations, but they would offer nearly 40 quintillion (40 and fifteen noughts) of them, each of which would have a period of 1000 characters (i.e. a thousand different configurations of the wheels relative to one another before the cycle started again) any one of which could be the 'core position' (starting point) for a given message.

In fact, as suggested earlier, the above is a *simplified* description of the *principle* of the machine, designed only to show the cunning of its designers and the genius of those who broke it. For break it they did.

Getting a set of the wheels was the first breakthrough. It enabled the cipher breakers to know what to look for. But investigations of the wheels also enabled the cipher-breakers to reduce the number of combinations which needed to be tested to a fraction of the theoretical range. Without the wheels, it is probable that the cipher would not have been broken.

But the real thanks then went to the Germans for providing a massive supply of collateral. They did this accidentally, thanks to their depressing passion for tidiness. The German military mind appears to be incapable of starting a message without reciting an elaborate introductory incantation. Just as clerks used to write 'We are in receipt of your favour of the 15th ult', so the Germans opened their top secret messages with gratuitous formulae. There was, of course, a range of formulae, depending on who you were, who you were writing to and the topic; but if the cipher-breakers knew where a message was coming from, they could have a pretty good idea about words and phrases to look for.

The combination of all these things meant that Enigma was first broken within months of the beginning of the war, and regularly from then on. It was still not easy. It was a daily race against time. Each day, the settings had to be determined by taking a guess at the content of a signal, and then working out the configurations of the wheels which would produce that set of values. These were applied one by one to the rest of the message. If a readable German text emerged, all was well; but there were a dozen different reasons why it might not: the whole procedure was based on guessing what the introductory formula had to be, and boringly predictable though the Germans were, there were many more ways of being wrong than right. Even so, in hundreds and hundreds of cases the cipher-breakers were successful, giving us

THIS (PREVIOUS) EXPLANATION
of THE ULTRA AFFAIR IS
WHAT CIPHER SPECIALISTS
would CALL, "A GAMBLE".

forewarning of secret weapons, plans of attack and so on.

The biggest problem with Enigma, in fact, was to know when to act on the information and when not to. This is a problem which afflicts all eavesdroppers. The problem is not that eavesdroppers never hear good of themselves – they can live with that – but that every time they take action, they run the risk of blowing the fact that they were eavesdropping.

What the Enigma people did, and what we did under similar circumstances with information from Operation Rafter, etc., was that whenever we found a piece of information we wanted to use, we invented an alternative source from which we could have received it. All references to the information would be subtly distorted to give the impression that we had got the information from a prisoner of war, a traitor or a spy.

**Erk**   see *Boffin*.

**Eye**   This word now means a private detective, but originally meant a security intelligence officer. The first security officers were called Eyes.

Many people reckon that the best way to measure a civilisation is by checking its consumption of soap. Maybe, but you can also measure it by checking its provisions for security intelligence, and it works even better. The longest lived civilisation the world has known, the Egyptian, was held together by intelligence gathering networks and the magic of written language, not by plumbing.

China was much the same. Its borders have remained largely unchanged for over two thousand years, despite the fact that its people speak many different languages and in some cases have much less in common with one another than with their neighbours over the borders. If there was one thing which held the country together, it was the written language. It transcended dialect, communicating the emperor's edicts to all corners of the Middle Kingdom and enabling local agents in those places to report back to the court.

Eye was a normal Chinese word for intelligence officer

in the Chinese State Papers. Centuries later, at the time of the Unequal Treaties, they used the phrase 'Barbarian Eyes' to describe the British agents posted round the country to watch what was going on and report on anything which represented a threat to the security of British interests. The Chinese had seen Eyes before, and knew what they were for.

The first security intelligence system of which we know much detail is the one in the court of the Great King of Persia, around 500 BC. The intelligence officers were known as the Eyes of the King, and they were everywhere.

The idea of having Eyes was so well established there that when Persian children played at being kings, the first thing the 'king' did was to appoint Eyes. We know this from Herodotus, who says that this was how Cyrus came to power. He first became king in a children's game, but he organised his Eyes so well that the game just went on and on until he took over the country.

The Persians also realised the importance of getting the intelligence back to headquarters. The Eyes communicated with the king by means of chains of bellowing messengers posted at earshot intervals along the great roads which ran from the capital, Persepolis, to the most remote regions of the empire.

Anyone who has tried the party game of passing verbal messages down a line knows that it is not a very accurate or secure way of transmitting intelligence, but it was a lot better than nothing. The result was that the Persian Empire, which was really quite a ramshackle affair, held together for some time despite military defeats.

By contrast, Alexander the Great's empire fell apart without ever being defeated. This may be because Alexander was not interested in plumbing, but more likely because he never set up a proper intelligence gathering system, or the couriers and roads needed to keep all parts of his empire in touch with one another.

The Romans learnt this lesson, and right from the start built roads whose purpose was not only to move troops but also to speed on its way the *cursus publicus*, the imperial post. This was the great secret weapon of the central government, carrying instructions on the way out and intelligence coming back. At first they used relays of mounted messengers, but Emperor Augustus realised that it was better to use a single messenger who travelled all the way in a horse-drawn carriage, changing the horses at intervals. It was not quite as quick, but it was a great deal more secure.

# F

**F Branch** was the part of MI5 which organised domestic surveillance. This meant that it looked after the dangerous organisations of Britain. It was the smallest and least important part of the Service.

When I first joined MI5, the main concern of F Branch was the CPGB (Communist Party of Great Britain) and the discussions they were having with trade union leaders about how to disrupt the country with strikes and so on. This was fair enough – these people were damaging the country just as treacherously as if they were selling information in a war; see *Bugging the CPGB*.

I also approved F Branch activity against the IRA. Whatever you thought about the rights and wrongs of the situation in Ireland, you couldn't have people going about letting off bombs in public places and killing and maiming innocent civilians. That is terrorism, and there is no cause so good that it justifies terrorism; see *Ireland*.

However, a lot of us felt very uncomfortable when the orders came down that we were to take the heat off the KGB and apply it instead to what was called 'the far and wide left'. This turned out to be an assortment of ratbag political groups like the Socialist Workers Party and Workers' Revolutionary Party, which despite their frightening names were about as dangerous as a pondful of ducks.

It was worse when it was extended to include organisations like CND, the Campaign for Nuclear Disarmament. The Nuclear Disarmers may have been misguided, but were certainly not treacherous. This is an important distinction. People are always going to be arguing about what is good for the country, and that is called political freedom. But political freedom does not include the freedom to betray your country to its enemies. That is treachery.

One of the hardest things in the world is to distinguish between a misguided patriot and a traitor. We thought we knew the difference, and for many of us the CND fell the right side of the line. We did not object to checking that the CND had not been penetrated, just as we did with the Red Cross and Oxfam and all sorts of other do-good organisations. But we did object to the idea that the CND was itself a hostile organisation, or that membership of it was simple evidence that a person was a security risk.

At that time, we had only recently completed a very successful operation which had crippled the KGB's effectiveness in London, and we wanted to keep up the pressure. But no. Resources were switched from K Branch (counter-espionage) to F Branch (domestic surveillance). When I last saw it, F Branch was the growth area in the Service, and that was something I didn't like the look of at all. It seemed more and more like a Gestapo.

**Family, indoctrination of**   If you interpreted the Official Secrets Act literally, a Security Officer couldn't tell his wife where he worked.

This was rubbish, of course, because the wives were constantly being dragged into MI5 activities. They were used for crowd scenes (see *Bugging the CPGB*) and they often drove around with us, especially after Hugh Winterborn and I pointed out that having women in the cars was good cover. In fact, in my case, my wife drove me around, particularly after I had lost my licence; see *Toad, the Ingenious Mr*.

Even so, deciding how much to tell was always a problem. It was not that the secrets were unsafe with our wives, it was that our wives were unsafe with the secrets. There was always the fear that the wives would be kidnapped and interrogated under torture to get information, and the best defence was to make sure they never had any information which was worth torturing them for.

In any case, we never told our families more than they needed to know. For example, my daughter Jenny knew that I was a scientist and a Civil Servant, and that was all. Until the Lonsdale affair, that is. For the details of how this blew my cover; see *Lonsdale, Gordon*.

**FBI** The Federal Bureau of Investigation has. no real equivalent in Britain, though it does, amongst other things, most of what MI5 does.

People who (like the British) live in a country with a central government sometimes find it hard to understand the workings of a Federal system, in which the legal and administrative powers are divided between the Federal authorities and the States. When Al Capone was taken to court for tax evasion rather than murder, this was because the FBI could get him for tax evasion, 'a federal rap', whereas murder is a State offence, on which the FBI could (theoretically, at least) take action only if the dirty deed was done within the District of Columbia.

The division of powers between the Federal government in Washington and the legislatures in the various States is laid down in the Constitution. Originally, the Federal government looked after foreign affairs, which included defence, immigration, customs and foreign trade, while the States looked after just about everything else – law and order, health, education and so on. However, as government activity became more complicated, the power of the Federal government gradually increased. In particular, it became responsible for everything which involved more than one State. This is why the crossing of a State line is so significant: a State crime may become a Federal crime the moment it is being committed in more than one State.

In addition, the Constitution itself is a Federal document, so that any breach of the Constitution is a Federal offence. This is why a lot of civil rights reformers have gone about the business of reforming civil rights by appealing to the Supreme Court. They ask the court to re-interpret relevant clauses in the Constitution to mean what they want them to mean. The Constitution is full of high-sounding phrases which may mean everything or nothing, so that the Supreme Court can sometimes act more like a Legislature than a court.

I say all this just in case anyone doesn't know it, because if you don't know it you will never understand why the FBI operates as it does. It was not originally set up as a security organisation. It was a police organisation, with a network of detectives and law enforcement officers whose job was to do law enforcement jobs which the individual States were unwilling or constitutionally unable to perform.

The first of these involved large scale business corruption and fraud, and this tradition has continued to the present day. During the First World War, the FBI got involved with security matters almost accidentally, as the only body in a position to act against German saboteurs operating in the USA. It performed badly, proving only that a more professional approach was necessary.

The turning point came in a totally unspectacular way in 1924, when J. Edgar Hoover was appointed director of the still ineffective and unimpressive FBI. Nobody could possibly have thought that Hoover would make it a job for life and turn the organisation into the biggest and most sophisticated law enforcement agency in the world.

One of the jobs which the Bureau was handling at the time was the enforcement of Prohibition. Prohibition was Federal business, not simply because it involved traffic across State boundaries but also because it involved the Federal Constitution. It had been enacted by means of an amendment to the Constitution – specifically, the Eighteenth Amendment of 1919. It had come in as the climax of a great popular campaign, inspired by the writings of Upton Sinclair and other would-be social engineers, which mobilised thousands of innocent victims of alcoholism with a dream of a sober utopia.

The amendment had not had quite the effect which had been intended. Instead of ridding the country of the curse of alcohol, it had merely turned a large legal industry into a large illegal industry. The respectable citizens who had previously grown rich on brewing and distilling were replaced by criminals who were growing even richer doing the same thing under less regulated and hygienic circumstances, and not paying taxes.

Hoover realised that here was a major campaign through which to build an enforcement empire, and he set about it with a clarity of vision which remains unparalleled in the history of modern private armies. From the start, the success of the campaign in achieving its purported aim, i.e. the enforcement of the Eighteenth Amendment, was incidental to the real task of developing the FBI into a self-perpetuating and self-sustaining organisation. In practice, however, these two aims were complementary: the same dedication and discipline which were necessary to the independent survival of the organisation were also ideally suited to an effective, incorruptible law enforcement agency. They became known as 'The Untouchables'.

Not least of Hoover's discoveries was the power of the dossier. One of the features of the American democratic system is the effective absence of a permanent civil service. In theory, all public appointments fall vacant every time there is an election, and while those in relatively humble positions can generally assume that their employment will be renewed by the incoming administration, those at the top can be equally sure that their jobs have been promised to somebody else. Knowing that this is the case, most top civil servants resign as a matter of course if their political masters are thrown out by the electorate.

Not so J. Edgar Hoover. The first time it happened, it was not too surprising: the 1928 election resulted not so much in an accession as a succession, with Herbert Hoover the anointed heir to Calvin Coolidge's throne; so it was naturally business as usual at the FBI. The atmosphere was entirely different in 1932, when Franklin D. Roosevelt defeated Herbert Hoover and was swept to power with the promise of the New Deal, but once again it was business as usual at the FBI with J. Edgar at his desk the next morning.

Precisely what J. Edgar Hoover had or did that made Roosevelt leave him in the job is not known, but there are plenty of theories. Despite his polio, Roosevelt was a womaniser, to say nothing of getting involved in some political activities which he was reluctant to be reminded of in public. Whatever the means, however, the end was clear: J. Edgar Hoover kept his job, as he did through the presidencies of Truman, Eisenhower, Kennedy and Johnson and into that of Nixon, during which he died (1972), still in control of the monster he had created.

He had been in control for thirty-three years, with fifteen still to go, when I first visited the FBI in 1957. The Bureau was still dealing with hoodlums as it always had done, but Hoover had found counter-espionage a game very much to his liking, and from being a small part of the Bureau's activities it had become one of the largest.

In the area of my own interest and expertise, they had little to teach us. Their scientific people did not seem to be as resourceful as ours: they had far better equipment, but made less use of it, so that in the end their advantage was dissipated. Furthermore, I could see that they were having problems trying to run a counter-espionage organisation within a police organisation, because dealing with spies is not the same as dealing with bank robbers and bootleggers.

The police connection affected their recruiting and training procedures and many of their daily routines, right down to their regular target practice with handguns in the basement of their Washington headquarters. We didn't do that sort of thing at Leconfield House.

However, the police connection did mean that they were able to teach us some useful lessons. For example, they used fingerprints as a routine part of their investigation of suspects, and the value of this was apparent.

But the feature of the FBI which I found most impressive was something which came straight from J. Edgar Hoover, and this was the sense of long-term mission and purpose. Whether it was a good mission and a right purpose is beside the point. I thought it was, but even if I had thought they were totally misguided, I would have had to admire their belief in their own destiny. It was this which has kept them out of trouble through more than half a century of very tricky, sensitive activities. The reputation of the CIA had risen and fallen with a sequence of coups and disasters, so that no one could possibly describe them as dependable or responsible. But the FBI had the reluctant admiration even of those who disliked it most. It could easily have become involved in Watergate, as the CIA did; but it did not. It could easily have harassed anti-war protesters or civil rights workers or any of hundreds of dissidents, as the CIA did, but it did not.

It was not that Hoover was tolerant or liberal. It was just that he knew a strategic error when he saw one. With him, the demands of long term strategy prevailed over tactical expediency. This is the mark of a mature organisation.

**Fibonacci system** Leonardo Fibonacci, also known as Leonardo da Pisa (1170–1240) was a mathematician whose main claim to fame was that he played a major role in introducing Arabic numerals into Europe.

His name appears most often today associated with the Fibonacci system, in which you ignore numbers which are 'carried' during addition. We write (Fib) before the line to remind ourselves that it is a Fibonacci addition. Thus,

$$(\text{Fib}) \ 999 + 222 = 111,$$
$$\text{and}$$
$$(\text{Fib}) \ 999 + 111 = 000$$

The Fibonacci system is widely used in codes, because it allows numbers to be added together without acquiring extra digits. (In the examples above, the answers would all be 4-digit numbers in normal addition.) For another example of calculations using the Fibonacci system; see *One-time pads*.

You may be wondering how a mathematical system can be useful if it gets the wrong answer. Leaving them out seems rather a crude and unhelpful way of getting rid of extra digits. The answer is that if it is followed by Fibonacci subtraction of the same number (that is, subtraction in which you ignore numbers which you have had to 'borrow') you get back to the correct original:

(Fib) $111 - 999 = 222$

Thus encoding and decoding using this system involves getting 'wrong' answers to two sums, but the errors cancel one another out and the final answer comes out right.

It is one of those minor miracles of mathematics, which must have seemed like pure magic when it was first noticed all those centuries ago.

**Files, altering of** There must very strict rules about altering files in security records offices. In theory, files should be inviolable. The only time when it is sensible to alter a file is if, for example, you find that some of the information in it is wrong. However, there have to be rules about making the corrections: any alteration has to be made in such a way that you know who has made the change, when and why.

That was the rule in the MI5 Registry, and most of us obeyed it very carefully. If we wanted to delete an entry, we had put a line through it in such a way that it could still be read, and write our personal codes and the date. This is why Ian Carroll, who ran the Registry, was furious when he found that the Director General, Sir Roger Hollis, had removed a whole page from a file without leaving any marker, so that, but for a lucky break, no one would have known who did it or when.

The file in question was on the Profumo case. This was a salacious tale of how a Minister for War, John Profumo, had shared a high class tart, Christine Keeler, with a Russian naval attaché, Eugene Ivanov. If you used that as the plot of a novel, nobody would believe you. Add the fact that the tart's manager, Stephen Ward, had a holiday cottage in the grounds of Cliveden, Lord Astor's country retreat, and that the Minister met the tart when she was swimming nude in the Cliveden swimming pool, and the whole thing was too good to be true.

Astonishingly, there was even more to it than this, because Roger Hollis had got the idea of trying to get Profumo to recruit Ivanov for MI5. Now, getting Ivanov wasn't a bad idea, but you don't ask the Minster for War to go recruiting Russian agents for you – that's a silly thing to do. What's worse, he had written and signed a letter about it, so that there was a record of his silliness in the file.

The whole affair had then become the subject of a judicial inquiry before Lord Denning, and Hollis must have decided it would be better if Lord Denning did not see his letter. So he took it out.

Not surprisingly, Ian Carroll was very angry about that, saying that there shouldn't be one law for the DG and one law for everybody else. He was right.

**Foreign Office**   This is an organisation dedicated to undermining the security of the realm.

Our job at MI5 was to protect Britain against subversion and espionage. Thus, whenever we identified somebody in the Russian embassy who was doing any subverting and spying, we tried to throw them out. Before we could do it we had to get the approval of the Northern Department Committee of the Foreign Office, who almost always refused permission. They believed that their main job was to stop anybody doing anything to upset the Russians.

Courtney Young, who was head of D Branch at the time, summed them up after our first meeting. He said, 'I've never seen such a hotbed of cold feet.'

Everybody was against us on that committee. First, there was the MI6 rep., who was always worried that the Russians would throw some of their people out of Moscow in reprisal. That was fair enough, except that the Foreign Office was so weak that they had let the Russians go on and on adding to their strength in London. The Russians had forty-five Intelligence Officers in their London embassy at the end of the war, but by the late 1960s this had grown to three hundred.

However, the FO people raised even sillier objections.
They kept saying that it would upset trade, as if the sale of
a bit of wheat was worth more than national security. And
anyway the Russians were starving at the time, and were
unlikely to cancel a wheat order to teach *us* a lesson.

Then the FO had grandiose ideas about being able to
negotiate with the Russians about missiles. They kept
saying that we must not upset things because negotiations
were at a delicate stage. The truth was that negotiations
were never at a delicate stage, because the Russians didn't
care a bugger about our missiles.

This was not new. It was the same weak-kneed attitude
which had resulted in the Munich agreement with Hitler.

**Friends**  When a person from the Foreign Office says he is
calling in the Friends, he does not mean that he is seeking
help from the Quakers. He means MI6.

# *G*

**GCHQ**   These are the initials of the Government Communications Head Quarters.

The spiritual origins of GCHQ can be traced to the celebrated Room 40 at the Admiralty. It was here, in World War One, that Reggie Hall collected together a group of intellectually brilliant people whose purpose was to apply the latest information-gathering technology to the waging of war. They made a decisive contribution to the Navy's role in the defeat of Germany. My father was involved with them; see *Wright, G.M.*

After the war, the Room 40 team was disbanded, but its contribution was not forgotten. In the rearmament program in the thirties, one of its founder members, Commander Alastair Denniston, revived its spirit in the formation of the so-called Government Code and Cipher School, located in Nissen huts at the back of the MI6 retreat in Bletchley Park.

This unspectacular investment probably paid off more handsomely than any other part of the rearmament program. Denniston collected another extraordinarily talented group, including Hugh Alexander, better known as the chess master C.O'D.H. Alexander. Their greatest achievement was cracking the German military cipher; see *Enigma.*

This time, the end of the war did not bring about an end in the operations; quite the opposite. Signals intelligence, SIGINT for short, was recognised as one of the most important aspects of defence preparedness in times of 'peace'.

So the staff and equipment of Bletchley Park were moved to Cheltenham, forming the basis of a new organisation, GCHQ.

GCHQ was assigned a monopoly in SIGINT work. This meant that all traffic, whether collected by GCHQ itself or by the monitoring stations run by the services, was channelled through a single set of analysts, the best in the country. This minimised (though it did not of course eliminate) the risk of important traffic being overlooked or misunderstood. (Often, two separate pieces of information of no apparent value can together make up an important item.)

The monopoly also provided the British government with an organisation to nominate as signatory to the SIGINT agreement with the United States. This agreement involved the sharing of information, and was possible only if the signatories at both ends were totally trustworthy and the distribution of material kept to a minimum.

The monopoly had, however, an unfortunate side-effect. Denied the resources to do much monitoring on its own account and forbidden by the SIGINT agreement from doing the follow-up analysis of monitored traffic, MI5 had effectively moved out of electronic surveillance. MI5 seemed to make a virtue of its ignorance of technology, while GCHQ had a contempt for everything else. The net result was that they had nothing to talk about. Communication between MI5 and GCHQ was conducted at a six monthly meeting between two middle-ranking officers, neither of whom was in a position to develop an effective liaison. This was the situation when I arrived at MI5.

My problem was twofold: firstly, I had to prove to GCHQ that they had something to gain from working with us; secondly, I had to prove to my colleagues in MI5 that they had something to gain from working with GCHQ.

MI5 started taking electronic surveillance seriously following my work on cavity microphones (see *Thing, The* and *Satyr*). The discovery of The Thing showed that the Russians were taking electronics seriously even if we weren't, and Satyr showed that we could do it too. Once this was proved, it was obvious that we had to work more closely with the people who were really equipped to do it properly: GCHQ.

With GCHQ, the real breakthrough came with my development of Operation Rafter, which opened up a whole new area of operations for them. The immediate outcome was the Radiations Operations Committee (see ROC), the first truly co-operative venture between MI5 and GCHQ, but the long term effect was to break down the barriers of jealousy and mistrust which had kept the two organisations apart.

It is perhaps significant that when I left the service twenty years later, my contribution was recognised more clearly at GCHQ than at MI5. As one of them said at my farewell: 'Most people are pleased if they are responsible for one major invention or innovation during their careers. Peter was responsible for seven.'

**GCMG**  (Grand Cross of St Michael and St George). In the protocol lists, this is the top order of knighthood. It is given to people like retired ambassadors. Now, let us say that a very senior ambassador has been dallying with the KGB, and we find out. If he was sent into early retirement without any GCMG, the Russians would say, 'Look at that, sent to Bournemouth without a GCMG. They must have known all about it.' So, to keep the Russians guessing, the GCMG is never withheld. Otherwise there would not be so many of them.

**Gehlen, General Reinhard**  The story of this man illustrates what happens when you apply the principle that your enemy's enemy is your friend. It is a principle that gets you some very odd friends. I am glad that I had nothing much to do with Gehlen, as he was a nasty bit of work even if he was very anti-Communist.

In the Second World War, he was head of the Abwehr (Military Intelligence) section covering the Eastern front, and built up a massive network of spies all over Russia. Their reports were systematically filed, and provided dossiers on thousands of important and potentially useful Russians.

On the collapse of Germany, he managed to take personal charge of his files, and let it be known in American intelligence circles that he had them. It was not long before the Americans took the bait. They reckoned that anyone who was an enemy of their new enemy, the Russians, was a friend of theirs. Within a year of the defeat of his earlier paymasters, the Nazis, Gehlen was back in business as the Gehlen Organisation, a private, US-funded anti-Communist intelligence organisation, operating out of premises in Pullach, a town near Munich. He brought back many of his old Abwehr colleagues and reactivated his networks in Russia.

But he did not restrict himself to his old wartime contacts. One of his early expansions was into Egypt. In the late 1940s, President Nasser of Egypt was involved in a continuing struggle against the newly established state of Israel. 'Any enemy of the Jews is a friend of mine' said Gehlen, and the Gehlen Organisation assisted Nasser in setting up *Mukhabarat el-Aam*, the Egyptian General Intelligence Agency.

This caused problems with the Americans, who were backing Israel. The problem was resolved when the Russians came down firmly on the side of Egypt. 'Any enemy of the Russians is a friend of mine,' said Gehlen, and proceeded to establish links with the Israeli intelligence service, Mossad.

Meanwhile, the Gehlen Organisation was proving a great embarrassment to Chancellor Konrad Adenauer and the West German government. However, there was a complication. Like J. Edgar Hoover in the FBI, Gehlen had made it his business to get dirt on the lot of them, so no one was very keen to move against him. Finally they came up with the answer: to take over the Gehlen Organisation and give it official status as the national security intelligence agency, leaving Gehlen in charge of it.

So it was that, in 1956, Adenauer suddenly declared Gehlen his 'beloved General' and West Germany became blessed with the curiously named BND, *Bundesnachrichtendienst*, the Federal News Agency.

**General Post Office, GPO**   The General Post Office was a British Government instrumentality for intercepting mail and tapping telephones. (I say 'was' because the tapping of telephones has since been privatised. However, the interception of mail is still handled by the GPO.)

Every major telephone exchange had a Special Investigations room equipped for putting taps on the lines to that exchange.

The main mail interception centre was Dollis Hill, London. There was a room there full of kettles for steaming open envelopes and bits of split bamboo for getting the letter out if the flap didn't come undone in the steam. They slid the bamboo in under the flap, grabbed the edge of the paper between the two halves of the bamboo and then twisted, rolling the paper up into a tight cylinder which could be eased through the corner of the flap.

After it had been read and photographed, mail was generally put back in the envelope and sent on to its addressee. They were not supposed to destroy it. However, it was quite tricky to get it back with the bamboo, especially if the paper was very flimsy, and if they could not get it back in original condition it had to be destroyed. People don't like getting letters which are all creased and curly.

Also, they were not supposed to keep it. They broke this rule once, with a letter which had been addressed to a leading Communist, but which actually proved to be to us! It read 'Dear MI5, if you steam this open you are dirty buggers'. Naturally, we kept it. Firstly, it was addressed to us, which made it legally ours, and secondly it broke the laws about sending obscene articles through the mails.

The Post Office had an effective monopoly on the carrying of letters and operating the telephone service, and hence provided a one-stop shop to approved security organisations. Today, organisations wishing to obtain complete surveillance must consult the relevant private courier companies and the now privately owned British Telecom, who bug telephones and supply copies of other people's faxes at market rates.

For a discussion of the origins of the General Post
Office, see *Walsingham, Sir Francis*.

**Germans**   I never really got to like the Germans. Their engineering is very good, and their theoretical science is first
class, but for two examples of how their discipline lets
them down, read *Enigma* and *Tidy mind, dangers of*.

However, the biggest problem in my day was that
all their services were riddled with agents. This was
not surprising. During the Nazi period, one of the main
groups opposed to Hitler was the Communists; see *Rote
Kapelle*. After the war, many of the Rote Kapelle people
became associated with the new Communist government
in East Germany, and their old comrades in West Germany
continued to communicate with them. Thus the East Germans had a spy network in West Germany from day one.

When you went through West German passport control, it was as likely as not that the person checking your
passport was also reporting to the East Germans. It was
the same in their security organisations: it looked at one
stage as if one was run by the Communists and the other
by Nazis; see *BfV* and BND. As a result, we didn't have
much to do with either of them, so that when we mounted
an operation there we generally acted on our own.

I went over there in 1959 to help MI6 mount an operation, and stayed with the MI6 chief. The MI6 Station Office
was in the embassy in Bonn, and the Head of Station
doubled as Passport Officer. MI6 people all have to have a
proper job, and looking after passports is a very common
one, because you can meet all sorts of people without
arousing suspicion.

He couldn't keep his MI6 stuff in the passport office. To
keep it out of sight they had built MI6 an office in the space
under the roof. If you wanted to get to it, you had to climb
up a ladder.

**Gibson, Harry**   Harry Gibson was an MI5 officer in the 1930s
who organised the nearest approach to a genuine penetration of the Russian service we ever achieved. It was not
quite as good as their Ring of Five, but he organised a Ring

of One, which was one more than anyone else did.

Gibson had been at school in Russia, where he had made a number of friends. He kept in touch with them, and when he became an MI5 officer he recruited one of them as an agent. This man became a senior member of Anastas Mikoyan's staff when he was Minister for Trade, and handed on some quite useful information.

All might have gone well except that his reports were sent to the Director General of MI5. They were supposed to be seen only by the DG himself, but they naturally passed through the hands of his staff. At this time, one of the staff members in question was a young man called Anthony Blunt, who was a Russian agent. Blunt passed the information to his controller, and shortly afterwards the flow of messages ceased abruptly. Blunt later heard from his controller that the Russians were grateful for the information and had dealt with the problem.

So ended the most promising mole we ever had in the Russian service.

**Gifts**  People who are in important positions ought to be very careful about accepting gifts. It they don't go off bang, they are liable to spy on you.

The ultimate gift was, of course, the Trojan Horse, where agents were hidden in the gift. This was something which we never tried.

The nearest true equivalent to the Trojan Horse was a class of operations based on getting surveillance devices into embassies in the guise of gifts. This was particularly necessary in the case of the Sovbloc embassies, to which we had strictly limited access. Basically, we could not get our people beyond the public areas of these embassies, and getting a device in was the only way.

We classified the donated devices as *discoverable* and *non-discoverable*.

The discoverable class was typified by the large presentation edition of a book with a radio microphone embedded in its tooled leather cover. Once the device was found there could be no doubt about its purpose, so that the operation was effective only until the moment of discovery.

A microphone in the binding of a book may sound crude, but even in my day miniature bugs were being developed which could be hidden almost undetectably in the most innocent-looking objects. Today, they are smaller still. The only real defence against them is that if half the world is being bugged, the other half has to be listening, and having tried both, I'd prefer to be bugged any day.

The non-discoverable class contained no hidden devices, so that there was in a sense nothing to discover. This class was typified by the ashtray with a shape designed to resonate well at audio frequencies and with surfaces which would reflect radio beams. The hope was that the gift would be placed on the table in a conference room, and we then directed a radio beam at it from a house across the road. The sound waves in the room made the ashtray vibrate, and the vibration of the ashtray made the reflected beam shimmer in time with it. Our radio receiver produced an electric current whose amplitude and frequency were governed by the shimmer, this current was then fed into a loudspeaker and presto, you would be listening to the conversation in the room.

The good thing about these devices was that it was impossible to prove that such gifts were Trojan horses, since the characteristics could easily occur accidentally. Thus almost any hard object has resonating surfaces which could be used in this way, but this would not prove that it was intended for this purpose. We found that the head of Lenin was not suitable as a resonator, but there was some future in giving the Russians replicas of the Kremlin.

In practice, however, it was found that such devices had few advantages over items which were likely already to be present in the rooms, e.g. filing cabinets, or the windows. The only problem was to find a position on the resonating object where its vibrations were as true as possible a replica of the sound waves in the room, without too many overtones and distortions.

The gift that goes bang was happily something we never considered sending anyone, but we had to devise defences against them. We pioneered the inspection of containers with X-rays; unsolicited packages arriving at sensitive destinations should always be X-rayed before being opened. GCHQ developed special soft X-rays to avoid fogging film; see *X-rays*.

Finally, there were modern equivalents of the case of Hercules, who died from the gift of a tunic impregnated with the venom of the Lernæan hydra. I regret to say that this was something which we did experiment with. I will never forget my horror on seeing an experiment at the Chemical Warfare Research Station at Porton Down: a sheep suddenly keeled over and died moments after being hit by a pellet carrying nerve gas. It was the only time when my two great loves, security and animals, seemed to come into conflict.

**Golitsin, Anatoli** Like most of the big breaks for Western intelligence in the early 1960s, the defection of Golitsin was a stroke of luck. He simply walked into the US embassy in Helsinki with his wife and children and said 'Here I am'. All we had to do was to debrief him, and we didn't do it too well. The trouble was that he was smarter than most of his interrogators, and knew it.

The information he brought with him was so incredible that they couldn't believe it. For instance, he said he had seen a lot of NATO documents which had been so secret that only half a dozen top people had had access to them. So they tested his claim, showing him a bundle of documents, including both the ones he claimed to have seen and others which he couldn't have seen, as they had been forged specially for the test. He was shown the whole lot and then asked which ones he had seen before. Golitsin passed this test with flying colours, picking all the real ones and passing over the forgeries.

For us, however, the most important thing about Golitsin was his report that there was a Ring of Five agents in top positions in the British Civil Service, including one in MI5. Given the accuracy of all his other information, we had to take this seriously.

For the most important outcome of the Golitsin serials, see *Hollis, Sir Roger.*

**GRU** These initials stand for *Glavnoye Razvedyvatelnoye Upravleniye*, the Russian military intelligence service.

The GRU is in many respects a more straightforward operation than its ugly brother, the KGB. Many of its activities are carried out by 'legals', e.g. military attachés whose job is to look after military aspects of diplomacy. This will include anything from attendance at military ceremonies to acting as liaison officers in joint military adventures with allied armies, but it also includes reading all the literature, including technical magazines and brochures prepared by arms manufacturing companies, and attendance at public demonstrations of new weapons, e.g. the Farnborough Air Show. This is exactly what the spy does, but in the case of the military attaché it is all above board. Everybody knows that they will try to find out as much as they can about the items on show, and the game is to turn it into an opportunity for spreading a bit of disinformation.

In addition, the GRU ran agents working undercover. Most of them were in armaments factories or military bases, and their job was to get information on new weapons, tactics and strategy. Thus their activities were much more practical than the KGB, who would do almost anything if they thought it would make trouble for us.

For more on my most important brush with the GRU, see *Lonsdale, Gordon.*

# H

**Hats, choice of**  When I first went to work in MI5, I found that they all came to work in bowler hats, just like other Civil Servants, so I got a bowler hat, too.

Unfortunately, I was also a part-time farmer, and had a Land Rover I used to drive about in. This vehicle was liable to carry various animals, mostly dogs, but occasionally a pig or two. I was driving along one day with my bowler hat on the passenger seat and some dogs in the back, when suddenly one of the dogs leapt over into the front and put a great paw through the crown of the hat.

Very fortunately, I had just received a present of a bini from an aunt who was a great knitter. Better still, she had sent a very long scarf to go with the bini, the two together being a complete uniform for a football fan. The scarf was in St Peter's colours, yellow and blue, and very long, so that I could wrap it round my neck twice and still have it hanging down to the hem of my overcoat.

**Head waiters**  If you go to a restaurant and put a microphone in the vase of flowers in the middle of the table, you need to have the head waiter in your pocket, because otherwise he is sure to take the vase away for some reason or another.

We had a list of co-operative head waiters at MI5 (see *Resources index*). They not only helped with the microphones, but also did some watching for us. They would phone up and say 'So and so has just booked a table', giving us a chance to bug the table if we wanted to. Of course, if it was somebody from an embassy, we usually knew, as we had been listening to the conversation ourselves. But there were times when somebody had made the booking on an untapped phone and we were very grateful for the head waiter's help.

Another thing they did was to phone and say 'So and so was here from 12.00 until 2.30'. They knew that we were always interested in where people were and as a contribution to our Movement analysis.

All in all, head waiters are very valuable people. They are also very discreet people, because they don't keep their jobs for long if they are not.

**Helicopters**   These useful aerial surveillance vehicles are hard to conceal, being both noisy and visible. The helicopter from which we surveyed the roof of the Russian embassy in London carried the colours of the Duke of Edinburgh.

**Helms, Richard**   Helms was one-time head of CIA. He was subsequently booted out for not telling the NSA, the National Security Agency, that he was bugging us (the British).

This might suggest that the NSA thought it was impolite to bug an ally. This is not so. The NSA were all in favour of the CIA bugging us; indeed, they would have done it themselves except that they had sworn not to under the SIGINT agreement. What made them angry was that Helms had not handed on the results to them.

**Hollis, Sir Roger**   Not many people have to worry about the loyalty of their bosses, and a good thing too. The suspicions about Sir Roger Hollis when he was Director General of MI5 bit deeply into the morale and effectiveness of MI5 over a long time. It was no fun for any of us.

There are some people who say that we, the people who tried to get Hollis properly investigated, were the ones who caused all the trouble. This is rubbish. Once there are suspicions, the only way to get rid of them is to prove them false, and that is all we were trying to do.

After all, we did not invent the suspicions. To my knowledge, people had been worried about evidence of penetration of MI5 since 1943, and Hollis had been mentioned as a suspect long before I came on the scene. (For a discussion of the early suspicions, see *Mitchell, Graham*.)

By the time I became involved, the suspicions were based on two lots of evidence, one from outside and one from inside the Service.

The best outside evidence that there was a mole in MI5 was information from Operation Bride (q.v.) and various defectors, notably Golitsin (q.v.). Golitsin gave us a mass of information about KGB illegals operating in many countries, and of these, one of the most important was the Ring of Five, which he described as a group of five exceptionally important agents, highly placed in the British Civil Service. He did not know their names, but he was able to tell us their code names, and where they worked. One of them was in a top position in MI5. With this and the Bride material, we were able to draw quite a detailed profile of the people we were looking for.

Two of the profiles matched with two known Russian agents, Guy Burgess and Donald Maclean. They had defected in 1951 and were known to be in Moscow, so there could be no doubt about them. Two more matched with suspects who were soon to be confirmed, Anthony Blunt and Kim Philby. But the last one, the spy in a top job in MI5, remained unidentified.

The information we had was in some ways like an identikit photograph. Identikit photos can show you the *kind* of person you are looking for, so that they are very useful for eliminating suspects; but once you have a room full of suspects, all with dark hair and big noses, the identikit cannot give any further help. It was the same with the profile of the Fifth Man compiled from the Bride material and information from defectors. Hollis fitted the identikit better than anyone else, but this by itself was no proof of anything.

The inside evidence that there was a mole in MI5 came from some bitter experiences with operations. Every major operation we had mounted against the Russians had had

PROBLEM — GOLYTSIN ONLY KNEW THAT THE AGENT WAS IN (QUOTE), "FIVE-OF-MI". NOBODY KNEW WHETHER THIS MEANT "MI-5" OR "DEPARTMENT-5 OF MI-6!"

disappointing results. It was not that the operations had gone wrong: technically, they were totally successful. But they did not achieve the results we had hoped for. A typical example was Dew Worm, an operation to bug the Russian embassy in Ottawa. It failed because, at the last minute and at considerable inconvenience to themselves, the Russians moved the KGB facilities from the room we had bugged to another one, leaving us listening to some typists talking about their boyfriends; see *Dew Worm*.

But why suspect Hollis? Essentially, it was a process of elimination. We analysed each operation which had been blown, working out what the Russians must have known in order to take the counter measures they did. Then we made a list of all the people in MI5, crossing off those who did not have the information and hence were eliminated as suspects.

This gave us lists of suspects for each leakage. By comparing the lists, we could see which names occurred the most frequently. The answer was clear: Sir Roger Hollis's name was on every list. The name of his deputy, Graham Mitchell, also loomed large, but Hollis was clearly out in front.

Of course, this proved nothing. In any organisation, the boss ought to win the who-knows-most-about-what-is-going-on competition. If there had been two names which were left behind by the process of elimination, I would have gone first for the one who was not the boss. Indeed, we did eliminate Graham Mitchell before homing in on Hollis, although he seemed a much less likely bet. But any other explanation was even more difficult to reconcile with the facts: it would have involved postulating not just one mole, but several.

In addition, there were strange little subtleties. In the case of Dew Worm, it was that we had initially reported that the room was bugged but not how we had done it, and at that stage the Russians just moved the KGB out of range of our microphones, leaving the microphones in place. Six months later, we gave up the operation and handed Hollis our report on it, giving the technical details. A fortnight later the Russians sent in the Sweepers, who went straight to the mikes and ripped them out.

Now, this evidence is certainly not enough to enable you, the reader, to decide whether Hollis was guilty. It should, however, give you enough to answer some less critical questions.

First, would you agree that, at least until a more likely one was found, Hollis had to remain a suspect? Secondly, would you think it worrying that a suspected enemy agent had been in charge of the country's security services? Third, if you feared that this was so, would you just keep quiet about it, or would you consider it your duty to get a message through to someone who could do something about it, like the Prime Minister? I answered these question yes, yes and yes. The immediate outcome was The Dossier, which I sent to Mrs Thatcher. It got nowhere, as outlined under *Dossier, The*.

The subsequent debate revolved around the question *Was Hollis a Spy?* the implication being that a not guilty verdict would enable us to close the file and get on with our business. Nothing could have been further from the truth. A guilty verdict would have been encouraging, marking the end of the long search for the mole and the beginning of a cleansing process. A not guilty verdict merely meant that the search for the mole was not over.

Then they changed tactics again, suggesting that it didn't matter any more? The implication was that it was all old hat, as if treachery were biodegradable, decomposing with the passage of time. It is certainly true that Russian agents can do a lot less harm in the nineties than they could in the seventies, but that is because of the decline of Russian power. It is not that the spies themselves are less dangerous.

Now, I just don't like the idea of having foreign agents in the Security Service, even if they are working for a minor or even friendly foreign power. It seems to me that our security services should be working for us. After all, it is the British taxpayer who is footing the bill.

If, therefore, we have uncontested evidence that the Service was penetrated and that the identity of at least one important mole remains unknown, it raises an uncertainty which is not resolved by sweeping the whole problem under the carpet. We need to know what operations they knew about, or organised, and which current people were recruited by them. It is all very well to say that asking questions like this can cause innocent people to fall under suspicion, but if you don't, then everybody is under suspicion.

Because I still think that Hollis was the Fifth Man, I am pretty confident about the present service. I know the worst that he could have done and I know that it is under control. But if it wasn't Hollis, who knows?

(For a lunatic answer, see *Cairncross, John*.)

**Howl-back**   This is the name of the horrible noise which sometimes comes out of a public address system. It occurs if a microphone starts listening to itself on a loudspeaker.

Every microphone 'hears' a constant background noise, made by the molecules of air beating against its diaphragm. However, the effect is so small that it is not normally noticed. If, however, the microphone 'hears' an amplified version of this sound coming from the loudspeaker, it recycles it through the amplifier and loudspeaker ... and again ... and again. In a matter of microseconds the inaudible sound builds to a howl.

It can be minimised by making sure the microphones and loudspeakers do not point at one another. The initial sound which generates the howl is minute, and unless the microphone and speaker are on line-of-sight, diaphragm to diaphragm, it is unlikely to occur except in ultra-sensitive equipment.

Howl-back was used by Sweepers to detect bugs transmitting at radio wavelengths. In the simplest case, all you needed was a receiver with a loudspeaker. You pointed the loudspeaker at the place where you thought the bug might be, and then adjusted the frequency of the receiver up and down the spectrum of wavelengths at which the bug might be working. When you hit its wavelength, it would set up a howl between its microphone and your loudspeaker.

However, this only worked if the transmitter was on. This was so if the device was battery-powered and permanently on, or if it was powered by some other internally controlled source, e.g. the current generated by sound waves hitting the diaphragm. But sweepers had to watch also for devices which were turned on and off by being irradiated from a distance. In such cases you had to discover the characteristics of the radiation required to turn it on, which was easy enough if you had got the gadget and could measure its components, but very difficult if the purpose of the exercise was to find the gadget in the first place.

Today, bugs are even harder to detect than they were in my day.

**Identity, mistaken** Some readers of *Spycatcher* were a bit puzzled about how the Watchers managed to mistake Lonsdale (a Russian illegal they had never seen before) for a known Polish Intelligence Officer. It sounded like incompetence.

What was really more surprising was that mistakes like this were so rare. The Watchers used to sit in their little rooms overlooking embassy entrances day after day, year after year, watching the people going in and out (see *Watchers*), or in the cars, doing the same thing with even greater difficulty and discomfort. They had to get very good at recognising people on sight, because although they had a mug book which could be used as a check, it was no good turning to a book containing thousands of photographs hoping you would immediately find a photo of the stranger just walking past the window.

Well, it seems that the Watchers who were put on the Lonsdale case identified Lonsdale as a particular IO from the Polish embassy who had not been seen for some time. They then watched for him at the Polish embassy, but he never turned up again; and when they checked with the mug book, they realised that they had been wrong all along.

You might say 'They ought to have checked immediately' but that is the trouble with checking facts. You can't check everything, so you check the facts you are not sure about. In the present case, the Watchers thought they recognised him, so they didn't check.

One of the things which gave them false confidence was that they had been told in advance to expect somebody from UB, the Polish intelligence organisation. This meant that as they watched and waited for Lonsdale, they were probably thinking of all the Polish IOs they knew. And then they saw what they had been told to expect.

In fact, the reason for thinking it might be a Pole was very far fetched. The person who gave the original lead to Lonsdale provided the information in anonymous letters to the CIA, and all we knew about him was that he wrote bad German. From this, the CIA had assumed he was Polish, and hence that his information would be about UB operations. There are so many holes in this logic that it is just a bad joke, but it shows how a mistake can grow.

However, even if it had not been a mistake, the Watchers should not have been told who to expect. This broke an inviolable rule: if you ask people a question, never tell them what answer you are expecting, as they always seem to oblige.

**Illegal**   see *Legal/illegal*.

**In place**   This phrase is used to describe somebody who is working for us as an agent, but whose value stems from the position he held when we recruited him. He therefore continues 'in place' in that job while working for us.

It applies particularly to foreign agents, e.g. KGB officers, who have been 'turned'. Thus, Oleg Penkovsky (q.v.) was run 'in place' for several years by both MI5 and the CIA.

**Indoctrinate**   In general language, this word usually has a nasty taste to it, as in the sentence 'The children were indoctrinated into believing that it was necessary to spy on their parents'. This has undertones of other evil concepts like brainwashing and thought police. Actually, this sense is very new, dating from World War Two. Until then, it was a perfectly good word meaning 'to teach', with a special connotation of teaching religious doctrines.

This is the way the security services used it. It was the normal word for letting somebody in on a secret. Thus if I said 'I have indoctrinated Angleton about Rafter', it meant that I had told Angleton all about the secret operation called Rafter.

**Intelligence Officer, how to identify**  If you were in a British embassy, it was easy to tell which of the staff were MI6: they were the ones with direct outside-line telephones on their desks.

This was not much help in identifying the Russian IOs, because you never saw them at their desks. If you got friendly with a Russian embassy staff member and asked for his telephone number, he gave you the embassy switchboard number.

You could still find out whether he was a spy if you wanted to, but the process was less direct. You phoned him up and waited to see what happened. If you were put through to his desk, he was not a spy. If he was a spy, he would have to be summoned from the secure section of the embassy, which had no switchboard lines into it; so you had to wait while he came to the phone.

The next step was to measure the length of time it took him to get to the phone. By careful analysis of such measurements, you could work out the position of his office or desk in the secure area. By carefully correlating this kind of information, we worked out the whole layout of the secure area, which helped a great deal in identifying the members of each group of IOs.

The same technique could be used the other way round. Having found that there was an IO with a given code name working in the embassy, you could give him a face and a real name; see *Movement analysis* and *Who's who at the embassy?*

**IO**  These initials stand for Intelligence Officer, a general term covering middle ranking members of espionage and counter-espionage organisations.

**Ireland**  I spent a lot of time in Ireland, and it was not pleasant. We all saw and did a lot of things there which I am never going to talk about, because it would just cause more trouble.

The real trouble in Ireland is memory. God knows there are a lot of people in the world who have been very unpleasant to one another, but in most countries they soon learn to live together, and after a couple of generations it is all over. But the Irish have been fighting the Battle of the Boyne for over 300 years, and if anything the bitterness is greater than ever.

Sometimes, when I saw what the Ulster Unionists did to preserve their position, and heard the things their leader Ian Paisley said, I found myself wishing they were not on our side, and would start feeling sympathy for the Republicans. But then the IRA would come along and let off a bomb in a shopping centre or some other place chosen simply for the publicity it would get, and I would feel like stringing the whole lot of them up.

That was the real tragedy. There were thousands of people on both sides who just wanted to live in peace and harmony, but any move in this direction was answered by a bomb or a bullet through a kneecap, and the next day the talk would once again be of violence. And, thanks to having separate schools, etc., the next generation was being prepared to carry it on.

I'm afraid it has got no better since I left.

# J

**JIO** It is an absolute rule of organisations that if you have two of them, you have to have a third to co-ordinate their activities and adjudicate on demarcation disputes. If the organisations in question are involved in security, this is particularly necessary but also particularly difficult: you can only act on what they tell you, which may be precious little.

The JIO was the Joint Intelligence Organisation, a Cabinet committee on which the heads of the security services sat. In theory, it was the channel through which we got our instructions from our political masters and they got the answers back from us, but in practice it rarely happened that way. Apart from anything else, it was chaired by one of the wets from the Foreign Office, and nobody wanted to listen to them, still less tell them anything important.

I was not at all surprised, therefore, that the Franks Committee was very critical of the JIO's contribution to the Falklands War, when its advice was so misleading that it nearly caused a total disaster. Fortunately it didn't, but the JIO has since been re-organised to make sure that doesn't happen again.

**John, Otto** Otto John was the first director of the *Bundesamt für Verfassungsschutz*, the Federal Office for the Protection of the Constitution, the West German equivalent of MI5; see *BfV*.

He was the absolute opposite of Reinhard Gehlen, who ran their equivalent of MI6. John had a very good record as a leading member of the resistance to the Nazis, and seemed in every way the perfect man to protect the new German Constitution. It was thus a great shock to everyone when he suddenly turned up in East Berlin, making broadcasts in which he was very critical of the West in general and the West German government in particular.

The assumption was that he had defected, and when he later returned to the West he was put on trial as a defector. In his defence, he told an astonishing story about how he had been drugged and kidnapped in Madrid by East German agents, and woke up to find himself in Berlin. They had then used various means, including drugs and threats to his family, to force him to make the speeches denouncing the West.

The court was not very convinced, and he didn't get his job back. But he only served a short term in gaol, whereas they might have locked him up and thrown away the key.

# K

**K Branch**  An alias for D Branch; see *D Branch*.

**KGB**  This is the *Komitet Gosudarstvennoye Bezhopaznosti* (Committee for State Security). It has no real equivalent in Britain. From our standpoint at MI5, the most important of its activities was overseas espionage and subversion, in which it was the Russian equivalent of MI6 or the CIA. However, it had a wide range of domestic responsibilities which in some respects paralleled those of the FBI: it looked after domestic political surveillance, the border guards and passport control.

Its oldest tradition was that of domestic political surveillance. In this, the KGB was the direct descendant of the Tsarist Okhrana, a political inspectorate with teeth. Its job was to see whether the decisions of the Tsar were being properly carried out in the far corners of the vast realm, and, if not, to do something about it. The job involved using a range of sticks and carrots. The main carrot was the one which secured the allegiance of the Okhrana rank and file: the offer of a secure, relatively well-paid job. The sticks were the sanctions which could be applied to enemies of the Tsar, including imprisonment, torture and execution.

The need for such a political inspectorate did not cease with the revolution. Indeed, it increased. Even in areas of the country where all military action had ceased, there were other enemies of the new State to expose and punish, bourgeoisie and kulaks. To organise all this required very special skills, skills which were easiest obtained by recruiting those who already had them, namely, the officers of

Okhrana. So it came about that after the revolution, many of the same secret police came to be operating from the same barracks and prisons, but with a new leader, Felix Dzerzhinsky, and a new name, Cheka, the Extraordinary Commission for Combating Counter-revolution and Sabotage.

The Bolshevik Cheka (1917–23) in turn became the Stalinist GPU and OGPU (1923–34), which became the NKVD (1934–46).

These were, however, fundamentally domestic organisations. Activities outside the borders of the Soviet Union in the 1920s and 1930s tended to be in the hands of the Comintern, the Third Communist International of 1919. The Comintern was conceived by Lenin as an evangelical international organisation dedicated to spreading the good news that the workers of the world had nothing to lose but their chains. The theory was that this good news would stimulate the workers of Western Europe to rise against their masters and usher in the Communist millennium. As it happens, successes were few, but it was these agents of the Comintern, many of whom were not even Russian, who recruited the people who were to form the great spy rings of the Second World War: the Rote Kapelle, the Rote Drei and the British Ring of Five.

During the war, yet another peril arose, this time from defeatism and subversion within the Red Army. To counter this, the Russians set up the organisation known as Smersh, so dramatically described in fiction that it is sometimes forgotten that its existence was fact. Its name was an acronym for *Smert Schpionam*, Death to Spies, and it was possibly the most brutally effective of all Russian 'security' organisations. It mounted a few offensive operations, infiltrating agents into German-occupied Russia to identify and murder collaborators and organise resistance groups. However, its main activity was domestic, identifying those who, for a variety of reasons, were looking forward to a German victory and even supplying recruits for German units.

There were plenty of them. Firstly, there were the

ethnic German communities, some of which saw the invaders as liberators; next, there were the nationalists, most notably the Ukrainians but also those of the Baltic States, for whom the Communists were just the latest in a series of unpopular Russian overlords; next, there were relics of Tsarist elements and those, notably the kulaks, who had suffered at the hands of the Communists. While most Russians were prepared to make common cause against the Germans, these various groups provided plenty of targets for a paranoid traitor-seeking organisation like Smersh. In many respects the war was just the excuse; Smersh's operation was another in the series of purges and campaigns aimed at destroying all internal resistance to the Communist State.

After the war, there was a general reorganisation in which the activities of the NKVD and Smersh were distributed between two organisations, the MGB (Ministry of State Security) looking after activities in relation to enemies outside Russia and the MVD (Ministry for Internal Affairs) to handle domestic subversion. The MGB carried on until 1953 when, following the death of Stalin, its chief, Lavrenti Beria, was found guilty of attempting to gain control of both organisations and shot as a traitor. The discredited organisation was then rehabilitated by the simple process of changing its name to the KGB.

In many respects, the KGB continued the tradition of the Comintern rather than that of the NKVD or Smersh. It was thoroughly international in its activities and its composition and it was more sophisticated in its approach than its brutal forebears. Its agents were liable to be suave and worldly. But in other respects it was a throwback, no longer making any pretence to be the vanguard of a great working class movement, but concerning itself only with the safety of the Soviet State and the confusion of its enemies. Technically it was more effective than any Western organisation with the possible exception of Mossad. While it had more than its fair share of defectors, the level at which it was penetrated by us compared favourably (or, from our standpoint, unfavourably) with most of its NATO competitors.

This is not to say that it was a civilised organisation. It maintained a division devoted to *mokrei dela*, wet affairs, which was their euphemism for assassinations. Recent wet affairs, however, have mostly been the executions of defectors from their own ranks.

I must admit to having had a sneaking admiration for the KGB. It is important for any professional to be able to distinguish between the means and the end. Since the end for which the KGB worked was the security of Russia and damage to almost everybody else, including the British, they were and remain my number one enemy. But it is stupid to deny that they went about their job in a very professional way, occasionally acting with a sense of humour which made the Great Game for a brief moment really seem like a game. But then somebody would pull a trigger and you could see that the guns were loaded.

**Knight, Maxwell**   When I joined MI5, Maxwell Knight was one of the legendary people, the greatest agent-runner MI5 ever had. And his reputation was well founded. He had been very successful in the thirties. The secret of his success was his uncanny ability at getting on with people. He could persuade them to do things they didn't want to do, which is the secret of being a good agent-runner.

I didn't trust him an inch. He was a consummate liar. You never knew whether he was telling you the truth or not. He certainly had some great successes, but I have a strong suspicion that in other cases he more or less made up the reports the agents were giving him; see *Driberg, Tom*.

I also suspect that he made a lot of money out of being an agent-runner. He seemed to be getting increasingly wealthy, when he was doing hardly anything. The only explanation that makes sense is that, with Driberg for example, he had made an agreement not to tell MI5 anything about Driberg being paid by the Czechs if Driberg gave him half the money.

# L

**Lawyers**  At MI5, we needed two sorts of lawyers. First, we needed lawyers to act for us, just as any organisation does, but we also needed them to help with our operations.

Being a solicitor for MI5 was particularly difficult as we had no existence in law. He couldn't go to someone and say 'Somebody who doesn't exist wants to buy your house' or 'If you don't stop that somebody who doesn't exist will blow your brains out'. Happily, most people understood that an invitation to 'take tea with the Treasury Solicitor' meant that we were on the warpath.

When I wrote *Spycatcher*, for example, it was originally going to be published by Messrs Hamish Hamilton, but they withdrew from the race after having tea with the Treasury Solicitor. The book then went to Messrs Heinemann, who first handed it over to their Australian people and *then* went off to take tea with the Treasury Solicitor, thereby minimising the risk of being clapped in irons.

We needed a completely separate lot of lawyers to help with operations. It would have wrecked everything if they had been known to be acting for us. For example, suppose that somebody had seen some people breaking into a house over the road and phoned the police. If the house was one which we were interested in, the police would have been told to refer all queries about it to Special Branch. Special Branch would have got in touch with us, and we would have had to decide on the action.

It might have been our people breaking in, or it might

have been the enemy doing something odd there. Either way, we would want to find out exactly how much the neighbour had seen and convince them that there was nothing to worry about, or, if that was not plausible, at least stop them talking about it. It was no good sending in the police, as they would have increased the suspicions and would probably have brought along the local press, the police being very keen on publicity. What we needed was somebody very discreet and reassuring, and the perfect choice was a local family solicitor. So we collected family solicitors, hundreds of them all over the country. Their names were listed in an appropriate section of the Resources Index.

**Laziness, danger of** One of our biggest intelligence coups might not have started but for the fact that Moscow is at work when the Canadians are in bed.

The Mounties intercepted an argument between a Canadian illegal code-named Gideon and his Support Officer in the Russian embassy in Ottawa. Gideon was saying that he had not been able to pick up his instructions from Moscow because of static. In fact, he just hadn't wanted to get out of bed in the middle of the night to listen to a lot of Morse.

His Support Officer did not believe him. He said that he knew Gideon was lying, because he had heard the broadcast coming through loud and clear in the embassy.

This incident gave us an idea. If Russian intelligence officers made a practice of listening to their agents' messages, this could help us to identify them. All we had to do was to check the frequencies and schedules of all the broadcasts coming from Moscow and find out, using Rafter (q.v.), which ones were being monitored in the Russian embassy.

The plan was very successful. We got help from GCHQ to get a signal plan for the broadcasts coming out of Moscow, and identified which ones were being listened to in the London embassy. Even if we could not understand what was being said, the length and timing of the messages was often interesting; see _Chatter_. In a few cases we were able to get possession in advance of the relevant code pads and read the messages themselves; see *Lonsdale, Gordon.*

It also helped us to identify the Support Officers; see *Who's who at the embassy?*

**Leads, bad** Intelligence officers waste an awful lot of time following bad leads. They can come from the best sources. I had one once from the then Director General, Martin Furnival Jones.

It seems that F.J. was at a dinner, and found himself sitting opposite Christopher Mayhew, a leading Labour MP at the time. Mayhew started baiting him about MI5's ineffectiveness in tracking down the Cambridge traitors, and said that we were talking to the wrong people. The clear implication was that he himself, as a person who had been at Cambridge at the same time as Philby and Blunt, had something to tell us. So F.J. bearded him after the dinner, and said he would like to send me round to talk to him. Mayhew agreed.

F.J. passed on the message to me, and I invited Mayhew to dinner at the Oxford and Cambridge Club. We talked about cabbages and kings over dinner, and then moved into a corner of one of the rooms upstairs where we had our coffee and port and some real talk.

Mayhew suddenly said 'What can I do for you?' I told him what F.J. had told me about the conversation over dinner. There was about five minutes silence, and I finally said 'What about it?' To my surprise he said 'I don't see why I should tell MI5 anything. It's your job to find things out.' And he stalked out of the club.

I don't know what he had been playing at during the dinner with F.J. He must have thought that F.J. wouldn't take it up, which was silly of him. Anyway, the next day I reported what had happened to F.J. He rolled his eyes to the ceiling and said 'Record it on the file and we'll forget it.'

Denis Healey didn't waste my time like that. I wrote to him asking if we could meet somewhere and have a chat about his experience of politics in Oxford University when he was there, and got a letter back point blank refusing to talk to me.

The Russians really knew how to waste our time with dud leads. For a good example, see *Double agent*.

**Learning to drive** It is pretty frightening going fast down a one-way street the wrong way, half on the pavement. However, provided you have a police pass and the car is in good condition and the driver knows what he is doing, it is not too dangerous.

The police passes were easy – we all had them. They didn't help you if you hit something, particularly if it was a police car (see *Toad, the Ingenious Mr*), but if the police tried to stop you running through a red light or breaking the speed limit or driving in the wrong lane, you just waved it at them and they let you go.

The MI5 cars were misleading. Most of them looked fairly scruffy, but they were in absolutely tip-top mechanical order. We had a special garage to look after them, where the people not only made sure they were A1 mechanically but also that they were the right colour and had the right number plates for the jobs they would be doing that week. They were very good at giving a car an old paint job.

The drivers had surprisingly few accidents. This was not because of any special training – they trained themselves, and the old hands helped the newcomers. But when we were recruiting we gave preference to people with experience of driving getaway cars and stunt driving. I used to love being driven by them. They really loved their jobs, and took great professional pride in not hitting anything.

**Legal/illegal** These terms were used (originally by the Russians, but we adopted them) to differentiate a professional spy we all knew about from a professional spy we were supposed not to know about.

Thus a Military Attaché was a legal spy. His job was to obtain military intelligence, which meant that he was clearly supposed to be a spy, but he was of no account since he did it openly. As a legal he was no danger to us, being unlikely to find or be given any information of strategic value. Military Attachés tended to dress up with chestfuls of medals and spy on the Trooping of the Colour.

An illegal, by contrast, was a person whose overt job was to do something else, but whose real job was to obtain military intelligence. Thus Gordon Lonsdale was an illegal. He was a Russian, with a wife and family who sent him wistful messages over the airwaves, and he was a full-blown officer in the KGB, not a civilian recruit; but to those who knew him in London he appeared to be a Canadian businessman working in the juke box business, with a keen eye for beddable women.

**Light, use in communications** Archimedes is said to have set fire to an enemy fleet by focusing the sun's rays on the ships, using a shield as a concave mirror. It is alleged that he stood on the walls of Syracuse, in Sicily, and set fire to ships in the harbour below, a distance of a kilometre.

This attractive story cannot be true. The flash point of ships timbers is approx 250°C (depending on the condition and finish of the timber), and it would require a shield of considerable optical accuracy to generate such a temperature in timber at this distance. If the timber were moving, as tends to be the case with the timbers of ships at sea, Archimedes would have needed also a tracking mechanism to cause the shield to follow the movement of the vessel. Today, it would be possible to devise such a system, but this was not available to Archimedes.

Assuming that the story has some foundation in fact, it is most likely that Archimedes was using the shield to convey items of naval intelligence to his own fleet.

If this is so, he can be said to be the inventor of the heliograph, a device which was used alongside the semaphore (q.v.) for telegraphy. It had certain advantages over the semaphore, most notably that it could be read without a telescope, and could be aimed very precisely, making it relatively secure. At its most sophisticated, the heliograph was used to transmit Morse messages.

Its main shortcoming was that it only worked when the

sun was shining, and it was ultimately replaced for all-weather communications by the Aldis lamp. This consists essentially of a very narrowly focused searchlight with a shutter, rather like a venetian blind, which can be opened and shut very rapidly. Messages are sent in Morse or similar codes.

The Aldis lamp has survived into the age of radio for communication between ships which are maintaining radio silence. It was widely used for this purpose in the Second World War. It is rarely of any use in espionage or counter-espionage communications.

**Lonsdale, Gordon** Some people imagine that counter-espionage is all shadow boxing and paranoia. It is certainly true that there are not many cases where one can show concrete evidence of the enemy at work, but this is what we had in the case of Gordon Lonsdale: a real Russian pretending to be a Canadian but talking Russian to himself when he thought he was alone, complete with wireless messages from Moscow, code pads, document camera and a string of informants and contacts.

We were able to watch him, a Russian illegal, in the act of carrying on his daily business of spying, even to the point of being able to decipher his messages as they came in over the wireless. I have still got his special camera.

It would have been even better but for the fact that the Special Branch insisted on issuing a press release and calling in the TV people. We had asked them to give us a couple of days to round up other suspects, but they were so keen on the lights and cameras going that they blew it.

This had another outcome – a personal detail which is worth adding.

After Lonsdale had been arrested, there was still some work to be done in his flat, searching for further equipment and evidence. I had a little Ford Estate car at the time, and my wife Lois had driven me to Lonsdale's flat to do some snooping around.

While I was there, the newspaper reporters and photographers arrived, having been given the address by the Special Branch. There were police on the door who stopped the reporters coming in, so they interviewed all the neighbours they could find while the photographers took pictures of the outside of the building.

That evening, when my daughter Jenny came home from school, she saw a copy of the *Evening Standard* with a large and very identifiable picture of our car on it, standing in front of a house under the headline 'Spy ring broken'. Needless to say, the first thing she asked was 'Daddy, what was our car doing there?'

Up till then, I had told her I was a scientist working for the Civil Service (see *Children*) but not which part of the Civil Service. She was sixteen by then, and quite sensible, and I decided that it was time to stop telling stories, so I explained that the government department I worked for was, in fact, MI5.

She found it all rather exciting. She had always known that my work was secret, of course, and knew what I had done in the war, but had thought it was still the same – radar and other aspects of military technology. Counter-espionage was much more interesting to her than any of that.

Of course, I still did not tell her any details about the operations I was on at any given time, but at least I did not have to be making up stories to cover me for every day of the week.

**Lying to Parliament**  Agents should understand the rules about lying to Parliament, as they will sometimes be involved in devising the lies, or in working out good excuses when the lies are blown.

Some people claim that Margaret Thatcher is the first Prime Minister to lie to the House of Commons, but this is rubbish. The rules have, however, changed recently.

It is true that most Prime Ministers until Thatcher did obey the basic rule which says that ministers must not lie to Parliament, but there has always been one major exception: it never applied to lies which are told in the interest of the State. All Prime Ministers have always lied like troopers in the interest of the State.

This was Harold Macmillan's excuse for lying to Parliament about Kim Philby in 1955. He told Parliament that Philby had been investigated for four years and nothing had been found against him, whereas the truth was that MI5 had put in a report saying that we had found enough about Philby to show that he should never have been allowed near the Secret Service; see *Philby, Kim*. Macmillan justified this by claiming that MI6 would have looked a proper lot of Charleys if he had told this to Parliament, and that this was why he had told the lie.

Certainly it is not a good idea to go around shouting about how bad your own security is; but the people who mattered – the CIA, for example – already knew all about Philby and MI6. To the CIA, Macmillan's lie simply told them that the cover-up was to continue, which meant that nothing would be done about the breaches of security which had allowed it to happen in the first place. It seemed to me that this made us *all* look like a lot of Charleys, and did much more harm to the interest of the State than the truth would have done. But that was just my view. At least Macmillan felt that he had to say that he was acting in the interest of the State.

Mrs Thatcher did something similar when she told Parliament that the Trend Committee had cleared Sir Roger Hollis of suspicion of being a mole. This was *not* what the Trend report said. It said that the evidence was insufficient to get a conviction in a court of law. Again, I wondered who she thought she was deceiving, or why it was in the interest of the State to deceive them, because the only interest she seemed to me to be serving was that of the KGB. But maybe she believed that she was doing the right thing.

The business of lying moved a lot further with the Ponting case. This was a complicated case (see *Ponting Case, The*) but the outcome was that the jury in the Old Bailey decided that, at least in the phrase, 'the interest of the State', the State was *Parliament*.

This was unheard of. If it had been allowed to go

unchallenged, somebody might have suggested next that the interest of the State meant the interest of the British people, or some other dangerous American idea. At this point, Mrs Thatcher solved the whole problem by passing a law which specifically said that, for the purposes of determining 'the interest of the State', the State was 'the Government of the day'. This settled the matter; so now ministers can lie on any subject if the truth would be inconvenient to them, which it often is.

I don't think it was necessary nor desirable to give the Government this much power. At a more practical level, it means that 'the interest of the State' and the list of Official Secrets will change every time there is a change in government. Red faces every five years.

**Maclean, Donald**  The unmasking of Donald Maclean was an outcome of the deciphering of intercepted Russian traffic known in this book as Bride. The decipherment was possibly the greatest achievement in the history of cryptography; a greater technical achievement, even if less spectacular in its outcomes, than the breaking of the German Enigma cipher.

The material was collected in the closing years of the Second World War, and scattered through it were references to the Russian agents operating in various countries. The ones we were most interested in were the 230 of them who were said to be in senior positions in the British government and Civil Service

Each agent had a code name or names (some agents changed their code names from time to time) and by putting together fragments of information, suspects could be sorted out and eliminated. Thus we might be able to get clues about the agents' identities from the kind of information they were supplying, from information on their whereabouts or movements, or little scraps of detail.

It was a little scrap of detail which was the undoing of the agent code-named Homer. From the information he was supplying, he was known to be a senior staff member in the British embassy in Washington, but this meant a suspect list of dozens. Then, early in 1951, a team working on the Bride material produced a fresh scrap: Homer's wife had been pregnant in September 1944. At one stroke, the dozens of suspects reduced to one: Donald Maclean.

What happened then illustrates one of the classic problems facing MI5 (or any such security service operating in a 'free' country). The evidence against Maclean was overwhelming in security terms: for a well-run security service, a suspected mole must be guilty unless proved innocent. The law works the other way. Even if the Bride transcripts could have been produced in court, they would have been no more than hearsay evidence, and in any case we were not going to blow the Bride operation by telling a court about it.

At the time, there were plenty of people who still believed that Maclean was innocent. After the event, of course, all sorts of evidence of his irresponsibility came to light, along with claims that the Foreign Office had him on a suspect list and were investigating him. But the reality was that he was in charge of the US Department, which is not the position you give to a suspected Russian agent, even if the suspicions are not strong. However, the Bride material was too damning to ignore, so he was put under surveillance, the hope being that he would be caught making contact with his Russian friends.

The Watchers watched in vain, and finally MI5 decided on confrontation. That was on Friday 28 May, 1951. The decision was made to call him in for questioning on the following Monday, 31 May.

At this point, the plan became unstuck. Somehow, a warning that he was about to be interrogated reached Maclean. The evidence about how this happened is once again circumstantial, but in Arthur Martin's view the sequence was clear. A message went to Washington requesting the MI5 representative there to brief the CIA on the action they were about to take. This was seen by Kim *of MI6* Philby. Philby then sent Burgess a cable which was on the face of it a message about his *Burgess's* car, which had been left in the embassy car park when he had departed under a cloud earlier in the month, but was really a pre-arranged warning. Burgess, as 'Roger Styles', turned up with a hire car and two tickets on the night boat from Southampton to St Malo, and within twelve hours of the decision to haul him in for questioning Maclean was safely out of the country.

As with Burgess, many people continued to believe that there was some innocent explanation for his disappearance, but when he turned up at a press conference in Moscow in 1956 his supporters had no option but to accept the inevitable.

It was an eventful year for the Ring of Five: back in London, Anthony Blunt was knighted by the Queen.

**Magnetic mines**  In 1939, within weeks of the declaration of war, Britain came nearer to losing the Second World War than at any time afterwards, even at Dunkirk and the Battle of Britain. The facts of this campaign are little known, because they were kept secret from the British people at the time – they might have caused panic – and they did not have the glamour of the great battles which were to follow. The weapon which nearly won the war for the Germans was the magnetic mine.

My own part in the story is a small one, but it was full of valuable lessons, so I will tell it as it happened.

It was a Friday in November, 1939, when I was told exactly what was going on. The Germans had laid magnetic mines in the Thames estuary, and they had been so effective that virtually no merchant shipping had got through to the Port of London during the previous fortnight. It was not just that the shipping was being decimated; it was being annihilated.

Steps were being taken to increase dock capacity in other ports, further from the bases of the German mine-laying vessels and aircraft, but in the meantime London docks were the only place where much of the food and war materials could be landed. Unless the blockade could be broken, Britain would be out of stock of essential materials in a matter of days.

Essentially, a magnetic mine was an underwater bomb whose detonator was connected to a magnetised trigger. The idea was that the [mass of metal] in any boat passing
MAGNETIC FIELD

overhead would attract the magnetic trigger and detonate the mine.

Obviously there were two ways of solving the problem: to change the ships so that they did not attract the magnetic triggers, or to devise something other than a ship passing overhead which would attract the magnetic triggers and cause the mines to explode without doing any damage. Eventually, we made ships safe from magnetic mines; see *Degaussing the* Prince of Wales. In the meantime, the quickest answer was to clear a path through the minefield by setting off the mines.

The traditional minesweepers were no good, as they were not designed to be proof against a magnetic mine. Instead, they decided to fly over them in a plane carrying a huge electromagnet which would generate a magnetic field great enough to make the mine think there was a ship passing over it. This was quite a tall order. The mines were moored at a depth of up to forty feet, and the plane could not reasonably fly much below fifty feet, so the field had to be strong enough to replicate, at about 100 feet range, the attractive power of a thousand tons or more of iron passing only a few feet above them.

The proposed device took the form of a large circular coil, some forty feet in diameter, strapped underneath a Wimpy – a Wellington bomber. The problem was that, if made of copper, the usual metal for such purposes, a coil large enough to generate the required field strength would make the aircraft too heavy to get off the ground. The only practical alternative was aluminium wire. And to make the coil as small as possible, the wire had to be made with a square cross section, so that the loops packed together with no wasted air space.

I didn't think that you could walk into a British wire factory on a Friday and ask them to produce several miles of square insulated aluminium wire, a specification quite unlike anything they had fabricated before, over the weekend. However, the magic of a Defence Procurement Order did the trick. The moment I produced it, nothing seemed to be too difficult, still less impossible. The wire duly arrived at the Admiralty Research Laboratory workshops on the Monday morning.

The huge coil was wound and fitted to the belly of the Wellington, and the whole contraption was ready for test flying. The main question was to know what field strength would be required to trigger the mine at any given distance. If it was too weak, the plane would fly over the mines without affecting them, while if it was too strong, the field might trigger the mine before the plane was overhead, causing the plane to fly to its own destruction in the explosion.

Fortunately, one of the mines had fallen in shallow water off Shoeburyness, and two Naval chaps, Lieutenant Commander Ouvry and Chief Petty Officer Baldwin, had gone out and dismantled it. This was one of the bravest things I ever heard of anyone doing. Not only did they risk setting off the mine, but there was also a risk that, like most new weapons, it had been booby-trapped to stop its secrets from being discovered.

Anyway, it had been found and disarmed, and was available for experiment. The idea was to put it on the ground and fly over it at varying heights, watching the mechanism to see when it responded.

My job was to do the watching.

If you have never had a largish plane fly over you at an altitude of less than fifty feet, you will have no idea of what it is like: the din and turbulence are beyond belief. But the mine just sat there and did nothing. So they made another pass ten feet lower, and then lower and lower again until I was lying on the ground beside the mine and felt that the propellers were trimming the hair off the back of my neck. At last, with the plane at an indicated zero altitude, the mine mechanism clicked.

Obviously the idea worked in principle but the field had to be even more powerful than we had thought. We modified the shape of the coil and increased the power supply, and produced an arrangement which did the trick.

Over the next few days, the plane flew up and down the Thames estuary, setting off mine after mine. Shipping started getting up the Thames again, and the crisis was averted. In the meantime, we had developed the procedure for degaussing by which we could stop the ships from setting off the mines. This was fortunate, as the Wellington was soon afterwards lost when, as we had originally feared, it triggered a mine prematurely and was destroyed in the resultant explosion.

**Marconi, Guglielmo**   Marconi was an Italian, and is generally credited with inventing wireless. Of course he didn't. Like every inventor, he was building on other people's inventions and discoveries. But his great achievement was to put it all into practice.

The theorists, Maxwell, Helmholz and others, had predicted that electromagnetic radiation would be propagated outwards into space indefinitely, but when it came to practical experiments they were finding it marvellous that the waves could travel all the way across a laboratory. Marconi trusted their mathematics and set out to show that the waves could indeed travel round the world.

He did most of his work in England in the period before World War One. In 1899, when he was only twenty-five, he established a company to operate a wireless telegraph between England and France. The success of this led him two years later to establish a similar link between Britain and [America] He was awarded the Nobel Prize in Physics in 1909.

The name, wire-less telegraph, is significant. Marconi's invention was thought of as a special sort of telegraph, carrying a message between two telegraph operators tapping away in Morse code just as in the normal electric telegraph, except that they would not need to have a wire between them.

The first important use of wireless was communication with places the wires wouldn't go, notably ships. Marconi started a huge company, Marconi Marine, which supplied complete wireless systems for ships: the equipment and the operators.

One of the major clients of the company was the British Admiralty. But the Admiralty people were not only interested in buying Marconi's equipment. Marconi also supplied a very powerful spy service for them. If Naval Intelligence wanted to get a spy into some place without attracting any attention, they would train him as a radio operator and Marconi would find a ship to take him there. This was the origin of Marconi's close connection with the Security Service.

Very early in the history of wireless telegraphy, people realised that a signal sent by the wireless telegraph would not be secure. Although it had a single transmission point just like an ordinary telegraph, it would have no single reception point. It could in theory be picked up by any receiver, anywhere, which was operating at the same frequency. They used the word broadcast to describe the transmission process. It was taken from a way of sowing seeds by throwing them in the general direction of a field, and was a pejorative term: it was seen as a problem with wire-less transmission that the message was broadcast, i.e. scattered indiscriminately to the four winds.

The telegraph operators used transmitters and receivers equipped to operate only on the frequency chosen for that service, but Marconi started making receivers which could be tuned to a range of wavelengths. As there was then no broadcasting to the public as we know it, these first tuneable receivers had no other purpose at the time than to listen in to other people's telegraph traffic. In other words, they were really just bugging devices.

The military, and especially the naval people, were immediately interested, and by the time the First World War broke out there were so many people around the world with tuneable receivers that ships had to maintain radio silence if their presence in some area was not to be noticed.

It was in this period just before the First World War that my father joined Marconi, starting an association between our family and the company which was to last for more than half a century. Thus it was as an employee of Marconi that my father was involved in early work on Radio Direction Finding (see *RDF* and *Wright, G.M.*); and it was on Marconi premises forty years later that I took The Thing apart and made it work; see *Thing, The*.

After the First World War, Marconi realised that the fact that wireless transmissions were 'broadcast' could be turned into an advantage. Many people could all listen to the same messages, and you could make them pay for the privilege. In 1921 the word was first applied to a wireless transmission aimed at anybody who wanted to listen. It seemed at the time a foolish idea: who would want to listen? But the wireless telegraph, carrying Morse, had by then been developed into the wireless telephone, capable of carrying voices and even music, and this made Marconi and others realise that it could be a medium of instruction, propaganda and even entertainment.

As with marine wireless, Marconi started by offering a complete service: his own broadcasting station transmitted at a predetermined frequency, and the public bought wireless sets pre-tuned to that frequency. Thus he sold a package, the broadcasting service and a device to enable you to listen to it.

This idea proved impractical, the domestic market being won by tuneable radio sets capable of picking up any station within the frequency bands it covered. This meant that broadcasting could not be funded as a service to paying listeners, and at this point Marconi decided to forget the service side and concentrate on selling the devices: transmitters and receivers. He sold his broadcasting station, 2LO, to the newly formed British Broadcasting Corporation.

In the late twenties, despite the evident success of broadcasting, it was widely believed that 'the wireless' had reached its limits, and that for long distance point-to-point communication wires – cables – were still the answer. This view was held particularly strongly by the people who made the cables, who had at the time the ear of the British government.

Marconi believed that wireless had a future even for long distance point-to-point communication, and that the future lay in the development of what were termed beams, highly directionalised transmissions focused like the beams of searchlights and thus travelling much further than broadcasts of similar power, which dissipated their power over 360°. The beams operated at much higher frequencies than the existing wireless broadcasting, what is now known as short wave radio.

Marconi poured all the energies of the company into demonstrating the new techniques. In a triumphant vindication of his claims, the firm transmitted a telegraph message to Australia by short wave beam, and it arrived quicker and in a less distorted state than was possible through the cable network.

Meanwhile, my father, who was his Chief of Research, was involved not only in this demonstration that short wave radio could provide an alternative to cables as the communications system for the Empire, but also how the short wave 'beams' could be adapted for radio telephony and facsimile document transmission and television. He was thus developing many aspects of the technology which became a reality over the next fifty years or so; but at the time, 1929, the world was not ready for them.

The cable people mounted a massive campaign in defence of their own interests. All sorts of plausible reasons were given for rejecting beam radio and continuing to rely on the cables.

This was nearly catastrophic for the firm. My father lost his job, and Marconi went into retirement, returning to his native Italy, where he died in 1937.

**Martin, Arthur** Around the time of the Lonsdale case, I was at a meeting with the Director General (Roger Hollis), the head of D Branch (Martin Furnival Jones), Arthur Martin (the D1) and some other departmental heads. Halfway through the meeting Arthur was called away, and his loyal colleagues started to stick their knives into him.

F.J. listened quietly to it all for a time, and then said

BY "BEAMS", THE AUTHOR SIMPLY MEANS "DIRECTIONAL" TRANSMISSIONS. NOT "NARROW BEAMS" AS PER LASERS AND SUCHLIKE, BUT RATHER, A TRANSMISSION WHICH MIGHT BE, SAY 30-DEGREES, INSTEAD OF 360-DEGREES.

simply 'That man is the best counter espionage officer in the world'. This makes Arthur worth remembering. His career is, in fact, the story of both the strengths and weaknesses of MI5 in the early post-war years.

Arthur had joined MI5 from Military Intelligence during the Second World War. He did all the original Bride cases (q.v.), which meant that he had caught Klaus Fuchs and unmasked Don Maclean.

He became fed up with the way things were handled following Maclean's defection in 1951. The Bride transcripts had given evidence of the Ring of Five, five moles in top positions in the security services, and suggested a list of forty people who ought at least to be interviewed. It was an impressive list, with all sorts of Sirs and Lords, including one called Anthony Blunt, who was the Director of the Courtauld Institute and Surveyor of the Queen's Pictures.

To the Establishment, it all sounded too preposterous for words. There was Arthur, who had not been to a proper Public School, wanting to interrogate a gentle, cultured art historian about being a spy for the Russians. The long and the short of it was that Arthur was not allowed to go near any of the suspects.

However, there was another argument against interrogation. This was that some of them might be guilty, and that interviewing them might cause them to defect and hence damage the credibility of the Service.

When you think of it, this was an astonishing Catch 22 argument. They were saying, let the spies stay in the Security Service because the Security Service might lose credibility if some of its members and ex-members were shown to be spies. It was a real case of polishing the outside of the jug. Yet that is what some of the geniuses in MI5, like James Robertson and Graham Mitchell, were recommending. Small wonder people started asking whose side they were on.

Anyway, Arthur got fed up with this and resigned, saying that he was going to join ASIO in Australia. Dick White, who was head of counter-espionage and therefore his boss, should have backed him, but failed to – Dick had a good intellect but was very weak when it came to facing issues. His only suggestion was that rather than join ASIO in Australia, Arthur should go to Malaya to work in the E Branch operation there. So Arthur spent the next few years in Malaya.

When he came back he was no more popular, partly because he still hadn't been to a Public School, but, more important, because he still wanted to get things done. Furnival Jones, who had a great respect for his ability and was by then running D Branch, put him in charge of D1, and he set about activating it, going on the offensive against the Russians. This upset his colleagues, because they preferred a quiet life; it also upset the traitors, who wanted to keep MI5 ineffective. So one way or another he didn't have many friends at the top. Of all the members of the MI5 Board, only Bill Magan supported him.

However, he had a lot of supporters lower down. It was around then that I arrived, and I was very impressed by him. He was the first person I had met at that level who could think. Many of us thought that he would go to the top, or very near it.

We were reckoning without the other people near the top. His immediate boss, Furnival Jones, respected his brilliance but really didn't like him. The others, led by the DG, Roger Hollis, were either jealous of his brilliance or for some other reason found his effectiveness objectionable. They managed to get his reorganisation of D Branch stopped, and imposed a new structure which was both frustrating and insulting to him. His response – predictably – was to resist the change, and within weeks his opponents found cause to move at a board meeting for his dismissal. They picked a day when Bill Magan was away, and it went through without a murmur.

I asked Furnival Jones about it afterwards, and he simply said that all the Board had agreed. But I could picture it: Hollis making the running and all the rest just nodding weakly. It was a tragedy from which only the KGB really benefited.

Happily, his old boss, Dick White, who had moved on

to run MI6, was not one to allow the country to lose a good man in this way, and took him on in an equivalent capacity. But he was never so effective at MI6 as he had been, and could have been in future, at MI5.

**Mata-Hari** It is really rather astonishing that anybody remembers Mata-Hari, because about the only memorable thing she did was to get shot. However, in the scandal-starved salons of World War One, the mixture of showbiz, sex and spying proved irresistible, and Mata-Hari has gone into legend as the ultimate *femme fatale* of espionage.

Her real name was Margarete Gertrude Zelle (or Margaretha Geertruida Zelle in Dutch, which she was). At the turn of the century, she went with her Scottish husband to the Netherlands East Indies, where she learned Javanese dancing. After a time she got bored with colonial life (her husband was an alcoholic) and returned alone to Europe. Here she adopted a new name, Mata-Hari, which means 'eye of the morning' in Javanese, and started a new life as a dancer, offering a repertoire of Javanese and other eastern dances. In 1905, she was the toast of Paris.

During this period she was recruited by German intelligence, and she became an enthusiastic agent for them in the years leading to the First World War. She danced in a Paris nightclub which was frequented by the military, and she accepted offers of bed and breakfast from a wide range of French officers. How she steered the pillow-talk to the topic of military technicalities is far from clear, and there is little evidence that she handed over any information of value.

Her activities continued despite the outbreak of war. She commuted between Paris and Madrid, making contact, both physical and intellectual, with the French officers in Paris and the German ones in Madrid. One of her German contacts was Admiral Canaris, later to be head of the Abwehr (German military intelligence in the Second World War).

In 1917 she was arraigned on a charge of communicating with the enemy. There was no question that the charge was true, and defence claims that she was a double agent acting on the instructions of French military intelligence were rejected. She was found guilty and was executed in November 1917 by a military firing squad.

**MI5** This is a non-existent British security organisation to which I belonged for many years. It is concerned with counter-espionage. Its proper name is the British Security Service, but its earlier name (Military Intelligence, Section 5) has lived on.

Many people do not understand why it remains non-existent, and why moves to legalise it have always failed.

Firstly, MI5 finds it very convenient not to exist. So long as it remains non-existent, it can do whatever it wants to do, including illegal entry, burglary, etc. If it were an official organisation, it would have to have its powers spelled out, and this would almost certainly reduce its freedom of action and hence its effectiveness.

Similarly, the Government does not want to make it official because they would then have to make a difficult choice: either they would have to tell MI5 to stop acting illegally (thereby reducing its effectiveness) or they would themselves become party to the illegality. They prefer to pretend that it doesn't exist.

At the same time, many of those who do not like MI5 like it to be non-existent, because if it were an official organisation, its powers would almost certainly include powers of arrest. It would then be on the way to becoming a secret police.

When MI5 wants somebody arrested, it is done by the Police Special Branch. When it wants to do ordinary things like owning property and be unpleasant to law-abiding citizens, it calls itself The Treasury; see *Treasury, The*.

For the structure of the organisation, see *A Branch* (resources), *D Branch* (investigations), *E Branch* (colonies) and *F Branch* (domestic surveillance). B Branch (personnel) and C Branch (protective security) are of less interest.

**MI6** MI6 is the non-existent British organisation responsible for positive security intelligence operations, i.e. espionage.

Its proper name is the British Secret Intelligence Service, but it remains better known by its earlier name (Military Intelligence, Section 6).

It did at one time exist. This happened by mistake during the *Spycatcher* trial. Sir Robert Armstrong was busily refusing to admit that it existed, but the sharp-eared judge pointed out that the good knight had made reference to its existence a couple of days earlier. Panic stations in the prosecution. However, they found an ingenious way out of the dilemma. Sir Robert claimed that his earlier statement only referred to the period when Sir Dick Goldsmith White was its head, and that after that (1969) it had ceased to exist again.

It is this kind of rubbish which makes one wonder about the British Civil Service. They behave like a lot of children playing a cops and robbers game whose rules they make up as they go along. Who do they think they are fooling? Who is impressed? The answer is, of course, that they fool and impress one another. But the tragedy is that, silly though the game is, it is played with real people, and the guns have real bullets.

MI6 was known as The Friends in the Foreign Office, and as SIS elsewhere in the Civil Service.

**Microdots**  Wireless has never been a very good way for agents to send information. It is not so bad for receiving it, but it was used for transmission only if other channels were not available. This was partly because the spy's lair could be traced by radio direction finding, and partly because wireless was a very public medium – you had to use cipher if you were not to have everybody else joining in your operations, and partly because of difficulties with pictures, which they often wanted to send.

This is where the microdot came into its own. The microdot was a photograph of a document reduced to 1/1000th or so of its actual size. A foolscap page became a piece of stripper film no larger than a full stop, and was stuck on to a letter or envelope in some naturally camouflaged position, e.g. on top of a real full stop.

MI5 were not so much interested in making microdots

as finding them. This was one of the problems I set the AWRE to solve, and they did. The technique they used was rather like the one they used for secret writing (q.v.), but since the chemical composition of the microdot could be predicted more certainly, a more specific search mechanism could be used. This was fortunate, as a microdot can be added to an otherwise innocent letter, so you really have to examine all incoming mail to intercept the microdots.

The process adopted involved neutron bombardment and was called neutron activation. If you are interested in knowing how it worked, there is a simplified account of it in the entry called *Neutrons, uses for.*

**Microfilm**   All security services maintain microfilm copies of important documents. At MI5 we made fresh microfilms of all files routinely at regular intervals, ever since the time some important ones were lost in the Blitz.

This is one reason why it is virtually impossible for a security organisation to obey an order to destroy any of its records. Back-up microfilms are held in ways which are designed to stop them from being destroyed by accident or by enemy action. Copies are always held in different places, and no one person can get access to them all. Unless you are very lucky, the chances are that further copies are being made as fast as they are destroyed.

For the same reason, you can't take seriously a claim from a security service that files have been destroyed. How do they know? It takes only one bloody-minded (or conscientious) officer to move in smartly and take fresh duplicates before the order can be carried out, and the whole destruction campaign is pointless.

In any case, the destruction of records goes against the grain. Asking a well-trained security officer to destroy a unique record would be like asking an art lover to destroy an old master. Sir Anthony Blunt, for example, couldn't have destroyed either.

If all this is so of physical records on paper and microfilm, it is even more true of computer records.

The reality is that anyone who demands that security

records be destroyed is naive, and anyone who believes it has been done is a fool, and anyone who says it has been done is a liar. One day, the records of the Cabinet and MI5 action in the *Spycatcher* affair will be available to historians. That will be the day that a lot of reputations will have to be revised.

**Microwave links**   Messages sent over a microwave link are very insecure. One of the main links from the Post Office Tower in London went straight over the top of the Russian embassy, and they were able to intercept the lot.

If you want to intercept a microwave, it is not difficult. The waves travel in a narrow beam from point to point, the points being the dishes on the various communications towers round the country. You can position yourself with great accuracy along the line of a link, which will then be at maximum power only a few metres above your head. Quite a small aerial will pick up enough of the transmission to monitor the messages.

You feed all the signals into a computer. The computer is programmed to search for the telephone numbers you want to bug. As these go down the airwaves as a digital message, they are easy to find. As soon as one of those numbers is dialed, the computer activates an intercept on that channel.

We did this in Ireland on the microwave link between Belfast and Dublin, and had considerable success; but we could only do it at the Belfast end. I wanted to set up a microwave intercept in the embassy in Dublin, where we could have heard the IRA traffic from most of southern Ireland, but the Foreign Office wouldn't let me.

**Middle East, effect of on agents**   It's funny, but all the people in MI5 like John Marriott who had had experience in the Middle East came back flabby. James Robertson was another. Something happened to them out there. Whether it was living in a hot climate for years I don't know, but they were very flabby – mentally, that is. They were not on the ball.

Marriott was the Personnel Director when I joined the Service, and he had to vet me. He was a Freemason, and he gave me the handshake when we were introduced, before he did any vetting. I'll bet all the Russian agents learned the handshake before joining. He told me his job was to make sure I wasn't a Communist or homosexual, and he had a clever way of finding out. He said 'Are you a Communist?' I said 'No'. Then he said 'Ever been a queer?' and I said 'No'. So he decided that I was a suitable person to join MI5.

That's what the Middle East does to people.

**Millimetric radar**  This phrase means 'radar operating on a wavelength of 1–10 millimetres'. For a discussion of why it was important, see *Centimetric radar*.

Radar working on wavelengths of 10 centimetres or more, could 'see' aeroplanes but could not see something the Navy wanted to see, namely, the snorkels of submerged submarines. For that we needed a radar working on an even shorter wavelength. I was working on this for the Navy when I was invited to work for MI5.

The problem was that if the radar was of the right wavelength to show a snorkel, it showed every detail of all the ocean waves, so the echo from the snorkel got lost in a maze of other echoes.

Our solution was to identify the Doppler shift in the echoes. The Doppler shift is the apparent change in wavelength if an object emitting a wave is moving relative to the receiver. It explains why car sirens and train whistles sound higher when they are coming towards you than when they are going away, and why you can tell how fast stars are travelling relative to us by checking the shift in the spectra of the light they emit.

It is worth understanding the Doppler shift, because it can be genuinely useful. Police speed traps work by the Doppler shift in radar echoes.

Let us suppose we have a siren emitting a series of very loud blips at one-second intervals. A person a couple of kilometres away hears them arriving one per second.

However, if the siren was attached to a racing car, the racing car will have travelled a long way in the five seconds it takes for the first blip to reach the observer. So blips reach the observer at shorter intervals.

If the siren is attached to an aeroplane travelling at the speed of sound, all its noise arrives simultaneously – a sonic boom.

However, you do not need to separate beeps for the effect to be heard. If the siren on the racing car emits a long note, all the sound it has emitted in five seconds may arrives in (say) three seconds. The sounds are just vibrations of air particles, and the number of vibrations emitted by the siren has not changed; but the person standing by the roadside hears them arrive in less time than it took the siren to produce them. They have suffered a concertina effect: their apparent wavelength is shorter and their apparent frequency higher. In the case of musical notes, this will mean that they have a higher pitch. In the case of light, it will mean that the colours will shift to the blue end of the spectrum. In the case of radar, the echoes will be at a fractionally higher frequency than the original beam. If the source of the waves is receding, the note will be lower, the light will be shifted to the red end of the spectrum, and the radar pulse will be at a fractionally lower frequency than the original beam.

In the case of our anti-submarine radar, all the main echoes from the ocean waves had the same Doppler shift, because the ocean rollers were all travelling at the same speed relative to us. But among them would be a small set of echoes with a different Doppler shift and hence a different frequency the echo from the snorkel, cutting through the rollers.

The Doppler shift caused by the velocity of the ocean waves was very, very small, nowhere near as great as that in the pitch of the note of the siren or the colour of stars. This was because we were talking of relativity, the relationship between the speed of motion of the source and the speed of light. However, by having very fine tuning, we were able to isolate the echoes of any given frequency and enhance or annul them. We annulled the frequency of the echoes off the waves, and the echoes off the snorkels stood out clearly.

**Miscellaneous information, what to do with**  An agent is bound to accumulate small scraps of information whose significance, purpose and even meaning is uncertain. He knows that all information must be filed, but is uncertain what to do with it.

In amateur systems, such material is collected in folders called Miscellaneous.

In the more sophisticated system run by MI5, it was collected in folders called List Files.

**Mitchell, Graham**  Graham Mitchell was Deputy Director General, under Sir Roger Hollis, when I joined the service. He was a key suspect in the hunt for the fifth member of the Ring of Five.

The suspicion that MI5 was penetrated went back a very long way. I got an inkling of this one day when I was talking with Evelyn McBarnet, one of our Research Officers. She produced a note book which had been left with her by another Research Officer, Anne Last, when she left the Service. The note book contained details, page after page of them, of suspicious events.

It seems that Anne Last had been worried that too many things were going wrong. Documents were disappearing, tape and wire recordings were being 'accidentally' erased, microphones being 'discovered' by the Russians within hours of installation, and so on. Such things could happen, she knew, even in the best organisation, but she felt that they were happening more often than they should. So she decided to keep a record of all the cases of which she became aware, hoping that some pattern would emerge which would identify the person or people responsible.

The list went on for page after page: events, times and dates, suspect lists. Some of them strongly suggested that safes within the office had been opened during the night; others were details of operations which had gone wrong as a result of a tip-off.

It was an intriguing list. She was not able to prove that

any one of these was an act of treachery or sabotage; the documents allegedly stolen from a safe *might* have accidentally been put into a burn bag instead of the safe; and the Russians *might* have discovered our new mikes by chance; but, in the end, she decided that it all added up to evidence of penetration.

Her note concluded: 'If MI5 is penetrated, I think it is most likely to be Roger Hollis or Graham Mitchell.'

When I saw this, I was appalled and astonished: appalled to think that it had been going on for so long without any official action, astonished by the fact that she had come to this conclusion without having access to the evidence which was leading us to the same conclusion. We knew nothing of more than a handful of her 'events'. For all practical purposes, we had come to the same conclusion independently, and on the basis of two separate sets of information.

On investigation, some of her events proved to have innocent explanations, and others were matched up with confessions of Anthony Blunt, who, for example, tipped off the Russians about our SF bugging operation against the CPGB Headquarters; see *Bugging the CPGB* and *SF*. But there remained too many which were still unexplained.

I found this very significant, because the senior women in MI5 demonstrated very good judgement. I am not talking about the Registry Queens, the debs who acted as filing clerks in the Registry. I am talking about the research officers and transcribers, women who dedicated themselves to the Service and got to know far more about the Service and its operations than many of the case officers.

They had an uncanny knack of being able to tell when someone was lying, even from listening to a distorted tape recording of a conversation. Some people call this intuition, but I prefer a scientific explanation: that some women have more finely-tuned ears, capable of distinguishing and interpreting subtleties of tone which other people can't hear.

So it was that Arthur Martin and I regarded Anne Last's

evidence as something to be taken seriously, and added items from it to the growing accumulation of evidence about the Fifth Man – the spy within MI5.

We had by then already come to the same conclusion as Anne. It had to be Mitchell or Hollis. Our evidence pointed more directly at Hollis, but for tactical reasons we decided to open the battle with an investigation of Mitchell. We needed official support, and it was more likely that Hollis would authorise an investigation of Mitchell than one of himself.

Hollis gave us the green light, but no facilities, and placed limits on our freedom of action which made it impossible for us to get anywhere. We decided that the only person who could help us was Dick White, a very sound former MI5 man who had moved over to become Director General of MI6. I had drawn up huge charts to show the relationship between the various bits of information. We spread them out on the floor of his office and soon had him crawling about, following the logical trail like a ferret. At the end of it he agreed that there had to be a proper investigation and that he would support our request for more help and facilities.

We were now able to take the initiative. We set up a TV camera behind the mirror in Mitchell's office, and were able to watch his activities through the day. They proved very boring. Hollis gave him nothing to do, and he did it very slowly. The only action was when he came over to the mirror and laboriously picked his teeth, which he did at least twice a day, pulling hideous faces at himself in the mirror and hence at us, monitoring the view from the mirror on closed-circuit TV. The flies on the walls must have had a good laugh.

In the end, the worst we could say about Mitchell was that he had not been very effective over the years. Indeed, one of his few initiatives was an unfortunate one: it was he who ordered the closing down of the Bride deciphering program in 1954. He was not doing much productive work for his salary, and was hence a sort of low level economic saboteur, but he was not the only Civil Servant of which *that* could be said. In any case, agents do not work that way. If you want to find the agent, look for a person who gets things done and gets them done well, the kind who get trusted and promoted. Mitchell had only been promoted by Hollis, whom he had followed up the ladder like a shadow.

However, the biggest weakness of the investigation was that we were not allowed to interrogate Mitchell. Interrogation was ruled out by Hollis. Why he ruled it out is another question.

As was normal with such investigations, the final report was not produced by us, the investigators, but by another officer, fresh to the case, who studied our material and drew conclusions from it. In our case, the writer was Ronnie Symonds, and he concluded that we had shown clear evidence of the existence of a spy in the upper echelons of MI5, but only the weakest of evidence that it was Mitchell. This left an awkward question mark, and Hollis knew it. He told Symonds to go away and produce a fresh report.

A few weeks later, the Blunt case broke. Anthony Blunt had worked in MI5 during the war, as assistant to Guy Liddell. Interrogation revealed something of the scope and nature of his activities.

In one respect we had won. We had claimed that leaks had occurred as far back as the war years and had not been properly investigated. This had been denied by Hollis, Cumming and others, but here was evidence that we were right. Had these leaks been investigated at the time, Blunt would have been unmasked almost immediately.

However, if we had won a battle, it had cost us the war. Symonds seized on the new information, and his second report, produced six months later, said that the highly placed spy in MI5 had now been identified as Blunt, removing the need for further investigation.

Arthur and I were aghast. At the meeting to discuss the new report, Arthur pointed out that while Blunt could be the source of the wartime leaks and the references in the Bride material, which dated from 1943–5, he certainly could not be the source of the more recent leaks. Nor could Blunt be the MI5 member of the post-war Ring of Five referred to by Golitsin, since he had left the Service at the end of the war, in 1945. So the high level spy remained unidentified.

Could Mitchell be involved? Arthur agreed that it seemed unlikely, but added 'Unless, of course, he was being used as a stalking horse by someone else'.

Shortly afterwards, his job as head of D1 was divided into two, the responsibility for investigations being passed to Ronnie Symonds. When he protested, he was sacked.

**Money** Counter-espionage costs a lot of money. It saves money in the end, because if you know what the enemy is doing you do not have to spend as much on defence; but you can never show people how much you have saved them, so they are never very happy to pay up.

At MI5, our real problem was that we didn't exist, and hence were funded from the Secret Vote, the British government's slush fund for illegal operations. In my early days with MI5, we spent most of our time working out ways of getting round this problem, trying to keep the Secret Vote for things we could not get anyone else to pay for.

This is how I first came to do jobs for MI5. I was on the Navy's payroll, but I was seconded to the private electronics firm of Marconi and working for MI5. My first major project for MI5, the development of Satyr, was done at Marconi's, with the help of six assistants and a new secure laboratory, all paid for by the Navy.

We could always get the Navy to pay for things by telling them that, if they didn't pay, we would give the project to the Air Force. The Navy were very worried that the RAF was getting all the rockets and making their surface ships redundant, so they were always pleased to help.

In general, governments like spending money on things they can open or be photographed with. Ships can be launched, weapons can be test fired, and a new building can be opened. Security is different. You can't get your photograph in the paper launching a new wiretap, and no one would want to be seen in one of the Watchers' cars. So MI5 got very little money, and we had to go begging round town to get our work done.

The AWRE (Atomic Weapons Research Establishment) was another very good place to go. They got as much money as they could spend, and no one asked what they spent it on. So they were happy to help us. The work they did for us was probably as valuable to the country as anything else they ever did. It included inventing ways to read invisible writing, to find microdots on envelopes, to crack the combinations of safes and to find out what was in a tin can without opening it; see *Writing, secret*, *Microdots* and *X-rays*.

**Morse** When Mr Samuel Finley Breese Morse (1791–1892), an American portrait painter, laid aside his brushes and devised the recording telegraph in 1837, he invented at the same time, almost as an afterthought, a system of dots and dashes to represent the letters of the alphabet.

If he had not done so, we would perhaps remember him for inventing the telegraph itself, or even for his portraits. As it is, we remember him only for the Morse code. Over a century later, the call-sign of the BBC broadcasts to Europe in the Second World War was the Morse code ···–, V for Victory, usually played on timpani.

Although designed to work within the limitations of telegraph equipment, where the receiver was a bell or buzzer, Morse was extensively used in radio communications. This was partly because of its technical simplicity. The on-off pattern could be produced with very simple equipment – in the last resort, a couple of bare wires. In transit to its destination, too, it was far less prone to distortion by interference, both natural and contrived, than the signal of normal sound broadcasting transmission. A haze of static would make it hard to distinguish *God Save the Queen* from *Pop Goes the Weasel*, but Morse would come chopping through the static. It was therefore particularly suited to applications where mathematical precision was required – as it was in the transmission and reception of cipher.

Today, digital systems are increasingly popular. Anything from the Mona Lisa to Beethoven's Choral Symphony can be analysed by a computer and recorded as a piece of digital information, a series of propositions to which the answer is either yes or no. The same goes for texts, but Morse is no longer the preferred code. Texts are handled in verifiable codes, e.g. the popular computer character code, Ascii.

Verification virtually eliminated transmission errors. Of course, if the content of the message was rubbish, it came out as rubbish, but at least it was the same rubbish which had gone in. In Morse there was no way of telling (other than from context clues) if a single dot or dash had been missed, but in a verifiable code a one-pulse corruption was noticed. A typical procedure was to arrange coding so that every character was represented by an even number of pulses. The missing of a single pulse caused the pulse count to be uneven, and the device reported an error. In addition, messages were 'zero proofed'. They were keyed twice, encoded as numbers, and the first set of numbers subtracted from the second. Any discrepancy between the two versions showed up as a number other than zero.

Today, things have doubtless moved on further still. Morse is likely soon to become a code for emergencies, when no sophisticated encoder is available. The last Morse message ever sent will probably be the one everybody knows: ···−−−···, SOS.

**Moscow**   We had terrible trouble with security in our Moscow embassy.

The first problem was to persuade the people there that there was anything wrong. After the Americans had found a bug in the Great Seal of the United States hanging over their ambassador's desk (see *Thing, The*), you might have thought that our people would have been worried. But they were sure that it was all secure.

However, we had evidence that some of our secrets were getting into the wrong hands, so we kept at it. Finally, we managed to persuade the Foreign Office to allow one of our best young officers, Duncum Wagh, to go to Moscow and carry out an audit of the security systems in the embassy. It was a good thing we did.

At that time, the cipher machines were in an upstairs room at one side of the building, with windows looking out over the wall at the building next door, about ten feet away. This appeared to be some sort of factory. I told Duncum to get some photographs showing as much as possible of the nearest section of the factory, if possible from several angles (see *Photographs of buildings, how to take*).

He took a good series of photographs from each of the three windows on that wall, the cipher room and rooms on either side. When we examined them, we were particularly interested in an array of television aerials on the roofline. They looked quite normal – the kind of aerials all Moscow factories would have – but when we looked closer we saw that the leads from them, instead of going their separate ways into the factory, all fed in through one window.

Further examination of the photographs showed that the aerials were not properly wired up. Some of them contained dummy elements which were not connected to anything. When we worked out the way the elements were really connected, we found that the whole array was in fact a set of disguised dipoles whose only purpose could be to act as powerful directional aerials aimed at our cipher room.

But what were they listening to? At this time the cipher machine we were using was called a Rockex, and it occurred to me that if the Russians were as clever as we were (and they generally were) they would be trying to pick up any very weak radio frequency transmissions which might be emerging from the apparatus itself or the cabling to and from it.

I arranged for some tests to be done on the Rockex, and sure enough found that, at the range from which the Russians were listening, they would be able to pick up an echo of the plain language message on its way into or out of the machine, just as we did with the French cipher in their London embassy; see *Stockade*. This did not prove that they were doing so, but it was enough to persuade the embassy people that something had to be done.

It was clear that the cipher machine must be moved out of range of listening devices. There was a very suitable room right in the middle of the embassy, but this would have upset the ambassador, because it was his dressing room. So we had to move the cipher room down into the basement.

The move itself led to further revelations. The old cipher room had to be completely redecorated, and during the process some pieces of plaster fell off the ceiling, revealing a fair number of microphones embedded in the concrete of the main structure of the building. The question was, how long had they been there?

I got two samples of the concrete, and took them to the Building Research Centre. I asked them whether they could date it. They could not give me an exact date, of course, but they produced results for the samples which suggested firstly that they were both the same age, and secondly that the estimated date for both was one which tallied with what I had feared: the time just before the embassy returned to Moscow from its wartime evacuation to Kuibyshev. The Russians had clearly seized the opportunity afforded by the near approach of the invading German armies to do a bugging operation on their ally's embassy, which is a good example of making the best of a bad job.

But what had they heard? In the early post-war years, there was no machine to listen to. All the ciphering was done manually, with one-time pads, so there was nothing to listen to but the scratching of pens.

Then somebody remembered the technique they had

actually used at the time. Enciphering and deciphering using one-time pads is a two-stage process: when enciphering, the message is first encoded as a string of numbers, using the code book, and then the code is enciphered, using the one-time pad. Deciphering is the same but in the other direction.

To avoid switching all the time from code book to pads, the cipher clerks worked in pairs, one working the code book while the other worked the one-time pad. Either way, the coded but not enciphered version was called out aloud, which to the listening Russians was as good as an *en clair* message; see *Codes*.

This discovery was interesting for three reasons.

First, it meant that every top secret message passing to or from our embassy since 1944 had probably been read by the Russians, which gave us all reason to pause for thought.

Second, it meant that the Russian defector Volkov had been speaking the truth when he said that the embassy's cipher was being read, and almost certainly had been in a position to say how it was being done, which he had promised to do if he got the chance. He never got the chance.

Third, the discovery of the microphones at least disproved the claims of those who had previously asserted that the embassy was secure. They could not deny the evidence of the microphones.

I then tested to see whether the Rockex machine could have been read with microphones, as we did with the Hagelin machines (see *Engulf*). The result showed that it was possible but difficult. However, the combination of the acoustic record and the radiations would have given the Russians everything they needed.

Armed with all this information, we were at last able to persuade the embassy people to take security seriously. So it was that the new cipher room, built in the basement, was altogether more scientifically planned that its predecessor. It was screened both acoustically and electrically, and for a time we believed that the machines were secure.

This confidence lasted until a visit from the Prime Minister. They were very concerned to ensure that the cipher machine was secure, and a special investigation was ordered.

One of the features of the building was the heating ducts. These were part of the main fabric of the building, and were effectively concrete tunnels about two feet square, large enough for a man to crawl along. These ducts ran all over the building, and we found that some of them actually ran under the floor of the basement cipher room. Thus they were an obvious security risk.

We opened one up – there was no secrecy about them – and our man crawled away into the darkness with a powerful torch. He had reached the point where he was under the cipher room when he noticed a hole in the side wall of the duct. Then he noticed a second similar hole on the opposite wall of the duct.

He was just sitting there wondering what it was all about when a small device on the end of a thin, stainless steel rod emerged silently out of one hole, paused for a moment in the middle of the duct as if to look around, and then continued on its way into the other hole.

With great presence of mind, our man reached into his toolbag and grabbed a clamp. When the probe reached maximum extension and came to a standstill, he quickly screwed the clamp to the stem of the probe, preventing the Russians from pulling it back. He was then able to get out a hacksaw and saw off the end of the probe.

We found that the device was a magnetic detection coil. We were not immediately sure how much it would be able to pick up but for safety's sake all the messages which related to or arose out of the subsequent visit of the PM were enciphered using one-time pads, before being keyed into the cipher machines.

It was fortunate that this was done. Tests were done later, after the captured probe was brought back to England, and it was found that there were magnetic emanations from the cipher machines which were strong enough to be read with these coils. Worse still, these emanations were produced in the part of the machine where the message was still in plain language. Once again, they were reading not the cipher but the plain language original.

Until we could design something safer, we decided to put the cipher machines on wheels and move them about every few minutes. This meant that the machines were constantly moving in and out of range of the various detectors, and unless the Russians had a very large number of them, very well placed, they would never be able to read more than a few words of any given text. These were known as the Wandering Cipher Machines.

In the end we persuaded the Foreign Office and the ambassador to move the cipher room above ground floor, even if it meant the ambassador losing his dressing room.

The next security problem was very different. One of the major activities of the embassy was listening in on Russian communications. This came under the category of Signals Intelligence, SIGINT, and was thus the job of GCHQ. So it was that GCHQ had a room in the front of the building, full of bugging equipment of one sort or another.

This room had an air conditioner in it, drawing fresh air through a duct on the façade of the building. One night, when this was being replastered and repainted by the Russians, the air conditioner caught fire, and we had to let the Russian fire brigade into the room to put it out. The firemen had no difficulty in destroying all the equipment in the room, putting us off the air.

The first question to ask when something like this happens is, was it all an accident? If it was not an accident, was it just luck that they set the fire in a very important room, or did they know that it was important.

We formed a working party of all the people likely to be involved. I was asked to chair it. We got the air conditioner sent back from Moscow, and the Home Office fire experts examined it. It was clear that the heat exchanger had caught fire; what was unusual was that the fire had started on the fresh air side of the heat exchanger, so it had nothing to do with any fault in the air-conditioning unit itself. It seemed most likely that an incendiary device had been introduced into the vent from the outside.

There were three possible explanations. The first was that the incendiary device was inserted on spec, just to cause a fuss, and that it was a pure chance that it landed in an important room. However, this was not the way the Russians worked. They did not waste time on fishing trips. The second possibility was that they knew that it was a high security area, but did not know why. This could have been the case, because they would have known that the door had a special set of locks. But there were many reasons for having a secure area in an embassy, very few of which were worth investigating.

It seemed evident that they knew exactly what went on there, and wanted to stop it. So we set about investigating whether the room was as secure as we had thought.

The door had a double locking system. There was a grill with a combination lock, which stopped the casual passer-by from getting close to the special high-security lock on the main door, which was opened by a key. The idea was to make it very difficult for anyone to get all the way in in a single raid. If they broke the combination they were in a position to start working on the main lock; for example, they could take X-ray pictures of the tumblers. But then they would have to analyse the X-rays and manufacture a key, needing a second trip to make an entry. But we would in the meantime have become aware that the combination lock had been illegally opened and would have changed the whole system.

In theory, it was secure.

However, we got a bit of a shock when we started investigating more closely. When the GCHQ people arrived in Moscow to set the room up, they needed a high security lock for it. As luck would have it, the New Zealanders had a spare lock which they were happy to dispose of, so this was the one which was installed. On further investigation, however, we found that the New Zealanders had lost one of the two original keys. So it seemed more than possible that the Russians had a key to the main lock.

But what about the safety grill with its combination lock? When we investigated this a bit more thoroughly, we found that they had not even bothered to break the combination. The grill was held in place with screws, and we found that it was possible to get our fingers through and under the grill on to the heads of the screws. For convenience, the Russians had oiled the screws and left them just finger tight.

It seemed overwhelmingly likely that the Russians had been coming and going at will, and knew exactly what was going on in the room.

We asked the operators of the monitors whether they set their receivers at zero when they left them. The answer was no. So whenever they got in, the Russians could have read off the frequencies which GCHQ were monitoring, and hence discovered what signals we were intercepting. They would have learned enough to know that it would be a good idea for them to destroy the room, and that is just what they did.

The last item in the Moscow story is an example of the aspect of Moscow security which I found most worrying of all. Whenever I had been involved in matters relating to the Moscow embassy, it had always struck me as astonishing that so many people had been compromised by the Russians, and then blackmailed. If we found that many, how many were there we didn't find? And how much information were they persuaded to hand over? So it was no surprise when I was finally involved in one of the cases.

The bones of the story are told in the entry under *Semstresses* ... I had no part in the Moscow end of the story, but I was involved later, in London.

The girl in the case was called Valya, and was the ambassador's wife's maid. According to the ambassador, who I will call Charlie, they had a beautiful, serious and passionate and long-lasting relationship in the linen room. However, when she produced candid snaps of the passion, and said that she was being pressured by the KGB to find out the name of the MI5 officer at the embassy, he realised that all was not well. He claimed that he did not tell her the name of the MI5 man. He then wrote to the Permanent Under Secretary at the Foreign Office, Dennis Greenhill, saying that he had got himself into a jam. He was immediately recalled.

In talking to Greenhill, he claimed that the photos had been taken in the embassy. This was an important point, as it had further implications for embassy security; so Greenhill called in Alec MacDonald, who was then Director of Counter-espionage, to interrogate him further. MacDonald reported that Charlie had been a fool but that it was all now in the past and no real damage had been done. And there the case might have rested.

The next development was, however that Charlie's secretary, who had stayed in Moscow, received a letter from Charlie enclosing one to Valya. The covering letter asked him to forward it on. The secretary forwarded it, but back to Dennis Greenhill in London, and at that point it was decided that he should be interrogated more professionally. I was asked to do it. I agreed on two conditions: first, that it was understood that this was a no holds barred interrogation; second, that I should be given unrestricted access to his personal file at the Foreign Office.

The file was brought to me and I carried it back to MI5. I went through it very carefully. There was no evidence of womanising. In fact, the only interesting item was a sealed envelope marked 'To be opened only by the Permanent Under Secretary.' I got permission from Greenhill to open it, and out popped the details of an arrangement for Charlie to come to Balmoral and receive his GCMG from the Queen. Evidently it was placed in the file so that it could be instantly activated when the need arose.

Anyway, there was Charlie's invitation to collect the top order of knighthood, along with his love letter to a KGB officer. The two documents were almost as bizarre a couple as the lovers.

My problem was that although Charlie realised that he had been a silly boy, he did not seem to realise the security implications. Given the number of well-publicised cases of blackmail which had occurred in the past, it was surprising that a senior British diplomat should not have been suspicious of Valya from the beginning. It was worse that he then failed to realise, despite overwhelming evidence, that Valya was herself a KGB officer, and that her story about being pressured by the KGB was nonsense. After showing such blindness, his further stupidity – in getting in touch with the lady again using diplomatic channels – seemed almost predictable. I knew that it was not going to be easy to get him to tell the truth.

I set up the interrogation room carefully, covering the desk with files, including his, and leaving his letter to Valya out where it was partially visible.

In due course he turned up at the front door of the War Office, and was shown up to room 055, where I was waiting for him. The girl took his coat and showed him to an armchair facing the desk where I was sitting.

I left him sitting there, getting more and more angry and tetchy, for about ten minutes. Then I stood up behind the desk and asked him when he was last in touch with Valya.

Clearly he hadn't seen the letter, because at first he sat there for some time squirming in his chair, and one could see that he was trying to decide whether to come clean. However, he finally admitted it, saying that he had sent a letter to her via his secretary.

I asked him what he thought he was doing communicating with her after he had seen the Permanent Under Secretary at the FO and the Director of Counter-espionage in Moscow. He tried to make light of it, saying that he couldn't see how it could matter.

At this point I lost all sympathy for him. If he could not see that the KGB could make capital out of evidence that the British ambassador was pursuing one of their agents with amorous intent, what could he see? I asked him why he should have the privilege of doing this sort of thing, when, if one of his junior staff had had such a liaison, he would certainly have lost his job and possibly landed in prison.

But the worst was still to come.

I was still puzzled by the photographs, and could not see how they could possibly have been taken in the embassy. There were technical problems involved and Charlie's story simply did not add up. I suggested to him that his statement about the pictures having been taken at the embassy was a direct lie, and finally he came clean.

It seems that he had gone to Leningrad with his wife. The Russians had arranged a tour of the Hermitage for her, but in the meantime he was to attend to other matters. When he returned to the hotel where they were staying, who should be waiting for him in the foyer but Valya, as beautiful as ever, explaining that as luck would have it she had a brother who owned a flat just round the corner, and he had lent her the keys.

By the time he had finished telling the story, he had persuaded me that his indiscretion was so blatant as to be totally inexcusable, and to require his instant removal from the diplomatic service. So he got his GCMG earlier than planned.

**Mossad** The Central Institute for Intelligence and Special Assignments performs espionage, counter-espionage, terrorist and anti-terrorist activities for the State of Israel. If ever there was a country which needed such an organisation, it was Israel, and if ever a country got what it needed, that was Israel, too.

The dream of returning to their ancestral homeland had stuck with the Jews ever since they had been scattered over the then known world following the destruction of Jerusalem by a Roman army under Titus in 70 AD. But it was revived as a real possibility nineteen hundred years later, in 1897, when Theodor Herzl founded the Zionist movement.

At the time, the area was known as Palestine, and was a

part of the Turkish Ottoman Empire. However, the Turks backed the losers in the First World War, and after the war Palestine became a British-administered territory under a League of Nations mandate.

This gave a great boost to the Zionist movement, largely as a result of the so-called Balfour Declaration. The 'Declaration' was included in a letter written during the war by the British Foreign Secretary, Arthur Balfour, to the British Zionist Federation, promising British support for the establishment of a Jewish state in Palestine in return for their support for the British claim.

Unfortunately, T.E. Lawrence, a British army officer who had led a military campaign to liberate the region from the Turks, had made a similar promise to the local Arabs to win their support against the Turks.

For the next thirty years the British administration pursued a hopeless policy of trying to please both sides, ending up pleasing neither. However, the horrific sufferings of Europe's Jews under the Nazis in the Second World War caused their claim to a homeland to win very widespread support. Finally, the United Nations ordered that Palestine should be partitioned and a substantial part constituted as the Jewish State of Israel. It came into being on 1 January 1948.

The hope was that the Arab population would be able to live in harmony with the new settlers, but within hours of its establishment, the new State was attacked by its Arab neighbours. The attack was beaten off, but it destroyed all hope of a peaceful settlement, and in the subsequent years relations between the Jews and the Palestinian Arabs varied only between bad and catastrophic.

This was the position as we saw it when I joined MI5.

The problems facing a security service in such a situation beggared description. A secret service was first set up in 1948, taking personnel from various pre-existing organisations, the main source being the intelligence services of Haganah, a para-military organisation which became the Israeli army on the establishment of the State. It covered, like its equivalents in other countries, espionage, counter-espionage and domestic security.

However, the problems of the new State were of a different order from those faced by the services in more settled countries. Perhaps their only advantage was that they could rely on virtually uncritical loyalty from the whole Jewish population of Israel and the support of Zionist organisations world-wide. Otherwise, everything was against them. The country was small and strategically indefensible. Its 30,000-strong army was outnumbered more than ten to one by those of its neighbours, all of whom except one, Lebanon, were pledged to its destruction. Its large Arab population was seen as a resident fifth column.

The territory gained in the Six Day War of 1967 had changed rather then solved the problem: it produced a set of borders which were militarily more rational, but increased radically the number of dissidents within those borders.

Thus the security of the State has not only demanded a powerful intelligence network to find out what was going on. It also required an operational unit able and willing to act, pre-emptively if necessary, if it saw the normal belligerence of its neighbours turning into threats to its survival. Such an organisation was called into being in 1951: Mossad.

The word simply means 'Institute'. There could in theory be a Mossad of Fine Art, but it is unlikely, as the word is now totally associated with security operations. Incidentally, they leave out the definite article: it is Mossad, not The Mossad.

The operational arm of Mossad was able to draw on people with experience in terrorist activities, notably from *Irgun Zevai Leumi* (National Army Organisation). This had been formed in 1937, offering a militant alternative to David Ben-Gurion's Zionists, both in defending Jewish settlers against the Arabs and attacking the forces of the British administration. A splinter group of Irgun, the Stern

Group (or Stern Gang to those of us who were on the receiving end) was formed in 1940 by Abraham Yair Stern. It was even more extremist and violent.

The moderate view was that the best way of getting a Jewish state was not by blowing things up but by massive immigration, legal or otherwise. This was the policy of Ben-Gurion's Zionists and their para-military organisation, Haganah (Ha Ganah, The Army), and it prevailed. With the end of the Mandate, Ben-Gurion became the first Prime Minister of Israel, and Haganah became its army. Irgun Zevai Leumi and the Stern Gang were disbanded, many of their members eventually joining Mossad and a few (e.g. Menachem Begin) turning into politicians.

Mossad also worked in co-operation with the *Sayaret Matkal*, the General Staff Reconnaissance Unit of the Israeli Defence Forces, a group trained for commando-type raids.

Mossad has thus either initiated or been closely associated with a sequence of spectacular forays into foreign territory, many involving assassination, kidnapping and sabotage. The most important pre-emptive strike was the move against an Iraqi atomic research establishment, believed to be on the point of producing an atomic bomb and hence upsetting the precarious political and military balance in the Middle East. The raid was a triumph of accurate intelligence and brilliant operational planning.

Another spectacular success was the Entebbe raid in July 1976, which rescued a group of Jews and others who had been aboard an Air France Airbus hijacked by Palestinians. They were being held as hostages at Entebbe airport, Uganda, and their hijackers were demanding the release of fifty-three Palestinians being held in Israeli jails. The rescue involved a 4000 km flight for three Hercules transports, an unheralded night landing on the airport, and then an engagement with the hijackers and Ugandan troops. By the time it ended, all seven hijackers and twenty Ugandan soldiers were dead, along with three of the hostages and one Israeli commando. ⟵THE Commander of THE Ground-ELEMENT.

A characteristic detail of the operation was that one of

the planes disgorged a replica of one of Ugandan President Idi Amin's cars, complete with plausible-looking occupants. The confusion caused by this car's appearance at the airport made a substantial contribution to the success of the operation.

Although involved in operations against foreign powers, Mossad has at all times devoted most of its resources to operations against its domestic enemy, the PLO (Palestine Liberation Organisation). The full scope of these operations will probably never be known, but they have certainly included the revenge killing of PLO terrorists and assassins and the assassination of PLO leaders. Perhaps more importantly, the infiltration by Mossad of the command structure of the PLO has enabled them to give the Israeli government and defence forces high grade intelligence about PLO activities. Conversely, however, concentration on the PLO has been said to have contributed to their failure to warn of other events, in particular the attack by Egypt and Syria in the Yom Kippur War of 1976.

**Motor vehicles**  If you have specialist motor vehicles, it is a good idea to make them inconspicuous.

When we needed a van to bring equipment into Cyril Mills' house at the back of the Russian embassy (see *Specific Heat Capacity*), we painted it in the colours of Bertram Mills' Circus, as this was the only kind of van which could go to Cyril Mills' house day after day without arousing suspicions.

By the same token, vehicles need to be garaged where they will not be noticed, and this vehicle was very conspicuous almost everywhere. So, being a Bertram Mills' Circus van, we kept it at Bertram Mills' Circus.

**Movement analysis**  This is the name of a technique we used to determine the identities of key members of the Russian embassy staff; see *Who's who at the embassy?* It was an essential part of a program which culminated in the expulsion of over a hundred Russian IOs in 1971.

The idea was that, just as you could get useful information from incomprehensible chatter (see *Chatter*), you can also work out what people are doing if you know where they are going. Movement analysis, therefore, was a huge collection of sightings: name, location, date, time.

Most of the entries came from the Watchers, who sat in rooms across the way from the embassies, identifying the people coming and going. This enabled us to match up real names and faces with code names; see *Who's who at the embassy?* But we also got information from other sources: these included other security services, newspapers and phoned tip-offs from headwaiters and other amateur agents.

All the information was carefully logged, as we never knew which bit of information was going to be crucial. Here is an example. We were once wondering whether two agents had ever met, and movement analysis suggested that they might have been at the same socialite wedding five years earlier. We got access to the press photographs, and there they were, chattering away together in the background as the bride was cutting the cake.

**Music, as code messages** Anyone who saw the film *The Lady Vanishes* – the real pre-war one, not the weak remake – will remember how Dame May Witty, as the sweet, elderly Miss Froy, hummed the tune which, she said 'contained a message, in code' and had to be got to London.

Maybe most people thought it a bit unlikely, but it wasn't. Tunes were used in the war to send simple messages to Resistance groups in Nazi-occupied Europe, and the Russians used them to send messages to agents in England.

We were able to show how it worked in the Bossard case. Frank Bossard was under suspicion for being the source of documents about guided missile secrets which the Russians were getting. We put him under surveillance, and found that he used to go once a week to the Left Luggage office at Victoria Station – the Brighton line – where he would collect a suitcase. He would carry it to a hotel, where he would take a room under a false name, spend an hour or so there, return the suitcase and hike back to his office at the Ministry of Supply.

We sent an officer to collect the suitcase. When we opened it up we found it was mostly full of films and photographic materials, but there were also two gramophone records. I played them, and found they contained eight Russian tunes, four on each.

I rang up GCHQ and asked them if any of the traffic from Moscow used tunes. They said that several did, and asked me what tunes I was interested in. I told them, and they said they would phone back in a couple of hours.

Well, it didn't take that long. They came back within ten minutes, saying that they had found one which had played five of the eight in the recent past.

Each of the tunes had a special meaning, of course. One of them probably meant 'Flee for your life', but we had him in the cooler before they could play it. It was direct proof of communication with a foreign power, so we just trotted him into court and he got his twenty years or whatever it was.

# N

**Name, what's in a?** In Grand Opera, a man becomes totally unrecognisable to his wife if he dresses up in a funny hat. It is much the same with security organisations: they believe that they become unrecognisable to friend and foe alike if they change their names. They are thus particularly likely to change their names if they want to put a nasty reputation behind them and become reformed characters. Thus South Africa's BOSS became NIS, the American OSS and OPC became CIA, and Russia's OGPU became NKVD and then KGB.

In Britain, MI6 became SIS (Secret Intelligence Service), but the older name stuck. This is partly because the organisation does not exist, and therefore cannot very well have an advertising campaign to launch its new corporate logo, like banks do. Much the same goes for MI5. If it had its name on a door, the name would probably be The Security Service. But the question is academic, as it does not have its name on a door. Nobody has ever called it by the initials SS, and it still is widely known as MI5 even to its own members.

The following is a checklist of names, pseudonyms and nicknames. More details of their activities are in each case given in entries under the first listed name:

*British*
GCHQ  Government Communications Head Quarters; formerly Government Code and Cipher School

JIO  Joint Intelligence Organisation

MI5  Military Intelligence 5; calls itself the Security Service

MI6  Military Intelligence 6; formerly MI1c; calls itself the Secret Intelligence Service; known to the Foreign Office as The Friends

SPECIAL BRANCH  The security division of the police force


## USA

CIA  Central Intelligence Agency; formerly OSS Office of Strategic Services, known as The Company

DIA  Defence Intelligence Agency

FBI  Federal Bureau of Investigation

NSA  National Security Agency

NSC  National Security Council

OPC  Office of Policy Co-ordination; absorbed into CIA


## USSR

GRU  Glavnoye Razvedyvatelnoye Upravleniye

KGB  Komitet Gosudarstvennoye Bezhopaznosti (Committee for State Security); formerly (or functionally related to) the Tsarist Okhrana, then the Bolshevik Cheka (1917–23) and the Stalinist GPU and OGPU (1923–34), NKVD (1934–46) and MGB (1946–53). SMERSH was one of its operations, but its participants acted as it if was an independent organisation


## Australia

ASIO  Australian Security Intelligence Organisation

ASIS  Australian Secret Intelligence Service


## Canada

RCMP  Royal Canadian Mounted Police

SIS  Security Intelligence Service (formerly the Special Branch of the RCMP)

*France*
DGSE  Direction Général de Sécurité Extérieur; for-
merly the Deuxième Bureau, BCRAM (Bureau Central de
Renseignement et Action Militaire) and SDECE
DST  Direction de la Surveillance du Territoire

*Israel*
Mossad

*Germany*
BfV  Bundesamt für Verfassungsschutz
BND  Bundesnachrichtendienst

*South Africa*
NIS  National Intelligence Service; formerly BOSS
Bureau of State Security

**Neutrons, uses for**  Neutrons are one of the three 'fundamental particles' in an atom (electrons, protons and neutrons).
They have the same mass as a proton but no charge. They
were discovered by Sir James Chadwick in Cambridge
University in 1932, and have been causing trouble ever
since.

There are several ways in which neutrons can be used.
If you bombard any matter with a stream of fast-moving
neutrons, the neutrons smash into the atoms and cause
them to break up. Some people use them as weapons: they
are particularly damaging to animal tissues, and this is
how a neutron bomb can kill people without necessarily
knocking down buildings.

At MI5, we were more interested in using them to detect
microdots and read invisible writing. The process was not
simple, but the basic principles are. The effect of neutron
bombardment varies according to the nature and arrangement of the atoms in the substance being bombarded, so
you can actually find out what a substance is made of by
analysing the bits which fly off when it is hit. Better still, if
you get a piece of paper with a microdot or secret writing

on it, the neutrons will have a different effect on the microdots and invisible inks than the effect they have when they hit the other parts of the paper. So the pattern of particles coming through the paper will be like a map of the locations of the different substances. This pattern can be intensified and turned into a visible image, rather like an X-ray.

If we are looking at invisible writing, the image will be the shape of the writing itself, so the hidden message can be read directly. In the case of microdots, the microdots will show up as blobs on the image, either brighter or darker than the surrounding areas. The piece of film can then be removed and its image enlarged just as we would with our own microdot messages.

Of course there is more to it than this: you can't just go and try it in your own kitchen. For a start, you need a nuclear reactor to provide a source of high energy neutrons. But this description shows roughly how it was done. It was pretty clever at the time.

**NIS, National Intelligence Service**  This South African organisation was founded in 1978 to replace the discredited BOSS (Bureau of State Security). Unfortunately they only changed the name, not the people, the activities or the methods, and nobody really noticed the change. Just as the Security Service is still widely known as MI5, so the NIS is still referred to as BOSS by almost everybody.

It has been very successful in promoting civil war and economic collapse in several neighbouring countries, notably the ex-Portuguese colonies of Mozambique and Angola, where it financed and armed local opposition to independence movements: e.g. UNITA against the MPLA in Angola. It was somewhat less successful in South West Africa, however, and even less so in Southern Rhodesia, now Zimbabwe. There its promotion of the existing rivalry between the ZANU (Zimbabwe African National Union) and ZAPU (Zimbabwe African Peoples Union) failed to prevent an unexpectedly smooth transition to majority rule.

It has few friends abroad, the nearest to a friendly

service being Mossad, with whom it shares some common enemies.

My own involvement with BOSS was about as indirect as you could get. After the General Election in 1974, the defeated Labour Party leader and ex-Prime Minister, Harold Wilson, alleged that there had been a dirty tricks campaign against him, and claimed that it was run by BOSS. This was only partly true. There was a campaign against him, but it did not involve BOSS. I know, because I was in it.

**Norman, Herbert**   This man's name was on many lists presented to Blunt for comment, and initially he made no response to it. It was the same when we presented the name in the form 'E.H. Norman'. However, when I tried 'Herb Norman', Blunt responded immediately, 'Ah yes, Herb.'

This illustrates an important general point in interrogation technique. It is easy to assume that people are holding out on you, and unquestionably Blunt did hold out on us about a great many matters. However, in this case it seems possible that the name genuinely failed to strike a chord.

Norman was a Canadian who joined the Canadian diplomatic service. He was their ambassador to Egypt, but committed suicide when told that he was to be recalled to Canada for questioning.

**NSA**   These initials stand for the National Security Agency, the American equivalent of the British GCHQ. Just as GCHQ employs more people than its better known cousins, MI5 and MI6, so the NSA employs more people than the CIA or the FBI. This is because of the nature of the work it does: monitoring, sorting, decoding or deciphering, analysing and correlating millions upon millions of items of SIGINT, signals intelligence.

Under the SIGINT agreement, the signatories (GCHQ for Britain and the NSA for the Americans) promised not to bug one another. This is why it was the CIA which bugged us, and MI6 which bugged them.

**NSC**   This is the National Security Council. It is sometimes regarded as the American equivalent of the British JIO, but it is in some ways more like the British Cabinet.

There is no equivalent to the British Cabinet in the American system. The President *is* the executive, and hence has much greater individual power than our Prime Minister. The President then appoints his friends to be Secretaries of State. He may listen to them, but basically they have to listen to him. In this respect they have even less independence and power than our Cabinet Ministers.

Against this, the Secretaries of State are also the heads of the various service departments, jobs which are done in Britain by the permanent Civil Servants, and in this respect the American Secretaries of State have more power than our Cabinet Ministers.

Thus both the JIO and the NSA can be described as meetings of the heads of staff of the relevant departments to advise their political masters on matters of military security. But the frontiers between the staff and the political masters are drawn at different levels.

**Number plates**  When fitting false number plates, agents should remember to make sure that the front and back plates carry the same number; see *Watchers, visual detection of*.

# O

**Official Secrets Act**  This is a law to enable British governments to conceal their mistakes. Any Civil Servant who may get access to information about major mistakes has to 'sign the Official Secrets Act' (which is a shorthand way of saying that they must sign a document saying that they had read and understood the OSA).

The Act says that it is an offence to talk about Official Secrets. However, as every piece of information gathered while on the job is an Official Secret (see *Secrets, Official*), the Act no only covers every mistake, but leaves you with precious little to talk about.

In my day, the Act said that it was all right to spill the beans if it was done in the interest of The State. Nobody was silly enough to believe that The State was the British public, who are subjects, not citizens, and have no rights in this or any other matter. But many people had the idea that The State meant Parliament.

This view was tested during the Falklands War. A senior member of the Ministry of Defence, whose job it was to prepare answers to questions in Parliament, found that an answer he had written was put aside by the Government and a lie substituted. He was very upset about this, and told the Parliamentary Opposition. He was then immediately arraigned under the Official Secrets Act, just as if he had given it to the KGB.

The case was tried before a judge and jury. The judge summed up strongly in favour of the Government, but the jury decided that The State was indeed Parliament. So he got off. (For further details of the case, see _Ponting case, the_.)

It didn't do any good in the long run. The Government immediately rewrote the Official Secrets Act to make quite clear that The State means the Government of the Day.

I was never taken to court under the Official Secrets Act. I could have been, since I had done security work in Australia, and Australia has a similar Act (part of the Crimes Act). If the British Attorney General, Sir Michael Havers, had asked the Australian one, Gareth Evans, to take the case over, it could have turned into a Crimes Act trial. Havers probably asked, but if he did, Evans very wisely said no, knowing that he would have lost.

So I was sued in a civil court – for breach of duty of confidentiality to the Crown. This was strange considering that all I did was to tell people that Her Majesty's realm was in danger and that Her Majesty's Government was doing damn all about it.

**One-time pads** The best code system known to us in the Second World War was one-time pads. They worked like this: first, you had a codebook which turned all the key words in the message into 2 or 4-digit numbers; then, you had a code pad consisting of pages of 4-digit numbers. To encipher the message, you added the two together.

Two four digit numbers can add to a five digit number, upsetting the tidy pattern of groups each of four digits. To stop this happening, they were added on the Fibonacci system, which ignored carrying or borrowing. For the way it worked, see _Fibonacci system_.

If you needed words which were not in the codebook (like the names of new people who had not yet been assigned code names and numbers) there were codes for the letters of the alphabet, and you spelled the word out, starting and finishing with codes meaning spell and end-spell. You could do the whole message this way, of course, but it would take a lot longer. (The main purpose of the codebook was to keep the message short, not to make it difficult to understand.)

The recipient used an identical pad to decipher the

message, subtracting the numbers given on the one-time pad to get back to the original numbers (again using the Fibonacci system), and then using the codebook to translate them back into plain language.

Any given message did not need to start at the beginning of a pad. The message would start with an indicator group, a sequence of numbers straight off the pad, indicating where on the pad the message started.

Let us say that the current one-time pad is looking like this:

| 4395 | 3945 | 4857 | 0394 | 9384 |
|------|------|------|------|------|
| 5963 | 9458 | 7364 | 4579 | 8742 |

The numbers with a line through them have been used. We make next number, 9384, the *indicator group*, and the message will start after that. We start by copying the sequence of numbers off the pad:

|  | *indicator group* | | | |
|----------|------|------|------|------|
| From pad | 9384 | 5963 | 9458 | 7364 |

Let us say that the message is 'London will be attacked tomorrow'. Using the codebook, we encode it as (say):

| Message: | London | attack | tomorrow |
|----------|--------|--------|----------|
| Coded message | 1334 | 5863 | 6923 |

Now we insert these codes under the numbers from the pad, and add the two figures together using the Fibonacci system of ignoring carrying:

|  | *indicator group* | | | |
|----------------|------|------|------|------|
| From pad: | 9384 | 5963 | 9458 | 7364 |
| Coded message: |  | 1334 | 5863 | 6923 |
| Fibonacci+ |  | ____ | ____ | ____ |
| Cipher: | 9384 | 6297 | 4211 | 3287 |

At the far end, the decoding clerk writes down the enciphered numbers as they come in over the radio, marries up the first group with an identical group on a current one-time pad, and copies the next numbers from the pad underneath the incoming cipher. He subtracts the pad number from the cipher, and dives for the cipher book to discover the message

| Cipher: | 9384 | 6297 | 4211 | 3287 |
|---|---|---|---|---|
| From pad: | 9384 | 5963 | 9458 | 7364 |
| Fibonacci— | ___ | ___ | ___ | ___ |
| Coded message: | | 1334 | 5863 | 6923 |
| Message: | | London | attack | tomorrow |

As shown in the entry on *Fibonacci system*, the two 'wrong' calculations cancel one another out, producing the right answer.

If they are used as intended, these codes are totally unbreakable. There is no relationship at all between the finished string of numbers and the original string of numbers, however powerful the computer used to analyse the numbers, and the same message would look totally different if sent a second time with a different pad or a different indicator group.

The only times we had any luck with one-time pads were when the Russians re-used them (see *Bride*) and when we found some pads before they were used (see *Lonsdale, Gordon*). In Lonsdale's case, we had difficulty with the first message we tried to read, because it clearly did not start at the beginning of a pad, yet did not seem to have indicator groups to show where to begin. Our initial fear was that he must be using new or different pads, but a return trip to his flat showed that he had used the ones we had copied. We then experimented with matching the middle of the message with various positions on the pad, and eventually found a sequence which yielded sense.

The first groups, which should have been the indicators, still made no sense. We subsequently discovered that Lonsdale had encoded them by adding his birthday.

**OPC**  Office of Policy Co-ordination; see *CIA*.

**Overseas operations**  Mounting bugging operations in a foreign country was very different from doing it at home. For a start, the telephone people were not as helpful, and you had a very different relationship with the police. If you were caught doing something illegal, you were really on your own, particularly if you were operating against the local authorities.

Of course, if you were simply helping the local authorities, it could be just like working at home. This was so in Australia, where ASIO had been set up on the model of MI5, complete with moles. In Canada, the security service was part of the Royal Canadian Mounted Police, the Mounties, who are a legal organisation. In theory, this should have cramped their style – the main argument for having MI5 as a secret organisation was that it gave it a freedom to act illegally which an official organisation couldn't have. But this never seemed to worry the Mounties. They burgled and bugged with the best of us. (For an example, see *Dew Worm*.) But later the security service was split off and set up separately.

It was a halfway situation in Ireland and Cyprus, where we theoretically had the authorities on our side, but we had to assume that most of the post and telephone people were spies for the other side. This meant that, although we could easily get warrants, we could not use legal telephone taps and mail interceptions. We had to improvise our own.

It was different again in Germany. There, we were not working with the local authorities at all – just the opposite. We used German wire and components, the idea being that if they found the mikes and wires we could just laugh it off, saying it had nothing to do with us. In fact, everybody would know it was us from the trade craft – our techniques would be written all over it – but we still did it. It was a routine procedure for all security services to use one another's materials and components. It was like using a false name – it became so automatic that you never thought twice about it.

# P

**Party walls**  Anyone who has lived in a terrace house knows that a party wall is not secure. The next-door neighbours can hear everything you do through it, and vice versa. But if they wake you up in the middle of the night making a great racket with drilling machinery, you should be extra suspicious.

The Russians were very careful about the party walls of their embassies. If a room adjoined a party wall, they would partition it into two smaller rooms, using the one adjoining the party wall for social chit-chat and the other, separated off from the party wall, for real business. This is quite a sensible precaution.

Flats present an even greater problem, since they can be bored into from above or below as well as sideways. Just about the only people who have their consulates and embassies in blocks of flats are the Swiss. They keep their secrets in banks, not embassies.

**Passports**  It is a good idea to have several passports in different names, because if your name is known you are liable to be noticed at passport control.

In my day, the main worry was West Germany. All the West Germans had friends and relations in the East Zone, and you never knew which side they were on. The Communists had infiltrated the government, security services and the whole civil service from top to bottom, and the chances were that the person who checked your passport as you came in was one of them. If I had come in as Peter

Wright they would have alerted their people, as everybody seemed to know that Peter Wright meant trouble. When I travelled as Peter Wright, I got held up at every passport control. So it was that Peter Wright never went to Germany. However, Paul Winchester went there quite often.

The second rule about passports is always to use the same one in any given country. They have little cameras under the desks in passport control, and photograph key pages of the passport, including the photograph of the owner. If they notice the same person coming and going under several names, they can get suspicious.

The third rule is to make sure that, on any given trip, all your documents are in the same name. You feel very silly if you have to produce a driving licence and some foreigner notices that the name is different from the one on your passport. For the same reason, it is a good idea to choose names with the same initials – having the wrong initials on suitcases can cause suspicions.

At MI5, all this was looked after by D Branch. They had a list of your names, showing which ones you used in each country, and which ones might have been blown. They made sure that you had the right passport and other papers for the place you would be visiting, and no other ones. People get very suspicious if they search you and find a whole lot of passports and driving licences in different names.

Ours were not false passports, They were all real ones, properly issued by the passport office. We would fill in the forms and send them round to a friend we had there. The only thing that was different was that we didn't have to produce birth certificates and so forth, as our friend would sign off all the forms without seeing the certificates. But if the Russians had got hold of the passport office records and checked our passports against them, they would not have been able to distinguish ours from real ones.

Most people have to put up with false passports. The most easily available alternative for most people is an Irish one. However, if it came to a choice, I would prefer to have a completely false one than an Irish one. Having an Irish one is asking for trouble.

**Penetration**  The dictionary defines *penetration* as the insertion of one of your own members into another body.

In the world of espionage, there are two ways of achieving penetration. The first is to put your own agent in, and the second is to find someone who is already in the enemy body, recruiting him as your agent and leaving him there 'in place' (q.v.) to do what you want him to.

Penetration is the best medium for espionage. It is easy to get people to sit outside an organisation's headquarters watching the folk coming and going, but you get a far better view if you have a friend in the boardroom.

Without any doubt, the best way is to put your own man in. Such people generally have undivided loyalties – their whole lives within the organisation they penetrate are a sham, and their real commitment is always to you. But it needs a lot of long-term planning. The great strength of Russian penetration of the West was their capacity to find people who believed in Communism, and who would then do anything they were told to.

All the great Russian spies in Britain – Philby, Maclean, Burgess, Blunt, Cairncross and so on, were of this sort. They were recruited as undergraduates and devoted their lives to the cause. They were told where to go and what was expected of them, and obeyed. Some of the instructions were quite bizarre – Guy Burgess was supposed to get married, which would have been a turn up for the books; see *Argentine meat, price of.*

Many of their sleepers are probably still waiting for instructions today. It is their Russian masters who have deserted the cause, not they. It must be very depressing for them, rather like being a contemplative nun and hearing that God has embraced Satanism and is no longer answering calls.

We never really managed to get our own people into the KGB. We had to wait for one of them to decide to change sides. Perhaps this was because our cause was just patriotism, and you can't be patriotic about somebody else's country. A lot of British students had portraits of Marx and Lenin in their rooms, but I doubt whether many Russians had portraits of Queen Elizabeth II and Sir Anthony Eden in theirs, or even hidden in cupboards. They might have had a portrait of the Czar tucked away somewhere, but this would not necessarily have made them potential recruits for the Free World.

There was a lot of penetration in Germany – both East and West Germany had infiltrated agents in one another's security services and government agencies, and they all thought they were being patriotic. But even there the East Germans seem to have done better than we did. They really *believed* in espionage.

The other way to achieve penetration was to use double agents and defectors, turning people who were already in high places and recruiting them to work for you. We used this a great deal, but I was never sure about it. Anyone who turned traitor once could turn traitor again. And could you be sure that he had really changed his loyalties? And might he not have another change of heart tomorrow? It was bad enough with people we had chosen as possible recruits, but even more dangerous with people who had come to us offering their services; see *Double agents*.

I have often wondered about the Serpent in the Garden of Eden. Was he a Satanic plant, or was he one of God's creatures who had been turned by Satan and was being run in place, or was he an agent provocateur being run by God? The Serpent was attempting to compromise the young couple within hours of their arrival, and it had probably been there for some time before that, perhaps since as early as the fifth day, which suggests a sleeper. But was he?

It is easy to say that a talking Serpent offering apples should have aroused suspicion, but God had not instructed the couple in the need for security. The serpent didn't have to blow their cover; it blew the fact that they had no cover. Finding themselves compromised, Adam and Eve had no option but to defect.

The subsequent history of the Middle East might have been very different had God decided at that point to abandon the whole operation and to make a fresh start elsewhere, with different personnel. That's what I would have done in His position. But maybe He had it all planned from the start.

**Penkovsky, Colonel Oleg**  Penkovsky was either one of the bravest heroes of the Cold War or a spectacular plant.

He attempted to defect three times: first to the American embassy in Moscow in 1960, where they concluded that he was a provocateur; second to a Canadian 'business-man' called van Vleet, early in 1961; and then to British 'business-man' Greville Wynne. At the third attempt he was taken seriously, and spied 'in place' (q.v.) for the CIA and MI6.

The principal arguments in his favour are the value of the information he gave us, which led amongst other things to the resolution of the Cuban Missile crisis, and the fact that he was tried and sentenced to be shot.

But was he really executed? and was the Cuban Missile crisis designed to be resolved? We may never know the answer to the first question, but the second one can perhaps be answered.

At the time, all the talk was about ICBMs, Intercontinental Ballistic Missiles, in which the Russians were said to have a lead over the West. It was in their interest to play down this lead, and how better to do it than the revelation of a plan to base IRBMs (Intermediate Range Ballistic Missiles) in Cuba. The West would conclude that they were deploying IRBMs because they did not have ICBMs capable of doing the job.

If so, then the operation was designed to be blown, and to make sure of this they sent Penkovsky to establish his credentials with some real information and then produce this great piece of disinformation. Next, they sent the IRBMs over as deck cargo on a ship, where they were bound to be noticed. They were duly photographed by US patrol aircraft. President Kennedy was thus able to have the great personal triumph of 'calling their bluff'. It was a bluff, but perhaps the real bluff was never called.

There is another powerful argument for this view. Penkovsky had been working for MI6 and the CIA for over a year, and all the top level officers in MI5 knew about him. I knew, for example, because I organised the microphones at the Mount Royal Hotel when MI6 and the CIA interviewed him there in 1961. Information based on his disclosures was very widely distributed – I counted 1700 names in Britain alone; and although the source was not named, the nature of the information would have alerted any mole who had seen it. Hence either there were no moles among the 1700 or he was a plant.

But we knew that there were moles among the 1700.

This is not an argument which would stand up in a court of law. It is just circumstantial. There are not many things in espionage which can be proved, because the possibilities of double cross and triple cross are infinite. But if the purpose was to lull us into a sense of security and ultimately make the SALT treaties and detente possible, it succeeded, as disinformation so often does. –

**Philanthropists**  A philanthropist is a person who helps other people in their hour of need. For example, after I had been treated very shabbily by MI5 and retired on half pension, Mrs Margaret Thatcher came to my aid and organised the publicity for my book *Spycatcher*. –

**Philby, Kim**  Everybody knows that Kim Philby was a KGB man, and many people wonder how he got away with it for so long.

Philby was very charming. I first met him just before he went to Washington to take up his position as head of the MI6 station there, when he came in to say goodbye to his friends in MI5. This may not sound odd, but he was almost the only MI6 person who could have done it – the only one to have any friends at MI5. Generally, the two services didn't fraternise at all.

This friendliness had made him very effective in the war, when it was important for the two services to work together. So long as we were fighting with the Russians against the Germans, he did a good job. And of course it meant that he had friends everywhere. That was his first line of defence. Nobody could believe that a person so charming, so very English, so much a member of the Establishment, could be a spy.

He was very charming to me that first time we met. I took to him immediately because he had a stammer, just like me, and was obviously very intelligent, unlike the usual MI6 man. I was not yet in the Service, just doing odd jobs for them, but he expressed interest in everything I was doing. Of course, I know now that he was wanting to get information about me and what I was doing to find out whether there was anything the Russians ought to know, but at the time it was very gratifying, like a personal pat on the back.

Six years later we met again under very different circumstances. In 1951, Burgess and Maclean had defected, and Philby had come under suspicion for tipping them off, but had remained on staff. In 1955, he had been dismissed by MI6, though nothing had been proved against him. So it was that, just three weeks after I joined the Service, my partner Hugh Winterborn came into my room and told me we had got the job of bugging the room in which MI6 were to interrogate him again.

We could have put SF on the phone, but we wanted a really clear recording, so we installed a proper microphone – an Activox, like the BBC used. The set-up was designed to look very easy and informal – a circle of armchairs round the fireplace – and we put the mike under the floorboards near the grate. This fed into an amplifier wired direct into the phone line, which took it back to the Seventh Floor of Leconfield House – MI5's monitoring and transcription room.

I monitored the session on earphones. It was the most pitiful interrogation I have ever heard in my life. For example, when they said to him 'Kim, you've never explained why there was that tremendous burst of traffic out of the Russian embassy in Washington when Maclean defected', he just stuttered and stalled. You could hear the cogs going round in his mind. Finally he just shrugged and said 'Ask the Russians', and they dropped the subject. No follow-up questions. They were out to let him off. One of the interrogators, Nicholas Elliott, was even feeding him answers. It was all the time 'Surely, Kim, the explanation is this . . .'

Listening to it, I was horrified. We all were. So we wrote a report expressing our worries, and when MI6 put in a report to the Prime Minister, Harold Macmillan, clearing Philby, ours was attached.

A few weeks later Harold Macmillan sold the whole thing down the river. He stood up in the House of Commons and said that there was no evidence against Philby, so he became a clean man.

I was shocked, but Hugh Winterborn just laughed and said 'You'll be shocked a lot more times yet'. He was right. Time after time I have been shocked by the way Britain's politicians and top Civil Servants will lie and deceive, not for operational reasons or for the public good but to get themselves out of trouble; see *Lying to Parliament*.

Eight years later, our worries were finally proved to be justified by revelations from the Russian defector, Golitsin, and an old girl friend of Philby's, Flora Solomon. He was interrogated again, and this time he confessed. The final interrogation was again done by his old friend Nicholas Elliott, on the curious grounds that Elliott might be better able to get the truth out of him as one old Public School boy to another. This attitude illustrated what was wrong with the security services at the time; see *Public School*. Elliott was immensely clubbable. He had no other merit.

Anyway, Elliott managed to organise the taping so badly that it sounded as if it was being conducted on a traffic island in the middle of Oxford Street. It took hours of careful work by our best transcribers, Evelyn McBarnet and Anne Orr-Ewing, just to get a transcript of it.

But even in defecting he had the last laugh. When we finally got the transcript, it was evident that he had been tipped off – he had all his answers planned. He also wrote and signed a lengthy confession, and this, too, was a mess of truth and lies, clearly calculated to cause us maximum anguish and doubt. He had known what was coming, and was prepared.

But then he turned up in Moscow in his new Russian officer's uniform, and there was no room for doubt any more. Even those of us who had been sure he was bent hated being proved right. That was a bad day for all of us.

**Phones, answering of**  The senior agent should never answer his own phone. The caller may be merely finding out whether he is in as a prelude to kidnapping him or blowing the place up.

**Photographs of buildings, how to take**  If you are taking a photograph of a building, always take two, moving a few paces sideways for the second one. If you do this, the two pictures can be used as a stereoscopic pair, and you will see a great deal of detail which is not visible in one. In particular, you will be able to see rods (e.g. the elements of dipoles) which are pointing in the direction of the camera, which will be virtually invisible in any one photograph. –

**Picking locks**  The police take a very dim view of people who are found to be carrying lock-picking apparatus. If you are found with it in your possession your legs don't touch the ground going into the cooler.

For the ordinary door lock, you need a set of skeleton keys. It is then just a matter of finding the skeleton key which fits the lock. Ordinary door locks – ward locks, they call them – are actually opened by the middle part of the key. All the 'wards', the odd-shaped bits which look so intricate, only stop the key from opening other locks. If you cut them off, the key will still open its own lock but will also open all others based on the same 'skeleton'.

For Yale locks we were given special stroking tools, bits of bent wire with which you stroked the tumblers into line. I always carried mine with me – and still do, for that matter. It was illegal, but I had a police pass which would have helped explain it away. I was very glad I had it with me the day James Jesus Angleton, Head of Counter-intelligence in the CIA, locked himself out of his car in Washington. I was able to open it for him.

Next in difficulty came Chubb locks. We could not pick

them. If we could get hold of the key for a few seconds we could take an impression of it in plasticine. Failing that, we could X-ray the lock and work out the shape of its tumblers from various X-ray views. Then we could work out what shape the key had to be.

The worst were Brahma locks. These have tumblers moving down the length of the lock, not up and down as in a Yale lock. The key has a sort of coronet of spikes, and you cannot find out about it even by X-raying it. You have to get hold of it before it is installed, take it apart and make a key. This doesn't generally help much – you don't realise you want a key to a lock until you are trying to open it. However, it helped us once. We found a lock that was about to be installed in an embassy safe, and although they were friends of ours we made a spare key for ourselves, just in case. It proved quite useful. But you can't rely on that sort of luck.

The fact is that the best way to open a lock is with a key. Leslie Jagger, who taught us all to pick locks, could open a Yale lock almost as quickly with a stroking tool as with a key, but he could still open it quicker with a key. The worst thing about picking locks is that you cannot really help scratching them, so the enemy knows you have been there. If you get in with a key, nobody need by the wiser.

Conversely, if you think a lock of yours has been picked, examine it for scratches. If you find some which were not there before, you can be pretty sure someone has been trying to get in. And, unless it is a Chubb or Brahma lock, you can be pretty sure that they succeeded.

**Ploughing** I believe that I am the only Senior Intelligence Officer since the war to have experience of driving a horse-drawn plough, and certainly the only one to have done it with a hyperactive horse. Perhaps this should be put in *The Guinness Book of Records*.

It was shortly after the war, and I was still working for the Navy, but seconded to the Marconi laboratory in Baddow. We had bought a small farm called Newlands, in the village of Widdington in Essex. We raised Aberdeen

Angus cattle and Large Black pigs, and decided to grow some oats in part of one of the fields. We had a plough, but our ponies were too small to pull it; so my wife Lois borrowed a large horse from some people in Henham, and rode it home. Then it was my job to do the ploughing.

I am sure that it would have been all right if the horse had been an ordinary, quiet horse, but this horse seemed to be wanting to get away from the plough, and as the plough was attached to it the result was that we went faster and faster, charging up and down until the whole field was ploughed; and not just ploughed, but laid waste.

Finding ourselves with more land ploughed than we needed for oats, we decided to grow mangel wurzels in the rest. If you think that the turnip is the most repulsive root vegetable in the world, you haven't tried swede, and if you think swede is the worst, you haven't tried mangel wurzel. However, to the Large Black pig, the mangel wurzel is strawberries and smoked salmon. They cannot see it clearly, because they suffer from a chronic problem with their vision, arising from the fact that their ear flaps tend to grow over their eyes. But they seem to sense the presence of a mangel wurzel, and the awareness drives them mad. I have seen our prize Large Black sow, Duchess, pick up a mangel wurzel and run headlong into a wall in blinded frenzy.

**Policeman, avoidance of**   Never make a policeman head of a security organisation. Policemen are good at keeping the peace, but peace and security are different things.

MI5 had a policeman in charge just after the Second World War. His name was Sir Percy Sillitoe. They got round the problem by not telling him what was going on. About the only positive thing he did was to agree that MI5 needed a scientific officer, the job I filled. So, come to think of it, perhaps even he had his points.

**Ponting case, the**   The Ponting case was not strictly a matter of security, but it was made into one by the actions of the British government. The key facts were as follows:

Ponting was a senior member of the Department of

Defence, one of whose jobs was to supply the Minister of Defence with answers to questions in Parliament.

During the Falklands War, he became concerned that the Minister was being less than frank with Parliament. The Minister was asserting that the truth would endanger the lives of British servicemen in the south Atlantic, but Ponting believed that the truth was being avoided because it would disclose the previous lies and incompetence of Cabinet.

In particular, Ponting was worried by an answer to a question relating to the sinking of the Argentinian cruiser *General Belgrano* by acoustic torpedoes from the submarine HMS *Conqueror*. He had believed that the national interest would be best served by telling the truth, and had prepared a truthful answer; but the Government persisted in their lies. He then disclosed the truth to the Opposition's spokesman for defence, Tam Dalziel.

At his subsequent trial under the Official Secrets Act, his defence asserted that the disclosure was covered by the clause in the OSA permitting disclosure if it was 'in the interest of the State'. They argued that 'the State' meant Parliament. The Crown, supported by the judge in his summing up, asserted that the State meant the Government of the Day. The jury found for the defence.

For a short time, Britain had a situation almost similar to that in America, where Congress is sovereign. However, the Thatcher government rapidly brought in amendments to the Official Secrets Act making it clear that the Act was to defend the interest of the Government of the Day; see *Lying to Parliament*.

**Property**   MI5 cannot own property, since it does not exist. As a result, its property is owned by a front organisation called The Treasury.

The Treasury's accounts are audited by the Chief Auditor, who is not party to the secret that MI5 exists (see *Secrets, Official*) and is therefore surprised afresh every year to find that Treasury owns a large number of apparently unoccupied houses in Mayfair, Belgravia and Kensington.

One of these days, somebody should let him into the secret.

**Prostitution**  It is well known that MI5 gained useful information by employing ladies who gave sexual favours to foreign diplomats and agents. It has been suggested that this means that we required our female agents to become prostitutes. This allegation is rubbish. We recruited prostitutes as agents.

**Public School**  The biggest single source of the problems in the British Security Service was the Public Schools. British readers must forgive this entry, which is designed for those (Americans, perhaps) who think that a public school is a school for the public.

Once upon a time, all the people in Britain who mattered were educated privately, by tutors, at home. These tutors would often be made available to other families within the same household – retainers, courtiers and hangers-on generally – so that these tutors came to be in charge of 'private' schools.

There were also tutors who set up schools which were independent of any single benefactor or patron, getting their pupils from the great houses up and down the country. Because entry was by fees rather than by private patronage, they were called 'public' schools.

The descendants of these schools still survive in Britain, and are still called public, although the level of fees ensure that the public is kept at bay. To show that the phrase is used in this rather odd way, we give it capital letters: Public School.

The schools are used to maintain the class system. The classes are kept apart by having distinctive languages, customs and schools. This is how each class recognises its own members, rather like a Masonic handshake.

Why does this matter? For many years, the Security Service recruited all its officers from the Public Schools. This was not regarded as odd: it was the same in the Army, the Navy, the Church and the higher levels of the Civil Service. A Public School background was considered not only a necessary but also a sufficient condition for getting a good job in any of the government services. You didn't need to check up whether a person had any brains, or was trustworthy, or patriotic, or was the right sort of person for the job. You just said 'Public School?' and if the answer was 'Yes' you gave him the job.

It worked reasonably well in most jobs. For example, it didn't matter much who was in charge of the Army and the Church. It meant you got a lot of atheists as bishops, which some people thought rather odd, but enough of the bishops believed in God to keep religion going, and they all had the right accents, which was what really mattered. It was the same in the Army. A lot of very strange people became officers, but not enough to stop the Army doing its job when it was needed.

But in security it was different. It only takes one highly-placed traitor to blow the whole organisation, and MI5 and MI6 between them had four we knew about (Philby, Maclean, Burgess and Blunt) and God knows how many we didn't know about. When we did fear that we had another spy in the Service (see *Tisler, Frantisek*) the Public School group all thought it couldn't be one of them, so they all suspected the Watchers.

That was not the only problem. When I joined MI5, the whole atmosphere of the office was just like a minor Public School. There was the same hero worship and bullying and sucking up to the masters and the prefects. They didn't want MI5 to *do* anything. They just liked the easy life – the big salaries and no questions asked. People who had some sort of conscience, who felt that we had a job to do for the country, were looked on as trouble-makers.

But it was the treachery that really got me down. I could never really understand it. Here were these people who always had the best of everything – money, social position, the best schools, and then all the plum jobs – and they were selling the country down the drain, while the ordinary people of Britain, who were treated with total contempt, were as patriotic as they come.

The women were not much better. The Registry was full of girls who would be Lady so-and-so when they got married, and that's what got them the job. Not competence, or efficiency, or integrity, but membership of the ruling class. As it happens, most of them hadn't the brains to be spies, but so long as they had the right accents nobody checked up.

Thank goodness that will have all changed by now.

# R

**Radar**  For a simple discussion of the principles of radar, see *Centimetric radar*.

**Radiations Operations Committee**  This committee made a major contribution to Britain's intelligence activities during the sixties. I was its founder and first Chairman, and bringing it into being is an achievement of which I am proud.

The committee was concerned with all sorts of operations involving electromagnetic radiations, but the most important of these was the interception, monitoring and interpreting of Russian radio and radar transmissions. It also covered our own development of, for example, bugging devices activated by irradiation from a distance.

The first remarkable thing about the ROC was that it was formed jointly by GCHQ, MI5, MI6 and the intelligence units of the three services. This will not seem odd unless you remember the jealousies which existed at the time. We sometimes felt that we knew more about what the KGB were doing than we knew about what MI6 were doing. Neither organisation told us much about what they were doing, but at least with the KGB we spent a lot of time and effort finding out for ourselves.

The ROC used to meet fortnightly, and would share information about our radiation-based operations: what we were doing, what success we were having, and where we needed help.

It was started after our first success with Rafter – to find out what broadcasts the Russians were listening to in their embassy; Engulf – to read the cipher off the Hagelin machines in the Egyptian embassy; and Stockade – to bug the French. Everybody realised that we had techniques which could be very useful in many areas, but we had to make the best use of limited resources and ensure we did not risk blowing the techniques by using them in some trivial operations.

Happily, there were people at GCHQ and in MI6 who were sensible enough to realise that rivalry in such matters would get us all nowhere, and my proposal for the formation of the ROC was thus approved. It allocated resources and decided on targets.

**Radio, principles of** Anyone who wants to be a spy or counter-spy ought to know the fundamental principles of radio. These would fill at least two books the size of this one, but a brief account, covering most of the aspects which are relevant here, is found in the entry entitled *Rafter*.

**Radio: intelligence without messages** Radio is a very insecure way of communicating. It is just too easy to eavesdrop. But the danger is not just that the wrong people may get the message. The transmission itself may give an enemy useful intelligence, even if it contains no message.

Firstly, of course, for every transmission there has to be a transmitter, so that you can sometimes get useful information just from the fact that a transmission is taking place. It means that somebody is there. As early as the first days of World War One, both sides monitored the airwaves, so that ships at sea had to maintain radio silence if they wanted to keep their presence in a given area secret from the enemy.

Next, if you have two receivers, you can fix the position of a transmitter with great accuracy. Essentially, you rotate a directional aerial until you find the direction at which the signal is at maximum strength, and this gives you a bearing on the transmitter. If you take a second similar bearing from another receiving point, the intersection of the two bearings gives the location of the transmitter; see RDF.

The first substantial advance on RDF, Radio Direction

Finding, came with the invention of radar, Radio Direction And Ranging, which enabled direction and range to be determined from a single transmitter/receiver. Radar transmits a pulse and measures the bearing and time lapse of the echo bounced off the distant object; see *Centimetric radar*.

In the Second World War, bombers had their own radar as an aid to navigation [and to warn of the approach of enemy~NIGHT~ fighters;] but often the enemy fighters used the transmissions from the radar equipment to guide them to the bombers. The bomber crews had a nasty pair of options: to keep their radar on, so that they got warning of the approach of a German fighter, but risked drawing attention to themselves; or to turn the radar off, thereby not drawing attention to themselves but getting no warning of fighter attack.

*[handwritten margin note: THIS ENTIRE BLURB REQUIRE CONNECTI OUR FRIE IS RED WRONG]*

All this information was got from radio transmissions which were just electronic noise: they either had no message or, in the case of the naval chatter, had a message, but it was irrelevant to the way it was used. Since people had been learning so much by listening to electronic noise for nearly half a century, it is strange that they were surprised to find that the Russians were doing the same in London in the 1960s.

We discovered that they were listening to our chatter through Operation Rafter (q.v.). Rafter enabled us to find out what frequencies the Russians were listening to, we found that they were not only listening to our Watchers, but also to the naval and military chatter – and learning a lot from it. However, Rafter gave us a whole lot of new opportunities. It worked like this:

First, we got GCHG to monitor the broadcasts~SIC~ coming out of Moscow which seemed to be aimed at agents; see GCHQ. From this monitoring, they produced signal plans, i.e. schedules of frequencies, times and call signs.

Next, using Rafter, we tested these frequencies at the relevant times, and found which ones the Russians were listening to.~?~ There were about two hundred of them.

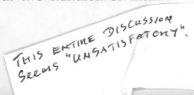

*[handwritten note: THIS ENTIRE DISCUSSION SEEMS "UNSATISFACTORY".]*

Although we could only very rarely crack the cipher (see *Lonsdale, Gordon*) the call signs had different patterns, distinguishing KGB agents from GRU agents, and we were eventually able to distinguish which were which.

But we could find out a lot more about each of the agents than this. For example, an agent who got very few messages was almost certainly a sleeper, getting just enough to keep the channels open; an agent who got very short messages, perhaps five groups, twice a week or so, was almost certainly a saboteur; and so on. Most of the messages were Morse cipher, but some standard messages took the form of tunes; see *Communication with a foreign power*.

Next, we were able to use this information to identify the Intelligence Officers within the embassy. The Watchers kept a log of the comings and going of the staff, so we knew who was in the embassy when the monitoring was going on; see *Who's who at the embassy?*

Finally, there were occasions when we were able to use Rafter on an agent who was ~~working~~ LISTENING. This was more difficult, as the detection range was limited. We could often hear them from the air where the effective range of the ~~transmissions~~ EMANATIONS from the ~~local~~ INTERNAL RADIO oscillators was much longer, but it was not possible to get a bead on the [transmitter] from a low-flying aircraft. All we could be certain of was that they were down their somewhere, listening to their incomprehensible but surely diabolical instructions coming in from Moscow. It was a strange feeling to listen to it.

**Radioactive markers** When we were trying to stop people stealing classified documents, we evolved a nice way of going about it with radioactive markers.

The idea was simply to put a stripe of radioactive material down the side of the document, and have a detector by the door. If anyone went out carrying one of these documents in his pocket or in a briefcase, the detector would sense the presence of the document and trigger a camera which would photograph the chap taking it out.

Unfortunately, we were never allowed to use it. It happened just at the time when everybody was starting to get scared stiff of radioactivity. The idea was referred to some safety expert who said it was dangerous.

Of course, it wasn't. At that time, people were saying that there was no bottom limit of safety when it came to radiation. In a way this is true – you can argue that any radioactive material is dangerous. But if you want to take this seriously, you had better go somewhere else to live, because the whole universe is full of natural low-level radioactivity. It is more sensible to regard levels which are close to the natural background radioactivity as being safe; otherwise, you deny yourself some valuable uses of radioactive materials.

We used material whose radiations had certain characteristics you could only detect on a special detector. This meant that we did not have to make it strong enough to drown out the background radiation. It was even less dangerous than the background. Even so, the chap who looked at it turned it down flat. I'm pretty certain he didn't understand what we were doing.

**Rafter** This is the code name for an operation which was perhaps the most successful of all those for which I was responsible.

I had been trying for years to persuade GCHQ to work out a way of finding out whether the Russians were listening to our Watchers' radio, but they always said it was impossible. Perhaps they really believed this; or perhaps they just couldn't see the point. Anyway, under an agreement they had with MI5, GCHQ had a monopoly on all SIGINT (signals intelligence) so that was that.

This changed following the Tisler affair; see _Tisler, Frantisek_. Everybody at MI5 wanted to know whether the Russians were listening to the Watchers, as this might have helped to explain the events which Tisler described (to say nothing of making nonsense of a lot of the Watchers' work). I got approval to do some experiments – 'approval' meant that they said they would back me if GCHQ kicked up a stink.

There were devices for telling whether there was a radio RECEIVER
being ~~operated~~ [USED?] in a building. Some had been developed by
the GPO in the thirties to hunt for people who had not paid
their wireless licences. But these did not say what frequency the radio was tuned to. ( HUNT RECEPTION FREQUENCY.)

These devices depended on the basic principles of radio.
To set the scene, I'll try to describe the basic principle on
which the success of this and other operations were based.

The main principle of radio is that every time an electric
current is turned on or off, a radio pulse is transmitted.
This happens around 500 times a second in the ignition
circuit of a car, for example, and cars used to cause a
horrible buzzing noise on nearby wireless and TV sets until
it was made compulsory to fit them with suppressors. And
we stop stray signals from getting into our sound systems
by 'screening' the leads – the fine-wire mesh round the
leads is the screening.

If a device is running on an alternating current, the
current is changing all the time, so the radio transmission
is continuous, with a frequency which depends on the
frequency of the alternations. This is how we generate
radio waves for communications. The range of practical
frequencies and wavelengths we use is divided into classes
with names:

| Typical frequency | Equivalent wavelength | Popularly known as |
|---|---|---|
| 0.1 MHz | 3000 m | Long wave |
| 1 MHz | 300 m | Medium wave |
| 10 MHz | 30 m | Short wave |
| 100 MHz | 3 m | VHF (e.g. FM radio) |
| 1000 MHz | 0.3 m | UHF (e.g. TV) |

These figures are related to one another. In each case,
the wavelength in metres multiplied by the frequency in
hertz (or cycles/second) gives the speed of light, in metres
per second ($3 \times 10^8$ m/s). Thus, if you know the frequency,
you can work out the equivalent wavelength, and vice versa.
My microwave oven operates at 2450 MHz, so the wavelength

of its radiations is just over 0.12 m, or 12 centimetres.

Whether the waves are produced efficiently, and are hence detectable at any worthwhile distance from the source, will depend on the currents involved, the frequency of the alternations and the size of the components. The size of the components is important because radiations are generated most efficiently if the waves can 'resonate' in a conductor, and they can resonate best if the conductor is at least half as long as the waves. So anyone who wants to transmit will put up a resonator designed to maximise the radiations, whose length is governed by the wavelengths being transmitted; in other words, an aerial. A receiving aerial does the same thing the other way round.

Most natural and accidental radio transmissions are too weak to be detectable. Transmissions from electric motors may interfere with nearby wireless and TV sets, and those from power lines can upset car wirelesses as you drive underneath them. But only a small fraction of the millions of potential radio sources produce transmissions which are detectable on ordinary wireless sets.

In the case of Rafter, the [stray] *precise* transmissions we were listening for were from what are called the local oscillators. These are essential [components] *circuitry* of the short wave superhet receivers used for short wave and VHF reception at the time. The local oscillators produced the very high frequency currents needed to 'beat down' the [transmission frequencies of the] incoming signals to the frequencies which could be processed in the receiver.

There was no question that such an oscillator would *does* generate radio waves. The only question was, would they carry far enough in a strength great enough to be monitored? GCHQ said no, but my calculations suggested that the transmission would carry at least a couple of hundred metres. We realised that they would not give direct evidence of the wavelength, but we hoped that by comparing it with the various *typical* audio signals on an ordinary receiver, we would be able to find some sort of match.

The scheme worked better than I had dared hope, but

*These are the same as the internal oscillators in a TV-set, which can be detected and located by the TV-Licence chappies.*

the key breakthrough was accidental. We had set up our receivers in a special van that had been developed for mobile radio work. It looked like an ordinary delivery van, but the body contained no metal, so that it was transparent to radio transmissions and receptions.

The first time we drove it past the Russian embassy we heard the telltale transmissions from a local oscillator, but were not able to match it to any particular broadcast.

A couple of days later, we were doing the same thing when one of the Watchers' cars drove by. At that moment there was a squawk from our receiver. The signal from the Watchers' radio was so strong that it had overloaded the Russians' receiver, and this had caused their local oscillator to squeal with pain. *— TO BE BADLY DISTORTED FROM ITS NORMAL FUNCTION.*

We realised immediately that we had solved the problem. All we had to do to test whether a *VERY* frequency was being listened to was to transmit a brief burst at that frequency, and listen for the squawk. In fact, it was better even than this. This technique was used by us directly to identify the frequencies which the Russians were monitoring, but indirectly for many other purposes, including identifying the agents in the embassy; see *Radio: intelligence without messages* and *Who's who in the embassy?*

In many ways, the most spectacular success of Rafter was in the Lonsdale case (q.v.). We had found his cipher pads, and this seemed to be a good opportunity to watch a Russian spy at work. The problem was to decide which of the many broadcasts coming out from Moscow were his. We solved the problem with a straightforward Rafter operation. We set up a listening post near his flat, and were soon able to identify the frequency to which he was tuning his receiver. We tuned one of our receivers to the same frequency, and were thus able to monitor and then, with help from his pads, to decipher the messages.

**RCMP** Everybody knows about the Mounties, the Royal Canadian Mounted Police. They wear bright red jackets and broad-brimmed hats and huge gloves, and they are handsome and brave, gentle with women and children and tough on baddies, and then ride into the sunset on huge white horses.

This is not the whole story. There were also Mounties who looked and behaved more like burglars; see *Dew Worm*. I got involved with them because at that time any MI5-like activities in Canada were handled by a department of the RCMP.

So long as the enemy was the Russians, all went well. However, in the 1970s, the activities of the department were switched to the Quebec Liberation Front, an organisation involved in the struggle for greater autonomy for French-speaking Canada. This caused a deep rift within the RCMP, since many members sympathised with the aims of the QLF even if they deplored its violent tactics, and others felt that it was unseemly for the Mounties to be involved in a dirty tricks campaign against other Canadians, even if they did speak French.

So the Mounties were called off and a new organisation, the SIS (Security Intelligence Service) was formed to harass the Francophones.

**RDF** (Radio Direction Finding) You use RDF every time you swivel the aerial to get the best reception on a TV set or FM receiver. You turn it until you get the best reception, and that means that the aerial is directed towards the transmitter.

In real life, RDF works not on the maximum point but on the minimum point. This is because a radio signal approaches its maximum amplitude very gradually, so the exact maximum point is ill-defined, whereas it approaches its minimum abruptly. In the diagram below, the maximum points are shown as the tops of domes of uncertain height, whereas the minimum points are the bottoms of clearly defined spikes.

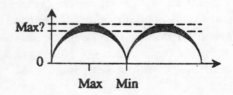

My father developed the equipment to do this very efficiently. The key to it was the development of an aperiodic aerial, which was terminated to minimise resonance by reflection, and thus identified the direction of the transmitter rapidly and accurately; see *Wright, G.M.*

The equipment was very simple. My father carried a set with him all the time, just in case he heard a broadcast which he wanted to source.

**Resources index** The MI5 Resources index was started by Alex MacDonald when he was in A1.

Before that, each time we planned an operation we would work out the people we needed and then set about finding them. It was very laborious. Alex realised that the same needs kept cropping up again and again, so he started compiling an index of all the reliable people we knew, giving details of what skills they had and what sort of parts they could play.

The index started off with all the people who did things for us – plumbers, solicitors and so on. They all went on the index. Next, the index showed all the establishments where we had friends who could be relied on to be co-operative, with the names of the friends; see *Head waiters* for a typical example. Then we collected the details of all the MI5 friends and relations, showing what skills they had or what parts they could play. Often, all we needed was a crowd, and it didn't matter who they were provided they were trustworthy. At other times we needed people with special skills, like playing the trombone or talking Armenian. Piano tuners were very useful.

The index not only helped us to find people without too much trouble: it also helped by warning us if a person was being used too often. When we were following Lonsdale we wanted a lot of women just to stand about on street corners, and it didn't matter if some of them were standing on the same corner night after night. We used a lot of the wives for that. But on other occasions we had to be sure that the person playing a part would never have been observed taking part in one of our operations.

There were three or four ballet dancers in the index, and

I know they were used at least once. I wish I remembered why.

**Ring of Five** Of all the many spy rings operating in various countries of the world, one which did particularly well for the Russians was in Britain, and was known as the Ring of Five. We knew a good deal about the members of the Ring from deciphered Russian messages (see *Bride*) and four of the five were identified over the years: Kim Philby, Donald Maclean, Guy Burgess and Anthony Blunt. However, the fifth has remained elusive.

Let us start from the facts on which everybody is agreed. The first one is that there was a ring, and that it had five members. The second is that the descriptions of four of its members, as given in the Bride material, match perfectly with its four known members. These two facts lead to a generally agreed conclusion: that there was a fifth member, and that the description of him in the Bride material can be taken to be fairly accurate, and that *on,* description was that he had an important position in MI5. *"Five-of-s* [from Golitsyn]

This conclusion is independently supported by evidence that there was a mole in MI5. Over and over again, a technically perfect operation yielded no useful results, and we found the Russians behaving as if they knew all about what we were doing. Two of these are described in the entries for *ASIO* and *Dew Worm*. By itself, this evidence is not conclusive. However, we must either believe that we made major mistakes on each occasion without realising it, or that there was a mole. The mole theory is the simpler explanation of the two, and hence (if we believe in Occam's Razor) to be preferred. ?

Nobody who has looked at the evidence is in serious doubt that there was a fifth man. Under these circumstances, it was odd that people objected strenuously to my suggesting that the Fifth Man was Sir Roger Hollis on the grounds that it undermined confidence in the security service. If I was wrong, all it meant was that the Fifth Man was still undetected and the peril he represented was thus increased.

Eventually, the logic of this seems to have dawned on

the Cabinet, and the result was a mischievous TV documentary purporting to prove that Cairncross was the Fifth Man. No one in his right mind who had studied the Bride material and interrogated Cairncross would cast him in this role.

Lord Trend, who headed the last enquiry into the Hollis affair, found that the case against Sir Roger Hollis would not stand up in court. If he applied the same rules, he would certainly find that there was no case at all against Cairncross.

**Rosetta stone**  This was the source of collateral in a classic case of code breaking; see _Collateral_.

**Rote Kapelle**  This phrase, usually translated as Red Orchestra, was the name for a Comintern-inspired network of spies, agents, informers and saboteurs assembled in the 1930s, which played a major part in the resistance to the Nazis in World War Two.

The significant feature of the Rote Kapelle was its internationalism. Although its instructions came from Moscow, its centre of activity was in German-speaking central Europe, and its leading operatives were sophisticated central Europeans. And Jews!

Strictly speaking, the Rote Kapelle was a relatively small group of dedicated activists who recruited and ran thousands of agents all over Europe. In this sense there were just a few hundred of them. But Rote Kapelle was also used as a broader term covering all the people who were recruited and run by these activists, and in this sense it had many thousands of members. At MI5 we used the broader definition, so that our list of members of the Rote Kapelle contained fifteen thousand names. It was unquestionably the most elaborate subversive organisation the world had ever known.

**Rules**  Every intelligence officer knows that rules are made to be broken, but a sensible IO does not break them for the hell of it. He obeys them until they get in the way of the job, and then uses intelligence to see how he can get round them.

This was the trouble with Malcolm Cumming, my boss

in A Branch when I joined the Service and who moved to
D Branch just in time to be my boss again when I joined
D3. He was a great one for breaking the rules, which was a
good thing, as we often had to. But he used to enjoy
breaking the rules so much that he did it just for the hell of
it. He was the kind of person who pulled doors marked
push and pushed doors marked pull on principle, as if it
showed he was boss.

# S

**Satyr**   When I started work for MI5, one of the first problems
we talked about was the job of producing an undetectable
bug. It was not just a technical problem; it was a logical
one. The bug must be able to pass a message to us, on the
outside. But if we were able to pick it up, why would the
enemy not be able to detect it, too?

The most vulnerable bugs were the ones which consisted of microphones feeding into transmitters, with the
whole lot powered by batteries and on all the time. They
could be discovered accidentally, as happened to ours at
the Communist Party headquarters in King Street; see
*Bugging the* CPGB.

The second most vulnerable bugs were similar, but
voice activated. Since they were not on all the time, they
were less likely to be discovered accidentally than the
first type; but accidental discovery was still possible, and
they were particularly vulnerable to detection by sweepers
using 'howl-back' techniques.

Wired mikes presented a quite different problem. Radiations from them were very weak, and could be further
reduced by screening. In practice, a very fine wire buried
in a few inches of concrete was electronically undetectable.
But the wires were still there, and there is no way in which
the presence of a wire can be concealed from someone
prepared to take the building to pieces to check. Despite
this risk, we still used wired microphones whenever possible. If they were installed the right way, they were less

likely to be detected with normal sweeping procedures than wireless mikes, and the signal was generally of far higher quality.

However, not many buildings could be wired. Furthermore, even when we could get a wired mike into a few rooms (as we could through the party walls of semi-detached and terrace houses) the Russians generally made sure that the interesting conversations went on in rooms well away from party walls.

It was clear what was needed: a wireless mike which could be turned on by us from outside.

It was while we were working on this problem that The Thing arrived (see *Thing, The*). It was clear in a moment that it was designed to do what we were trying to do. The only question was, how well did it work? The answer, once we discovered how to operate it, was 'not at all badly'. It was ahead of ours in some ways – for a start, they had got theirs working, whereas ours was still at the development stage – and we were able to get some good ideas from it. Nevertheless, the device we developed, while using some of its features, was a notable advance on it.

The device was known as Satyr. To the outsider, the most visible components of Satyr were the aerials, two umbrellas suitably wired to make them into highly directional parabolic transmitting and receiving aerials. The transmitting aerial was coupled to an oscillator tuned to 850 MHz, and was aligned on the device itself, which could be up to 200 yards away. When this was turned on, it produced a carrier wave of 850 MHz radiation strong enough to generate a minute eddy current in the aerial of the device. This eddy current was modulated by the movement of the diaphragm of the microphone, roughly as in The Thing, and this modulated current in turn generated a radio wave slightly different in form from the carrier wave. This was received by the second umbrella aerial, and fed into a receiver which annulled the carrier wave and amplified the modulations.

From its first demonstration, even the anti-scientific people in MI5 realised how useful it was going to be. It was put into quantity production for use by all the British intelligence services, and the Americans bought twelve sets which they then copied with modifications for their own use.

**Schlieffen plan** The Schlieffen plan is mentioned in all the histories of great secrets and brilliant strategies. This is odd, because it was not a particularly brilliant strategy and was scarcely secret. In addition, it is generally described as a German strategy to defeat France by outflanking the French defences and going straight for Paris. This misses its essential point: that great truths lurk in the pages of railways timetables.

Although it was used in 1914 (unsuccessfully) and 1940 ~~(with partial success)~~ it actually dates back to the 1890s. The Germans' traditional enemies, the French and the Russians, had concluded an alliance. The Germans were confident that they could beat France *or* Russia, but were not so sure about beating them both at once; and the alliance brought with it the prospect of Germany fighting just such a war, a war on two fronts. Count Alfred von Schlieffen was the German staff officer who worked out how to win such a confrontation.

*NOT AT ALL!*

Where other plans called for doubling the size of the German forces or working out the best way to divide them between the eastern and western frontiers, von Schlieffen's was based on a time and motion study.

His first observation was that it would take at least a month for the French (and six months for the Russians) to mobilise an army capable of offensive action. The best they could do in the meantime was to create a line of defence. *(WRONG— IN BOTH CASES!)*

This was based not on spying or high level intelligence work, but on a study of the railway timetables and route maps. From these, von Schlieffen worked out the maximum carrying capacity of the various railways over which they would have to travel. His conclusion was that the Germans did not actually have to worry too much about defence, as nobody was going to take the offensive against them. *(THE FRENCH OFFENSIVE WAS LAUNCHED "IMMEDIATELY", AND THE RUSSIANS WITHIN 2-3 weeks.)*

His next observation was that because the French

THE FRENCH OFFENSIVE WAS
EASTWARD, TOWARD ALSACE &
LORRAINE. IT WAS A TOTAL
FAILURE, BUT LEFT MAJOR FO
IN THE WRONG PLACE.

Connect

railway system was almost entirely radial – radiating from
Paris, that is – it would take many days to bring reinforce-
ments from other parts of the frontier. They would all have
to go via Paris, where there would be fearful congestion.
If, therefore, the German forces were concentrated at one
point on the line, they would initially have a massive
superiority over any forces the French would be able to
mobilise against them, and this superiority should last
long enough for them to capture Paris. Once Paris was
captured, the various units of the French army would be
effectively cut off from one another, and the invaders
would be able to force a capitulation without engaging
more than a small part of the French army.

His observation of the Russian railways was that it
would take even longer for them to get into a position to
take offensive action, so that Germany would be safe from
a stab in the back while they were disposing of France.
Then, having dealt with France as an entrée, they could
have Russia for the main course.

↗ IT WAS
EXCEPT
FOR EA
PRUSS

By contrast, the German railways had been planned
from the start with military strategy in mind. Indeed, the
Prussian railways had been run by the army, and all the
drivers and signalmen were non-commissioned officers.
There were parallel double-track railways on both banks of
the Rhine, for example, which enabled whole armies to be
switched from one part of the French frontier to another in
a matter of hours, and from the eastern frontier to the
western in a couple of days.

So, what went wrong?

The first stage of the Schlieffen plan never went wrong:
neither Russia nor France made any offensive move against
her in the opening days of either war.

As is well known, the second stage was foiled in 1914
because von Schlieffen had thought only of trains. Thus
although the German forces reached the Marne on sched-
ule, the French General Joseph Gallieni, realising that it
was too late for his troops to get there by train, sent them
to the front in 600 taxis.

OUR AUTHOR OMITS THE "SMALL MATTER" OF THE
TRANSIT OF NEUTRAL BELGIUM BY THE GERMANS.
THE GERMANS HOPED TO PASS THROUGH BELGIUM
WITHOUT HINDRANCE ... BUT THE BELGIANS DECIDED TO
FIGHT...

The war dragged on for four years, but even so the Russians were reluctant to go on the offensive? and finally surrendered following the Revolution; so the German *? That's Fucking* nightmare of 'war on two fronts' never materialised.? *RuBBISH*

In 1939, the plan [was used once again.] As an added safeguard to Stage One, the Russians were neutralised by the Molotov-Ribbentrop Pact, and the timing was revised to take into account taxis and other twentieth century innovations. This time Stage Two went right, with Paris falling within a month while a great part of the French army watched helplessly from their outflanked positions along the Maginot Line.

On 30 June 1941, the Germans moved into Stage Three, attacking Russia, and once again came unstuck by an error in timing. The invading army should have captured Leningrad and Moscow by Christmas, but they ran a month late and the Russian winter closed in on them before they could capture either. The Russians got a breathing space, regrouped and from then on the ultimate German defeat was inevitable.

The von Schlieffen plan had many messages in it for intelligence officers. The main one was the importance of lead time.✓

Von Schlieffen realised that the side which took the offensive always had the advantage over the side on the defensive, since the attackers chose the time, the place and the manner of the engagement. As we were a counter-espionage organisation, we were by definition defenders, compelled to react to enemy activities rather than to take initiatives. Nevertheless, there were two ways in which we could in fact go on to the offensive.

The first was the frequent introduction of new techniques for surveillance, so that they were constantly having to change their procedures to avoid our scrutiny. These techniques could be both new technology, as with Rafter and Engulf, and new sources of information, as with Movement analysis.

The second way in which we could do something which

was nearly as good as going on the offensive was by predicting their next offensive and working out a defence against it before they had showed their hand. For example, it was very satisfying to work out how to break into a cipher machine or develop a new way of picking up tell-tale radiations, but we had to move on from there. We had to assume that the Russians would know that we had that success, and would be working on a new generation of machine designed to counter the technique we had developed. We thus had to put ourselves in their position and predict the form the next generation of device would take. That way we would be able to have our new attack mounted within days of the new machine going in.

**Secret, Official** An Official Secret is any information which is declared to be secret by an official. In particular, it includes:

(a) any information about an organisation which does not exist or the name of a servant of a non-existent organisation or any act committed by a servant of a non-existent organisation;

(b) any information that may be gathered during working hours by a person who is employed by an organisation which does not exist; and

(c) any information which is embarrassing to the Government of the Day.

The main items in category (a) are MI5 and MI6 and their respective activities. Items in category (b) include the contents of *The Times* crossword if completed during office hours, which it is each working day by all senior members of MI5. Items in category (c) include previous statements by the Government of the Day; see *D-notice*.

An Official Secret should not be confused with an ordinary secret. An ordinary secret is something people do not know and often wish they did, whereas an Official Secret is something people know and often wish they didn't.

I know far too many Official Secrets. A few which are not widely known, especially concerning operations in

Ireland. I do not talk about these, as it could cause trouble to agents who may still be in the field and to operations which have not yet been blown.

However, most of the Official Secrets I know are widely known or at least guessed at, e.g. that the MI5 canteen serves fish on Fridays, and I see no reason not to talk about them. I believe, as the Americans do, that once something has been in the papers it is pretty silly to call it a secret, official or otherwise.

**Sellotape** This product (also known as Scotch Tape, and for which the generic term is cellulose tape) is the best known protection against the opening of letters. No way has yet been found of removing Sellotape from an envelope and replacing it without leaving tell-tale marks. The Sellotape should be laid over all seams in the envelope or package.

**Semstresses, insufficiency of for the gaining of superior knight-hoods** Our embassy in Moscow had on its staff a number of Russians employed as domestics and personal servants. One such attracted the attention of our ambassador, and the attraction developed into a passionate relationship among the laundry baskets.

The ambassador was then given early retirement and the title of Grand Cross of the Order of St Michael and St George.

Do not imagine, however, that all you have to do to get early retirement and the GCMG is to roll in the linen with Russian semstresses. The first additional factor was that an enterprising Russian photographer happened to be in attendance on at least one occasion, and took some candid snaps of the happy couple.

Even had this been all, the ambassador might well have remained an ordinary knight for many more years. However, investigation disclosed that the semstress was a KGB officer.

To get early retirement and a shotgun GCMG, therefore, it seems that one must have photographic proof that one has been rolling in the linen with a semstress, and the semstress must be a serving KGB officer.

Note also that one does not get the GCMG for _detecting_ a British diplomat in the act of conveying secret information to a semstress, whether that semstress is a KGB officer or not.

For further details, see _Moscow_.

✕ **SF (Special Facility)**  This term was used by the British telephone service to describe a service they invented in 1942 which they offered to those of their customers who wished to bug another customer's premises. It converted that customer's telephone into a bugging device.

Normally, when you put a telephone handset back on its cradle, it disconnects the mouthpiece microphone from the lines to the exchange. SF was a very simple device whose effect was to stop the disconnection of the line, so that the mouthpiece microphone remained active all the time. It then picked up any conversation within range and transmitted it to monitors at the exchange or on a line tap.

If that was all it did, it would have been easy to detect. A quick test on the line would have shown that the mouthpiece microphone was still active. It had to be a lot more clever than that, but I think it best if we don't go into it too much.

If you wanted to know whether there was SF on a phone, you took off the baseplate and checked the input condenser. In those days, phones had a condenser across the incoming wires to stop stray signals coming through the circuit. As SF was essentially a stray signal, it could only work if this condenser was disabled. They did this by putting a fibre washer on one terminal of the condenser so that it was no longer active.

SF was leaked to the Russians very early on by Anthony Blunt, but the Russians never told anyone else how it worked; see _Bugging the CPGB_.

Then there was the SF at the Egyptian embassy. The Russians came there to sweep the place, and were in the cipher room with SF on the phone. We listened to them doing the sweeping, and they must have known about the SF on the phone, but they never touched it. For the reason why, see _Disinformation_.

If your phone had SF on it, you could see the tiny washer sitting there, and remove it. I used to check my phone at home every few months, but I never found SF on it. We also used it on our Director, Roger Hollis, and Deputy Director, Graham Mitchell, when we were investigating them, but we only got it on their office phones. This was because we had to get an order signed by them to get SF on ordinary telephones, and we didn't think they would request an order for bugs on their own phones.

The only person I knew who ever asked for SF on his own phone was Victor Rothschild. He was a top scientist – he was running all the Shell company research laboratories at that time – and he did a lot of work for MI5. He suggested that SF was the easiest way to bug his room when he was interviewing people for us, like when he was interviewing Flora Solomon about Kim Philby. We put SF on the phone in his study. Maybe he just wanted to see what the device looked like, or to show it to his friends. He had friends *everywhere*.

It was no good putting SF on the Russian phones, because they simply took it out. Once the technical chap who looked after their phones for us went on holiday, so we put SF on the phone in their hall. Within an hour it was out.

**SIGINT** This word is an acronym for Signals Intelligence, and is the jargon word for intelligence operations involving the monitoring and deciphering of enemy wireless communications.

There was an agreement between the Americans and the British about the collection and processing of SIGINT, known as the Sigint Agreement. Its main positive clause was one which said that the two sides would share information. The second clause said that, in order to be successful and safe from penetration, the activity should be concentrated at either end in a single top-security organisation, and the organisations nominated were GCHQ for us and the NSA for the Americans.

A by-product of this arrangement was that for the first ten years after the Second World War MI5 virtually pulled out of SIGINT work. This meant that when I started I had to be very careful not to do the kind of work which only GCHQ was allowed to do, or at least not to be caught doing it.

**Sillitoe, Sir Percy**   see *Policemen, avoidance of.*

**Special Branch**   This is the branch of the police force which handles publicity. The main reason for its existence is that MI5 doesn't exist, and hence cannot make public appearances.

Once we had found a spy, we would tell Special Branch all the facts and they would organise the TV and press events, e.g. the arrest and the subsequent appearances of the spy in court.

**Special Facility**   see SF.

**Specific Heat Capacity**   Those who have studied Specific Heat in school physics courses may wonder why it would ever play a part in counter-espionage. But forgetting about Specific Heat was the undoing of one of our greatest achievements: the bugging of the Russian embassy in Kensington. It happened like this:

We had got in early on the job, installing the microphones before the Russians arrived to take up residence. The original idea had been to take the wires along the service pipes leading out to the street, but we were aware that such an obvious route would be regularly and easily checked by the Russians. We therefore decided to take them out through the rear of the building.

The house whose garden backed on to the garden of the Russian embassy was owned by Cyril Mills, one of the sons of Bertram Mills, the circus man. Cyril had been our representative in Canada during the war, and lived most of the time in Canada, but he came and went in London, looking after his circus, and no suspicions were aroused when a large circus van arrived and backed into his garage, which adjoined the house. Actually it was full of drilling machinery. We drilled a tunnel the length of Cyril's garden, under the garden wall, and up the Russian embassy garden to the back wall into their basement.

The microphones had been installed in all the important rooms, and the wires terminated in the same back wall of the basement. Our tunnel ended the other side of the wall, so it was a simple job to bore through and connect up the ends of the wires.

It would have been good to leave the tunnel open, but we realised that if we did this the tunnel would immediately be detected by the Russians, as they were for ever looking for tunnels with their mine detectors. Most mine detectors work by noticing sudden changes in the density of the soil, so we had to make our tunnel the same density as the soil.

We contacted a friendly cement company, and explained that we needed a cement of exactly the same density as the Kensington subsoil. They supplied it, and when we had finished installing the wires we backfilled the tunnel with the cement.

The Russians moved in, and we watched as they went up and down the garden with their mine detectors, detecting nothing. We had won.

Then it snowed. The garden disappeared under a gleaming white sheet of virgin snow, disturbed at first only by the feet of pigeons; and then ... across the sheet, running straight down our garden, under the wall and straight up the Russian garden to the embassy, a line of melting snow. We had forgotten to make sure that the cement matched the Specific Heat Capacity of the soil.

**Spy, how to become a**   Spying is not just an activity, it is a state of mind. My father had it. I was with him on the south coast of England one day in the late 1930s, and we saw some great towers being built, obviously for a very special sort of radio installation.

To my father, seeing a puzzle like that was the same as being asked to solve it. He took one look at them and said 'Let's find out what those bloody things are doing?' It did not take much to work out exactly what they were for and roughly how they worked. We just looked at the elements in the aerials and measured them off by eye, and asked a few innocent questions of people working on them. By the end of the afternoon we knew that they were both transmitting and receiving and worked on wavelengths too short for useful communication, so it had to be a system for locating arriving aircraft be means of radio echoes, what was later called radar.

I shared my father's curiosity, but I found myself asking a slightly different question. If we were able to drive up in our car and find out so much about the latest secret weapon in a war which we knew was coming, what about the Germans? Would they know all about them, and be planning to bomb them in the first hours of the war, or to jam their transmissions?

That was perhaps the moment when I knew that my great love was not to be spying, but counter-spying. So, while my father worked mostly for Admiralty intelligence and MI6, I ended up working for MI5.

**Spycatcher**    *Spycatcher* wasn't my title for the book. I wanted to call it *I was There*. But my publishers wanted a more memorable title, so *Spycatcher* it was.

I liked *I was There* because it said what made the book different. All sorts of people had written books about the Security Service, but they were full of second hand stuff. The authors had taken a lot on trust, and some of them seem to have swallowed a lot of government disinformation.

By comparison, the message of my book was quite simple. It ran like this: secrecy is essential to the ability of an organisation like MI5 to do what it was set up to do. However this poses a risk: the secrecy regulations that can keep prying eyes out of proper, duly authorised activities can also be used to keep prying eyes out of improper activities.

To take a not impossible example. Say that I had discovered that one of our officers was using his MI5 tuition in picking locks to burgle the homes of the rich and famous, and was stashing their valuables in his safe at the office. Technically, this was an Official Secret like any other, that is, information gained during my job with the Service. Should I keep mum about it?

The book went on to say that this sort of thing had been allowed to happen. People in MI5 were using the cloak of secrecy to conceal their own illegal and, in some case, treacherous activities. And I knew it was so because *I was there.*

The British government's 'answer' was to try to stop me talking about it; see *Spycatcher trial, The.* They did not deny that the illegal and treacherous activity was going on – not one of the important facts in the book was even challenged, still less refuted – and did nothing about the security weaknesses I had disclosed, but dragged me through the courts as if I was a traitor. Even when they lost the case, all they did was to stiffen the law against disclosing it. This was either knavery of folly. Sooner or later, we will learn which it was.

In the end, the case was won and the book was published. Thanks to the publicity given to it by the trial, it turned from an ordinary spy book into one of the best sellers of the century, selling in its first five years the astonishing total of eight million copies. Never has an attempt at the suppression of the truth been such a devastating failure. But no heads rolled in the British Establishment.

The bookcase by my bed has a whole shelf containing nothing but editions of *Spycatcher.* They include French, German, Spanish, Italian, Dutch, Danish, Swedish, Norwegian, Japanese, American, and Canadian. There are even Icelandic and Nigerian editions. My favourite these days is a Large Print edition printed in the USA.

There is still no British edition.

**Spycatcher trial, The**  The *Spycatcher* trial was a sad episode in British history. Of course I was glad that I won. But I was sad to see a country I loved made ridiculous in the eyes of the world. And, make no mistake about it, that is what happened. The British press had some success in concealing this from their readers, even making out that it was a glorious defeat, like Dunkirk. But anyone who read the American press, or the press anywhere else in the world with the exception of Britain, saw the glee with which the British case was torn to shreds and the Cabinet Secretary shown to be a liar and a lackey; see _Armstrong, Sir Robert_.

Where did it go wrong? Ultimately, it was the wrong case in the wrong court. It would not have taken a great lawyer to predict that this Australian court would not like being treated as an arm of the British government, or to have warned that it is a well established principle in law that a civil prosecution cannot be used as a substitute for a shaky criminal prosecution.

This is what the British government did. They approached the whole affair as if it was a prosecution in a British criminal court under the Official Secrets Act. They expected the court to permit them to withhold evidence in the interest of British national security. This would have worked in the Old Bailey. It might have worked in a British civil court. It might even have worked in an Australian criminal court, if they had been able to persuade the Australian government to prosecute me under the Australian Crimes Act, which has sections which are very like the Official Secrets Act. But it could under no circumstances work in an Australian civil court. Since it was their decision to fight the case and their choice to fight it in an Australian civil court, it was hard to understand.

Even so, I found myself having some sympathy for poor old Theo Simos who was their chief barrister. Time and time again he had to change his tactics and eat his words because of new instructions and new revelations emanating from London. He was made to look incompetent, which he is not. I hope he was well paid.

Then there was the judge, Mr Justice Powell. In Britain, he was made out to be a rabid Anglophobe and his court a kangaroo court. He wasn't, and it wasn't. All he was doing was expecting the British government to follow the rules laid down for any plaintiff in a civil court; to remember that the case was not Regina v. Wright, but a Foreign Government v. Wright. That was not prejudice, it was the legal fact. As it was, he bent over backwards to allow them to recover from their mistakes, but they never took the hint. As for his court, so far from being a kangaroo court, it was

a very good example of the best traditions of British justice.
The only irregularity was a plaintiff who wanted equality
before the law to be suspended.

Just one quotation will illustrate why the British government lost the case. Mr Justice Powell, faced with yet
another of their constant changes in tactics said:

> I am quite unable to predict from one day to the next
> what is the attitude of the plaintiff in this case; what
> submissions will be persevered with and what course is
> to be taken. The situation I am placed in is, I believe,
> intolerable.

People who give judges reason to make statements like
this cannot be surprised if they lose their case.

However, this is not to take any of the kudos from my
admirable counsel, Malcolm Turnbull. When I was first
told about him, I felt that he was the right man for the job.
When I met him, I knew that he was. Again, he was
painted in the British press as a left-winger, which was a
travesty. He was a member of the Australian Liberal Party,
which is the Australian equivalent of the Tories, and had
actually stood for pre-selection for one of their safe seats.
But, like any good Tory, he has a deep commitment to
justice, and he saw that justice was being denied.

He handled the case brilliantly. Of course, he had some
luck. He could not have expected the British to bungle the
case as they did. He did not arrange the fiascos which
occurred whenever the official line was changed. But Turnbull quickly adjusted his tactics to seize every advantage he
was given. In such a case, good luck and bad luck are the
difference between noticing and not noticing what is going
on around you. And Turnbull showed a flexibility that left
the learned silks floundering in disarray.

For me, the trial was an ordeal. It was not that my own
part was too taxing. I made a statement to the court, and
the British government, in a rare moment of good sense,
must have decided not to cross question me properly.

They knew that a cross questioning would force me to reveal further facts, still more damaging to them and to Britain, which I had no wish to reveal; not that I felt loyalty to them, but I did to Britain. So when Theo Simos rose to cross question me, he clearly had no instruction about what to ask, and all that happened was a day of very boring quibbling.

But it was still an ordeal. The outcome remained uncertain to the end. I knew, and Turnbull knew, how the British could have made things much harder for us, and seemingly endless weeks of wrangling and threats are not the best way to spend the time when you are in your seventies.

Even when Mr Justice Powell dismissed the British government's appeal, they did not give up graciously, but insisted on repeating their humiliation by appeal to the High Court of Australia.

On Thursday, 2 June 1988, the High Court unanimously dismissed the government's appeal. The _Spycatcher_ trial was over.

**Stockade**  It all started as a technical challenge. One day, I asked the people at GCHQ if anybody had bothered to check whether there were any stray signals on the tele-printer graph wires coming out of the embassies. They said they hadn't, so I said, 'There are a lot of embassies in London; let's pick one and try'.

At the time there was a great deal of fuss about Britain's entry into the European Economic Community, and the Foreign Office wanted to know what the French were saying to one another. General de Gaulle was President of France at the time, and wanted to bitch things up for us. He didn't like the British, ever since he had trouble with Winston Churchill. De Gaulle remembered the case of his two right-hand men, Labarthe and Musellier. When he was away in Dakar on one occasion, they tried to overthrow him and take over the Free French movement themselves. The plot was discovered by MI5, who found that Labarthe and Musellier were members of the Rote Kapelle, reporting to the Russians, so they were thrown into gaol, and de Gaulle survived as leader. But Churchill commented later that he ought to have let them overthrow de Gaulle first and then put them in gaol. De Gaulle never forgot or forgave.

We therefore decided to try it on the French embassy. The Post Office faulted one of their phones, and I dressed up as a technician and went in to mend it. (Actually, it was not real dressing up. The technicians who mended the embassy's phones did not wear caps, they wore plain clothes, grey flannel trousers and so forth. So that's what I wore.)

I didn't get into the cipher room, but I saw enough of the layout of the place to believe that it might work.

The principle was simple enough, based on the fundamental physics of radio. If you want to read about it, there is an explanation in the entry for *Rafter*. We hoped that the input into the cipher machine would create a radio wave which would produce an echo in the output wires. It was not impossible, but would depend on a lot of luck. The power of the transmission from the input cable might be too low, and the current generated in the output cable too small to be detectable. This would be particularly true if the cables were properly screened – the wire mesh you see on cables in sound systems. What we hoped was that some of the communications equipment would have unscreened weak spots which would be producing detectable echoes in the telephone wires leading out from the embassy.

In the French embassy, they had two levels of cipher, low grade for ordinary classified traffic and high grade for the really confidential stuff, whose distribution was restricted to the ambassador and the top embassy staff. We felt we had a good chance of getting the low grade cipher, but the high grade cipher was in another room, on the far side of a partition wall. However, it would be an interesting test of the technique even if we only got the unimportant stuff off the low grade cipher.

We set up shop in the Hyde Park Hotel, just opposite

the French embassy. I had contacted H.T. Mitchell, head of the department of the Post Office which was then responsible for tapping telephones. I had explained that we needed a broad band radio frequency tap on the telegraph line from the French embassy. This involved putting a radio frequency choke on the lines. We had to be sure that the tap didn't affect the transmission and hence alert the French.

We also had contacted Major Denman, who ran Palmer Street. This was the GCHQ intercept station for telegraphic traffic in and out of London. They were monitoring the traffic twenty-four hours a day, and were able to tell us when the French were using their line for cipher material.

Mitchell placed a tap on their lines, and we fed the signals into an oscilloscope.

We quickly found a stray message which clearly ought not to have been there. It was exactly as we had hoped – the original *en clair* version of a low-grade cipher message, accidentally transmitted by the wire connecting the teleprinter and the cipher machine and picked up by the output line. However, there was also another set of signals, very much weaker but clearly visible as small variations in the big pattern. We quickly made a signal analyser which annulled the big pattern, leaving only the tiny peaks of the echo signal, which we could then amplify and analyse.

When we isolated these signals, we found ourselves looking at a message, again *en clair*, from the ambassador to General de Gaulle. This was the high grade diplomatic cipher, ORIGINATING ~~transmitted~~ from the teleprinter line, radiating through the partition wall and being picked up on the telegraph line.

For the next two years, the British Foreign Secretary had the pleasure of getting, every morning, the French ambassador's inward and outward mail as well as his own.

There are several lessons from this success: One is that you should screen every wire carrying an *en clair* version of a secret communication. Another is that it is worthwhile to stop and think from time to time – this operation happened only because we did a bit of lateral thinking. It needed no special equipment and cost next to nothing.

The third is that all the intelligence in the world will not help you unless you use it properly. The FO were tickled pink at getting the French traffic – you would have thought that it was the greatest victory since Waterloo – but they still mucked up the negotiations so badly that the French won every point.

However, it could not last for ever. In fact, the surprise was that it lasted as long as it did – two years. The Americans came and studied our techniques, and then ran a similar scheme against the French embassy in Washington. Then, suddenly, French sweepers descended on both embassies and screened every lead in the place, totally eliminating the echoes.

We wondered how our activities had been discovered. However, I later found that they probably had not been. I was talking to Marcel Chalet, deputy head of DST, the French security service, and he told me how they had found a Russian transceiver in their cipher room. It was in an electrical fuse box, disguised as a fuse. They realised that it was designed to detect and re-transmit weak local signals, and tested to find what local transmissions it might be detecting. It was, of course, just what we were picking up – *en clair* versions of their ciphers, radiated from unscreened leads. Hence the sudden activity.

Finally, there is a general point to be made about Operation Stockade. I have been asked why I ever told the story of it, blowing what was until then not widely known. There are really two reasons, one positive and one negative.

The negative one is that it doesn't matter a damn. The techniques I developed were frontier stuff in their day, but nowadays the problems and the solutions are totally different, largely because of the development of computers.

The positive one is that it illustrates an important point about developments in science: if you have a good idea, it is always worth trying it. If this experimental attitude had not prevailed, Operation Stockade (and Operation Rafter and a number of other operations I mounted) would never have gone ahead. The initial response of the experts was that there were all sorts of theoretical reasons why it couldn't possibly work, so there was no point in trying.

I remembered that Marconi had had a similar problem. The experts told him that wireless waves would not travel across the Atlantic. They showed conclusively that there was a hill of seawater three hundred miles high in the way.

Fortunately, Marconi believed that there was only one way to find out and that was by trying it. And that is how he, rather than other physicists of perhaps greater brilliance, came to be the first to transmit a message across the Atlantic. If this book persuades just one budding physicist to perform just one experiment which the experts say is bound to fail, it will have done a good job – even if the experts are proved right.

**Sweden** Nobody can talk Swedish except the Swedes, and it is silly to try. If you are pretending to be Swedish, and somebody speaks to you, it is best not to hear. It is even difficult to make the noise the Swedes make when they are talking English. Their English is technically correct, but they have an intonation which makes everything come out flat and boring; rather like Sweden, in fact.

I had to be Swedish to get on to the dock when we were listening for radiations from the cipher machines on the Russian cruiser *Ordzhonikidze* in Stockholm harbour. To minimise the risk of having someone try to talk to me in Swedish, we went down to the dock one night, got into the warehouse where our listening post was, and never came out until the cruiser sailed and the job was over.

It was thirsty work, shut in that unventilated room at the height of summer. We wouldn't even open the windows, because there were Russians walking up and down outside. But the Swedes had predicted the problem, and stacked the room with loads and loads of excellent lager beer.

I got there through the activities of the Radiations

Operations Committee (q.v.). Although they were neutral, the Swedish SIGINT people kept in touch with GCHQ and shared information about things they were doing to the Russians. They were probably in touch with the Russians, too, to share information about things they were doing to us. Anyway, they had told GCHQ that they were going to mount an operation against the Russian cruiser, and had asked whether we had any ideas. GCHQ had consulted the ROC, and the ROC sent me to help.

We detected some radiations, and they were definitely coming from the ship, because they faded and finally stopped as it sailed away, but that is just about all we discovered. We came back with miles of film of oscilloscope traces of the radiations, but we were not sure they were coming from a cipher machine. If they were we never captured the cipher, still less cracked it.

The trouble with radiations was that there were so many of them about. It was easy to sit there for weeks listening to some radiations, hoping that they were going to tell us something useful, and in the end we might find that they were just coming from a faulty power point.

**Sweepers**   Sweepers are people whose job it is to check a room or building for bugs. They use metal detectors, Geiger counters and other radiation detectors, and special devices designed to generate howl-back (q.v.).

This is a very specialised business, and although the Russians had people in their embassies to do routine checks, the top team was based in Moscow and was sent in to check any building where a problem was suspected. It may sound easy to sweep a room, but it is not. A metal detector will find all the floor nails as well as the device hidden under the floor. Walls are liable to be full of the remnants of old wiring, disused gas and water pipes and so on, and sweeping each room in an old building for every possible sort of bug is a major undertaking ... unless, that is, you know what you are looking for, and roughly where it is.

This is what often surprised us about the Russian

sweepers. They would arrive by plane, go straight to the embassy, move in on the precise room we were bugging, and select precisely the sweeping technique that was appropriate to the bug we had installed. This was not competence or good luck: it had to mean treachery.

*How did he knew this* [handwritten marginalia]

# T

**Tea** Non-existent organisations cannot invite people to tea, but if a non-existent organisation like MI5 wishes to invite somebody to tea, it issues the invitation through the Treasury Solicitor. Being 'invited to take tea with the Treasury Solicitor' is thus the British euphemism for being subjected to pressure by MI5.

**Telegraphy** This word was coined in 1794, but people had been playing with telegraph systems without knowing it for centuries before that. Telegraphy simply means the transmission of a message so that it can be 'read' a long way away, and it was thus fundamental to intelligence organisations from the earliest times.

For example, when Theseus went from Athens to Crete to rescue the maidens from the Minotaur, he agreed to telegraph the outcome to his father, Aegeus, who was the King of Athens at the time. The agreement was that he would signal success by hoisting white sails. This cunning strategem went wrong when Theseus, worn out from his affair with Ariadne on Naxos, forgot to hoist the white sails. Aegeus saw the black ones, assumed the worst and immediately committed suicide by throwing himself from a high rock into the sea.

Getting a coded message wrong in this way is always a risk. However, Aegeus got the Aegean Sea named after him, which was some compensation.

Rather over two thousand years later, we find Galileo putting his latest invention, the telescope, to practical use

THE LIVERPOOL EXCHANGE COMMISSION
A WIRELESS STATION FROM MARCONI, FOR
THE IDENTICAL PURPOSE. IT W
INSTALLED IN A HOUSE ON
RATHLIN ISLAND (AND IN LIVERPO

to take advantage of a similar system. The galleys coming home to Venice, loaded to the gunwales with treasure and spices, carried flags to show what they had on board. This was critical intelligence, as a boatload of pepper would send the price of pepper down on the Venice pepper exchange, while if a boat loaded with pepper was expected, but turned out to have none, the price would shoot up. Galileo used to climb up to the top of a tower with his telescope, and get at least an hour's advance notice of the contents of the ships on their way in.

By the eighteenth century, the British navy (and others) had developed quite complex signalling systems using flags. Each flag could either be used to represent a letter of the alphabet or could be a complete message in itself. It is signals in this form which were used in Nelson's day, leading to the classic story of him avoiding the order to disengage by putting his telescope to his blind eye and declaring that he saw no such signal.

A few of the flags are still widely used for specific traditional purposes, e.g. the Blue Peter is still flown by many ships when they are ready to leave port, and the yellow quarantine flag is still an internationally recognised indication that a ship has infectious disease on board. But the use of strings of flags to spell out whole sentences only survives as a game.

The word telegraphy was coined on the analogy of telescope, and was supposed to mean far writing. It was first applied to the invention we know today as the semaphore.

Although Guillaume Amontons (1663–1705) conceived the idea of the semaphore some years earlier, it was not till 1794 that Claude Chappe (1763–1805) built the first working examples. The semaphore consisted of a post with two windmill-like arms which could be positioned to spell out the letters of the alphabet.

Within a few years, line-of-sight chains of semaphore stations were set up on hills all over France and some neighbouring countries, and they played a major part in enabling Napoleon Bonaparte to continue to influence French affairs during his exile on Elba. After the defeat of the French at Waterloo (first news of which reached England on the legs of carrier pigeons belonging to *The Times* newspaper), semaphore chains were established all over England.

Each station had two transmitter-receiver units, one facing in each direction along the chain. Each unit consisted of a semaphore together with a telescope trained on the semaphore in the next station. Ideally, the message was verified by being repeated back to the source station, but in busy times, particularly if signals were passing both ways along the chain, verification was impossible, and transmission errors were frequent.

The semaphore could be operated at night by silhouetting the arms against a flaring fire.

Initially, the terms semaphore and telegraph were interchangeable. Later, the word semaphore remained with the original device while the word telegraph became a generic term for all sorts of communications contrivances of bells, whistles and lights, as well as the drums of Africa, and the smoke signals of the American Indians. It then narrowed again to mean (unless otherwise specified) the electric telegraph. It is worth noting, however, that the name Telegraph Hill on a map almost certainly indicates a hill on which a semaphore station was once located.

The invention of the electric telegraph is generally attributed to Samuel Morse, who then invented the Morse code as a means of turning a message into a pattern of electrical impulses which could be fed down it; see *Morse*. The date given is 1837.

For once, the main promoters of the new invention were not the military, but the railways, who desperately needed such a device for traffic control. But its value for ordinary communication was appreciated from the start. An early much publicised application was the catching of a murderer who was seen boarding a train in Windsor and was captured within the hour on arrival at Paddington, his description having been sent down the railway telegraph wires.

The electric telegraph was so much better than every other form of telegraph that the word came to apply only to this sort of communication, though its broader sense survived in terms like 'bush telegraph'.

The electric telegraph was the most visible of all means of communication, being symbolised by the wires looping from post to post across the country, forging a physical link. It was thus the absence of wires which was the most remarkable feature of the new communication system pioneered by Marconi; hence its name, the wireless telegraph. But the words soon went their separate ways, telegraph staying with the wires and Marconi's device becoming first the wireless and then the radio.

We still talk about telegraph poles, although the wires in question have carried little except telephone traffic in the last half century. But nobody in the world uses the word wireless any more – except me, that is.

**Thatcher, Mrs Margaret**   Mrs Thatcher was one of the biggest disappointments of my life. When she first came to power, I said 'Thank God, at last there's a Tory with some spine who will stand up to the Russians and the chinless wonders in the Civil Service'. I was also glad that a scientist was going to head the country. I don't think there had ever been one before. It seemed that she was one of us, and I backed her wholeheartedly.

I am still not sure how it went so badly wrong. Of course, the idea that she was a scientist was all a bit of a farce – she was no more a scientist in her thinking than I am a bishop. Less so, in fact, because I think I could have made a good bishop.

I had hoped she would tell the upper crust where to get off, but when she departed there were still just as many of them as ever at the top of the Civil Service, still making just as much mess of everything. However, what affected me personally was the way she was fooled by the Russians. We will probably never know exactly how it was done but somehow she was persuaded to take a line of action about me (and other concerned patriots) from which nobody could benefit but the KGB.

If there had been any outcome which could have been to Britain's benefit, one might have said that the action against me was just a good idea which went wrong. As it was, there was no way Britain could win. This was the tragedy of the trial for me. I had to fight the case, because I was personally under attack. But in defending myself against this attack from an incompetent and vindictive British government, I was portrayed as an enemy of Britain herself, the country I love above all others, Britain.

People say I ought to be grateful to Mrs Thatcher, and without any doubt it was only because of her actions that my book, *Spycatcher*, was so successful. But I didn't pay her to do it as a publicity stunt, and I don't think my publishers did, either. I think the whole affair started with some bad advice from the Treasury Solicitor, and before she realised how bad his advice was she had gone beyond the point of no return.

**Thing, The**   This was the name given to a device found in the Great Seal of the United States of America on the wall behind the desk of the American ambassador in Moscow. It was evidently a microphone/transmitter, but the embassy staff immediately realised that it was unlike any microphone they had ever seen.

The device was sent to America for examination, but the CIA scientists concluded that its performance was so poor that no worthwhile information could be gained from it. They reckoned that it might tell you whether something was going on in the room, but it was not sensitive enough to transmit speech in an intelligible form. However, they found it hard to believe that the Russians would go to the trouble of installing so useless a device in the ambassador's office, so they sent it to me for a second opinion.

It arrived carefully packed up in a box like the ones sets of chess men come in. When I took it out, I immediately saw that the diaphragm was broken. The Americans were very sheepish about this. They admitted that it had already been broken when they packed it up – apparently one of their experts had put his finger through it. This illustrated the problem they had with top secret work. It had to be done by the experts themselves – they could not risk bringing in any of the technicians who normally did the practical work – and the experts were not very good with their hands.

It took me about ten weeks to discover how it worked. Its operating frequency could be calculated by measuring the length of its aerial, and turned out to be 1800 MHz. At first, I assumed, as the CIA had done, that this was also the frequency of its signal. This would be so if it had worked on the normal AM (amplitude modulation) principle, where the signal modulates the amplitude of the carrier wave. At this frequency, I found, as the CIA had done, that it was impossible to tune (that is, impossible to separate a modulation from the carrier wave pattern).

I suddenly realised that we had been looking at it wrongly. The modulation was not generated by the electromotive effect, as in a normal microphone, but by capacitance.

If you know (or don't know but don't care) what capacitance is, skip the next three paragraphs. Otherwise read on.

A capacitor consists of two metal plates separated by an insulating layer, generally of air. The plates are so close that they are well within one another's electrical fields, but they are not actually in contact, so no current will pass across the gap.

However, if a capacitor is placed in a DC electrical circuit, there will for a short time be a very small flow of current in the wires either side of the capacitor. What is happening is a flow of electrons to one plate and away from the other: the capacitor is being charged. If you can imagine a pump trying to pump water round a closed pipe in which there was a rubber diaphragm: no water would flow round the pipe, but as the pump was switched on there would be a very small flow as water moved to stretch the diaphragm. If the pump was then switched off, the diaphragm would try to return to its original position, causing a very small flow back round the circuit.

In the case of a capacitor, the amount of charge it can store depends on the distance apart of the two plates. If, therefore, they are moved with respect to the other, the amount of charge they can hold will change, and surplus electrons will flow round the circuit. More important still, if the plates are moved to and fro, the surplus will be first at one side of the capacitor and then the other, so the movement will generate an alternating current in the circuit whose characteristics will depend on the characteristics of the movement of the plate.

This is roughly what was happening in The Thing. One of the plates was fixed, while the other was formed by the diaphragm of the microphone. Microscopic movement of the diaphragm produced a current which varied according to the nature of the force which caused the vibration – the sound waves in the air.

This discovery explained why we had not been able to get it to work. We had been trying to make the device as sensitive as possible by achieving maximum separation of the plates. If it had been a normal microphone, this would have been the right way to go about it. However, to maximise the capacitance effect, the plates had to be as close together as possible, without touching. It also changed the expected frequency of the transmission. So I retuned the receiver to 800 MHz, and the next moment had it working. It was one of the great moments of my life.

I was at the time working on a microphone for the same purpose, and was able to use (and improve on) some of the ideas in The Thing. For the outcome, see *Satyr*.

**Tidy mind, dangers of a**   $H_2S$, was the code name for a special radar carried in RAF bombers in World War Two, which showed the country below them laid out like a map. The source of very high frequency waves for $H_2S$ was a magnetron, which was tuned by bending its 'straps'; see *Centimetric radar*.

One of the puzzles of the war was that, although the

Germans had captured H₂S equipment from bombers they had shot down, they never seemed to have learnt quite how it worked. After the war I was sent to Germany to find out why.

I asked the German scientist who had been in charge of the $H_2S$ investigation project what their approach had been. He said that they had been astonished by the magnetrons, as they knew they must be devices for generating a lot of centimetric waves, but they had never worked out how we managed to tune them precisely enough to produce the exact frequencies required by the system. But he then explained that they had never found one in perfect condition: every one had been damaged in the crash, causing the straps to be bent. They had straightened them out, but the devices had still refused to work . . .

It never occurred to their tidy minds that the operation of a war-winning device could depend on the exact shape of the *bends* in a wire.

Similarly, many Germans found it hard to take the Russian tanks seriously, because the finish looked so rough. However, the tanks seemed to work rather well, and they finally realised that, although the outsides were not very pretty, they were very precisely machined where it mattered.

Our people had a difficulty the other way. In 1942 we found a huge new German radar installation called the *Mammut* (mammoth), and noticed that it transmitted with a very stable frequency, much more stable than was needed for ordinary radar work; so our tidy-minded people thought it must be for long-distance guiding of bombers. However, our expert, R.V. Jones, asked whether they had ever checked the stability of the ordinary German early warning radar. When they did, they found it was just as perfect as the new one, and much more perfect than any of ours.

**Tidying up**    Breaking and entering often makes rather a mess. If you want people not to know you have been there, you have to have plasterers and decorators standing by to make good the damage. We had very good ones at MI5.

They saved my bacon more than once. The worst case was an occasion one night when we were wiring up the Polish embassy. There was a gang of us in the roof cavity of the house next door to the embassy, feeding the wires in among the joists and rafters. I had suggested that we should all take our shoes off as an added precaution against making any noise. It was not that the people who owned the house would have been upset – they were away. But if the Poles had heard noises coming from next door when they knew the people were away, they might have done the neighbourly thing and told the police.

Anyway, there we were all beavering away, crawling along the bare joists and making no sound except the odd grunt and the swish of wires being pulled through holes. I was having difficulty feeding a wire into an awkward spot, and to get into a better position lodged my foot against an old nail sticking out from the side of one of the joists. Suddenly the nail broke clean off, and next moment there was an appalling crash as I went through the plaster, ending up with both feet dangling into somebody's bedroom and a good deal of their ceiling on the floor.

This was followed by an equally sudden silence, finally broken by Hugh Winterborn's voice: 'It's a good thing you'd taken your shoes off, Peter.'

We sent off a message to Leslie Jagger of A Branch, who arrived with his redecorating team. Thanks to their quick drying plaster and paint, we had the whole room tidied up, replastered and repainted before the milkman came the next morning.

**Times, The**  A once-great London newspaper, now foreign-owned; see *Vilification*.

**Tisler, Frantisek**  There are occasions when bad news can be turned to good account. The Tisler case was an example.

Tisler worked as a cipher clerk in the Czech embassy in Washington, but was also working for the CIA. He produced a report which, on the face of it, was all bad news. He told us how a friend of his, an agent called Pribyl, had been chatting with another agent in the back of a London taxi, and had noticed that they were being followed. However, after a few minutes the other car unexpectedly gave up the chase. He enquired with the Russian embassy, and they told him that it had indeed been an MI5 car, but it was being driven by a new recruit as part of his training. It was just luck that they had chosen his taxi for tailing experience.

How did they know? It was bad enough that they had recognised the car as one of ours, but they also seemed to know who was driving, and why. They clearly had access to accurate and detailed knowledge of the Watchers and their activities. At MI5, everybody suspected a mole among the Watchers. This was what they always suspected when anything got leaked. But I had another idea.

I had for a long time been wondering whether the Russians were monitoring the Watchers' radio, but no one had been very interested. It was like the old poem:

> In the first place, said the sages,
> the thing cannot be done;
> In the second, if it could be,
> there would not be any fun.

The Tisler affair showed that there would be plenty of fun if it could be done, and I was given the go-ahead to put my ideas into effect. For the outcome, see _Rafter_.

In the end, therefore, the Tisler affair turned out very well indeed.

**Toad, Ingenious Mr** I regret to say that at one stage I was known in the family as _Ingenious Mr Toad_. Readers of _Wind in the Willows_ will remember Mr Toad's disastrous foray into motoring, which led amongst other things to the lines:

> Who was it steered it into a pond?
> Ingenious Mr Toad.

Now, let it be clearly understood that I never drove anyone into a pond, least of all my family. The only time any of the family landed in anything was when my daughter Jenny landed in a dung-heap, but that was her fault, because she had saddled up a Red Poll calf called Poppy and was trying to ride it.

The Mr Toad business started with an unfortunate occasion when I turned a corner near Great Waltham and ran into a stationary police car which was parked there to watch for speeding motorists. My police pass allowed me to do many things, like going the wrong way down one-way streets, but it didn't allow me to biff into police cars. The police said it was a bad piece of driving and I lost my licence. Worse still, my family, instead of rallying round and agreeing that it is easy not to spot a stationary police car, simply called me Ingenious Mr Toad, implying that the police were right.

Another name I was given by my family was *Pasha*. It seems that they thought that I just sat in my chair like an Arab potentate, giving orders and expecting everybody else to follow them. They said it was because I was used to having laboratory technicians around me all the time. In fact, I did not behave at all like a Pasha. I was always willing to agree to anything provided I was brought a cup of tea.

**Traffic**   Jargon word for radio communications. Traffic is normally used to mean enciphered Morse.

**Traitors, how to deal with**   What do you do when you know somebody is a traitor but cannot prove it? We had this problem many times, most notably with Kim Philby and Anthony Blunt.

With Kim Philby the course we took was undoubtedly wrong, as it led to his defection, taking with him the priceless information he had stored in his head.

But what about Anthony Blunt. The whole problem needs very careful thought.

The affair falls into three periods. From around 1952 to 1964, people in MI5 who knew all the facts about Blunt were convinced of his guilt, but had no proof. After 1964, when he confessed, there was a period when he was being interrogated (largely by me) on the basis of immunity from prosecution. This second period ended when he was denounced as a traitor in Parliament by Margaret Thatcher in 1979.

The first period was more or less fruitless. He was interrogated eleven times by various interrogators, but none of them got any sense out of him.

Then, in 1964, the American Michael Whitney Straight not only named him but offered to stand up in a court of law and denounce him. At this point we had to make a difficult choice: to take up Straight's offer and put Blunt on trial, or to offer him immunity from prosecution in return for a promise to give us all the information he had.

As is well known, we gave him immunity, and many people have said that this was wrong. Their argument is that we got very little out of him despite his promise, and in the meantime he went on living a life of luxury, surveying the Queen's pictures and being the respected Director of the Courtauld Institute.

I would argue that it was the right decision, for two reasons. The first is that a court action would have got nowhere, and the second is that the procedure we adopted was the one which was most likely to improve our chances with any future traitors.

The argument against court action is simple enough. There was no evidence on which he could be arrested. In time of war, people could be detained in custody under the regulation popularly known as 18b, which allowed imprisonment without trial for those suspected of subversive activity. But there was no war on at the, time, so Sir Anthony would have remained at large throughout the trial. If it went badly for him, he could simply defect (as Philby did when he realised that the game was up).

We knew that he would not want to defect; despite his treachery, he remained a lover of the life he led in England, Queen and all. But if people had cut up rough with him, or if he thought that life in England meant life in a British gaol, he would, we believed, defect. Indeed, he didn't have to defect to Russia. He was very much _persona grata_ in many countries and could have gone almost anywhere.

But even if in some way we got the case to court, it would be thrown out, leaving us with red faces for having been silly enough to put so distinguished a gentleman in the dock. The only evidence we had against him which would be admissable in court was the personal testimony of Whitney Straight. Blunt would simply deny everything, and the jury would have to decide between the word of an American who was a confessed traitor with nothing to lose and a blue-blooded Englishman with royal associations. We would surely lose, and the loss would make it far harder for us to get anything from him.

More important, however, was the implications of the case for future security operations. If there was one thing we had learned (or should have learned) it was that the real danger to Britain was people in high places, and it seems that almost no place was too high to be looking.

But how were we to find these people? In the past, we had relied a lot on breaking ciphers, but it was increasingly clear that we ought not to rely on this too much in future. Nor ought we to rely on defectors to identify the highly placed moles or traitors. The reality was that the only chink in the armour of the really sophisticated intelligence network was the members themselves, who had information in their heads which was of value to us. It was far more important to get this information than to take vengeance on the traitor.

The best strategy was thus to show that it was easy and safe to confess. Not only was this the stategy most likely to encourage confessions, but it would also be the one most likely to make the members of the network mistrust one another, minimising the network's effectiveness.

I believe that the course that was taken – to give him immunity to persuade him to talk – was the right one. I just do not believe that there was any way of breaking Blunt other than the way we did it. It is certainly true that we got less from him than we had hoped, and less than he had to give if he had really told us everything. But we got a great deal more in the 'immunity' period than we had got in the long interrogations of the previous years, and a lot more than we got from Philby, whose 'confession' was devised to be as mischievous and time-wasting as possible.

I believe that Blunt was the toughest of them all, tougher than Philby or Maclean or Burgess. He stayed and sweated it out through all those years. Meanwhile we, too, were in trouble – we knew all the time that he was a spy but could do nothing about it until Michael Whitney Straight came on to the scene.

So we finally interrogated him under immunity from prosecution, the clear understanding being that his role would not be revealed. In my view this was a right decision. Not only was it appropriate for dealing with Blunt; it was also the only way of dealing with future cases which had any likelihood of success.

I therefore believe that Mrs Thatcher was unwise to have disgraced him in Parliament. It may not have been a breach of the promise he had been given, which was that he would not be prosecuted; but it was certainly a breach of the spirit of the agreement, and will discourage anyone in future from trusting the Government's word. If this means that this avenue for action is now closed to the Security Service, it cannot but result in damage to the security of the country.

**Transceiver**   A transceiver is a radio device which is capable of both receiving and transmitting, generally using the same circuitry. Examples are walkie-talkies, and cellular telephones. At MI5, however, we were most interested in transceivers which were used as bugging devices. A transceiver could detect the very low-power signals transmitted accidentally from devices within a building and re-broadcast them so that we could monitor them somewhere outside.

A transceiver had to have a power source. The French found a very clever Russian one in their Washington embassy. It was in the fuse box, and it was a fuse – with a transceiver built into it. So it ran on the mains electricity.

**_Transponder_**  A transponder was a cross between a radio beacon and a transceiver. Like a radio beacon, it transmitted signals which could be used for navigation or location finding, but like a transceiver it responded to incoming signals. Whenever it received a signal, it 'replied' by transmitting one. We could use a transponder for tracking cars.

Transponders were used in the first IFF (Identification, Friend or Foe) radar in World War Two. Allied planes were equipped with transponders tuned to the frequency of our ground radar. When a radar beam hit the plane, the transponder would transmit a signal at the same frequency, and slightly more powerful than the normal radar echo would be. On the radar screens on the ground, allied planes would register as stronger signals, and hence brighter dots on the screen, than the weak echoes from enemy planes.

**_Transcription_**  Before you start bugging rooms and tapping telephones, make sure that you have plenty of people to do the transcribing. Every hour of tape takes three to five hours to transcribe, and it is skilled, exacting work.

In our case it was also desperately secret, done in a special secure area on the Seventh Floor at MI5 headquarters, Leconfield House. It was no secret that we were tapping phones, nor was the problem that they were handling secret material – though they were. The real secret was who was being bugged. Some of it was obvious – for example, the phones at the Sovbloc embassies and the Israelis – but there were always a few politicians and leading public figures on the list, and there would have been hell to pay if they had found out.

The quality of the material was uneven. A direct telephone tap was generally very easy to understand and transcribe. Conversation captured by SF was of much more varied quality, since the people were not necessarily near the phone. If we were using a bug, it might be almost as clear as a phone, or (if we were using a badly placed probe mike) completely unintelligible.

How ever it was captured, most of the material came

into Leconfield House by phone line, and was recorded by Post Office technicians. They then handed the records to us.

Listening to bugs makes one realise how much the human ear sorts out the sounds which reach it. The microphone doesn't. If there is anything else going on in the room, like somebody handling crockery, it can drown out the voices.

It also makes one realise how important the stereoscopic effect is. I invented a procedure to introduce an artificial echo into a tape recording. This gave the sound more body, and actually made it possible to understand sounds which were impossible to recognise in the raw state.

Most of our recording was done on acetate disks. This was not because tape recorders were not available, but because it was much easier to 'dab' a disk. There was no way in which we could transcribe the whole of every disk, so we 'dabbed', listening to sample sections and marking for transcription the ones which were interesting. It was much harder to do this with tape or wire recorders.

Later, we used sleeves, rather like the cylinders of the old dictaphones, which were re-usable (like tape) but easily marked to show the position of interesting bits.

The transcribing was all done by women. They were much better at it than men. But even they varied, so we gave them hearing tests, and assigned the hardest jobs to the ones who had the best hearing.

**Treasury, The**  A front organisation for MI5 and MI6; see *Property* and *Tea*.

**Trojan Horse, The**  This operation revealed fundamental weaknesses in Trojan security intelligence. The key facts were as follows: Troy had been besieged for ten years, but the inhabitants woke up one morning to find that the enemy had apparently decamped, leaving behind a large wooden horse.

Opinion was divided. Capys and Laocoön advocated throwing the horse into the sea, burning it, or at least boring through its timber flanks to check its contents.

However, Laocoön shortly afterwards had the misfortune to be taken by a sea serpent, and this lowered the credibility of the hardline faction, while giving support to the view promoted initially by Thymoetes: that it was a peace offering from the departing enemy.

Some people say that this view should have been recognised as rubbish, there being no other case in history of a departing enemy leaving a gift in this way. But the Aegean area is noted for its elaborate gift-giving rituals, and it is possible that 3000 years ago this was a local custom.

However, this does not explain, still less excuse, the laxity of the Trojan security. The horse was known to be hollow, since it had given out a great hollow sound when struck by Laocoön's spear. This ought to have alerted the military authorities to the danger; yet they allowed it to be dragged into the city.

In the literature, much is made of the fact that an independent clairvoyant, Cassandra, warned of the danger. While it is true that this lady did utter warnings and that these warnings proved well founded, intelligence services cannot be expected to act on unsubstantiated clairvoyant traffic.

We should now consider the affair from the Greek standpoint.

The first point to note is that the whole operation was very dangerous. Success depended on the Trojans behaving in a very stupid way. Disaster would have occurred had the Trojans:

(a) left the horse out on the beach for a few weeks;
(b) sacrificed it to Poseidon or Irene as a burnt offering;
(c) opened it up to see what was inside;
(d) placed a guard on it to raise the alarm if anybody emerged from it.

The next point to notice is that it is normal to use expendable colonial troops for such risky forays, but the list of the participants in the Horse operation is significantly different: Thersandrus and Sthenelus were the leaders, obviously chosen for their experience in covert operations; Acamas, Thoas, Neoptolemus and Machaon were tough fighters; but an odd choice was Ulysses, the 'man of many devices' (*polymechanos*), while the detachment also included Epeos, who devised the operation, and Menelaus, whose failure to keep his wife under lock and key had led to the war in the first place.

There are only two explanations for the participation of so many top men: the first is that the scheme was devised to be decisive one way or another: if successful, it would lead to the destruction of Troy, while if unsuccessful the Greeks, having lost such an important segment of their leadership, would surrender. However, the presence of Ulysses and Epeos supports another explanation: that Greek Intelligence had ensured the success of the operation by massive penetration of the Trojan High Command.

Was Thymoetes a plant? Virgil clearly thinks he was, though he does not quote his source for the information. In any case, he was writing much later, possibly using information released under the Thousand Year rule, and some of the clay notebooks may have been damaged or even deliberately altered by interested parties. The Trojan security services have long since closed their files on the affair, and it seems that little purpose would be served now by a public enquiry.

The phrase 'Trojan Horse' is still popularly used to describe a variety of subversive devices and tactics. The professional will recognise, however, that the term should be used only for a very specific type of operation, one in which the enemy unwittingly assists our agents to penetrate his defence works in a portable hide. Such operations are rare, so the lessons of this one are particularly valuable. However, for some near parallels, see *Gifts*.

# V

**Vilification**  During the *Spycatcher* trial, the British government launched a major disinformation campaign, which was designed to discredit me. Vilification is a useful device, and had it been skilfully used it could have been very effective against me.

Their campaign was in four stages.

The first stage, which occurred in the pre-trial period, aimed to make out that I was a very junior officer who was at no time privy to any worthwhile secrets. This was stupid of them, as it was never credible.

In the second stage, they made out that I was mad. Again, the contrary evidence was overwhelming, and little more was heard of this.

The third stage occurred during the trial, when they claimed that I was doing it for the money. This was based on the fact, never denied by me, that I had taken a share of the royalties on *Their Trade is Treachery*, written by Chapman Pincher on the basis of information supplied by me. However, everybody who mattered knew that I had first published my own story in an edition of one free copy for Mrs Thatcher (see *Dossier, The*), scarcely the action of a get-rich-quick secret-seller.

All the stories were, however, lapped up and printed by the lackey London press, particularly Rupert Murdoch's *Times* and *Sun*. It is good to record that the British-owned London newspapers had a better record for resisting government pressure, or at least checking the stories before printing them.

After the trial, the British government had the book read by dozens of experts who marked and checked every factual statement in the book which could be wrong. There were thousands and thousands of them – names, dates, background details, but all they came up with was a pitiful little pile of irrelevancies. Making the best of a bad job, they sent lists of these 'errors' to venal editors and hacks, and they duly turned up in 'Letters to the Editor' columns, feature articles and reviews. But it all added up to nothing. The essential truth of the book was never successfully challenged.

In my day at MI5, we would have done a lot better than this.

# W

**W., Peter**   In his book, *A Matter of Trust*, Nigel West calls me Peter W. (e.g. p123). I suppose I should be grateful, as it keeps me out of the index of his misleading book. But it is puzzling – I am the only person whose anonymity was respected by Mr West. But no doubt he or his bosses had a good reason for doing it.

**Walsingham, Sir Francis**   (1530–90). This man can be called the Father of the General Post Office (q.v.), as he devised all the basic procedures for intercepting mail.

He lived in stormy times, getting into trouble with Bloody Mary, and as a result living abroad throughout her reign (1552–8). When Elizabeth I came to the throne in 1558, his potential value as a spy was recognised, and he was employed in the service of the new government.

His biggest contribution was his understanding of the importance of communications. He realised that no plotting could go on without communication, and that finding out about a plot in good time was better than foiling it later. He therefore devised an organisation devoted to intercepting mail and reading ciphers.

To ensure that his organisation got all the mail for examination, he persuaded Elizabeth to create a crown monopoly in the carrying of mail, and his interception organisation became known as the Royal Mail.

His best-known operation was one he mounted against Sir Thomas Babington and Mary Queen of Scots. Their mail was not only opened, deciphered and read, but was then re-sealed and sent on. Thus the conspirators continued to communicate and incriminate themselves more and more deeply, enabling Walsingham to pick the perfect moment for arresting them and exposing the plot.

His other great achievement was obtaining full details of the plans for the Spanish Armada. When Sir Francis Drake, playing bowls on Plymouth Hoe, said that he had time 'to win this game and to thrash the Spaniards too', he was not being bold or foolhardy: he was relying on excellent intelligence about the Spaniards' travel plans, which he got from Walsingham.

As so often happens to loyal members of the Secret Service, Walsingham received no thanks, and died two years later in poverty.

**Warrants** If you want to tap phones or intercept mail in Britain, you have to get a warrant from a Minister of State. This is usually the Home Secretary, but if you need one urgently at a weekend you go to the nearest convenient Minister of State.

The Post Office were very particular about warrants, but if we could show that somebody was about to escape from the country, they would act immediately provided we promised to get the warrant the next day.

We had bulk warrants on the most important targets. This included the headquarters of the CPGB (Communist Party of Great Britain), all the Sovbloc embassies and a lot of other embassies, especially of the terrorists, e.g. the Libyans. With embassies, we had to get the approval of the Foreign Office.

Then there were the Israelis. We had had a bulk warrant on them ever since the days of the British mandate over Palestine, before Israel became a State, when they just had an office in Regent Street. The Foreign Office was very pro-Arab, so we could always get a warrant against the Israelis from them. They were worried about the Israelis taking things into their own hands.

We listened mainly for people phoning in to Mossad agents there. The Foreign Office were always wanting us to pass on any information we got about diplomatic matters, but we were very cautious about doing so, as they would have been sure to have leaked it and caused a political storm. The Foreign Office people are not renowned for being watertight.

Apart from these, there were actually not many active warrants at any given time, not more than three hundred. This was partly because we had to give good reasons when we asked for a warrant, but mostly because we didn't have enough people to open all the mail and listen to all the telephone conversations.

**Watchers**  Intelligence work demands patience and vigilance over long periods of inactivity. Most of the Watchers spent their time sitting in drab rooms equipped with binoculars, telephoto camera, a log book and an overflowing ashtray. The alternatives were worse – sitting in a car, watching for something to happen. Usually, nothing happened at all.

What makes good Watchers? They are the kind of people who can be standing in a street and you walk past them and do not notice they are there. They have to be absolutely inconspicuous. I tried it from time to time, but I was no good at it – I stood out like a sore thumb.

MI5 had very good Watchers. There were fifty of them when I joined the Service, and two hundred and fifty by the time I left. They operated from a house in Regents Park.

One of their main jobs was manning our Static OPs (Static Observation Posts) in houses overlooking the entrances to embassies, etc. They used to watch everybody going in or out, keeping a log of their movements and photographing anyone they didn't recognise. They had astonishing memories for faces; some of them would immediately recognise a Russian who turned up at the embassy but hadn't been seen there since a single visit five years previously.

If they were in doubt about a face, they could check with our mug book. This had pictures of all the Russian IOs we knew about, thousands of them. There was a copy in each Static OP.

All the regular staff and visitors at the embassy had code

numbers, and all the Watchers would do was to call the number over the radio to Control. There was no acknowledgement. This gave the Russians no way of knowing from the message whether anyone was going to try to tail that particular IO. *Iu a House — whY Not TeLePHoNe?*

The log of comings and goings was vital for us in identifying the Intelligence Officers; see *Who's who at the embassy?*

Next, there was the job of watching places where we had no Static OP. This included places where we thought agents were going to be meeting their controllers or making drops, and many of the embassies. Whenever possible, the Watchers would rent a room to work from, but often they had to work from their cars, which was very unsatisfactory (see *Watchers, visual detection of*) or in the open air, which was worse.

There was not so much following of people as you might expect, because it is not easy. The Russian IOs used to spend hours making quite sure they were not being followed. They had obviously seen the American film where the man in the white hat asks the railway booking clerk where the man in the black hat has booked to, because they always booked to the next station after the one they were really going to.

We found that following people in city streets only worked if the people being followed had no idea they were being followed and made no attempt to shake you off. Otherwise you had to be lucky as well as clever and athletic to keep up with them. There were just too many ways to get away.

Following cars was the best bit, careering down London streets, crashing the lights, clutching your little slip of paper telling the police that you were not to be booked. The trouble was that generally we didn't want the people to know they were being followed. Following cars without being noticed was even harder than following people on foot.

The Watchers cars looked very ordinary, but had

souped up engines and special suspensions which meant that they could go pretty fast. We had a garage in Clapham which maintained them mechanically, as well as repainting them and switching the number plates at frequent intervals.

**Watchers' radio, Russian monitoring of**   When I first suggested that the Russians were listening to the Watchers' radio, one of the questions asked was 'How would they know which messages were ours, since they are disguised as taxi or ambulance calls and are on wavebands which are crowded with similar calls to and from real taxis and ambulances, and are not acknowledged?'

This unfortunately showed the easy way of picking them. Ours were the only messages which were not acknowledged.

**Watchers, visual detection of**   One day, my partner Hugh Winterborn and I decided to go out and test how good the Watchers were at watching without being detected. We went round the embassy district, and took down the numbers of all the cars which we thought might be full of Watchers. We sent the list to the Jim Skardon, who ran the Watchers.

The message came back that we had picked the lot, and they asked how we had done it. We explained that we had just looked for cars which had three men sitting in them. There aren't many times you will see three men sitting in an ordinary car in London.

In one case we had the additional clue that the false number plates at the front were different from the false number plates at the back.

I asked why there had to be three Watchers. The answer was very simple: a driver to watch the road, a navigator to watch the map and a Watcher to watch the Russians.

We said that it might help if some of the Watchers were women, but they said that the wives wouldn't like it. This seemed to me an inadequate answer. All they were doing was sitting in the cars. But my suggestion didn't get any support.

Then we organised some special trials. We got one group of Watchers to try to follow one of our people, and another group were told to identify who was being followed, and who was doing the following. They got it right every time. The third time, we actually filmed them doing it, and showed them the film, just to show how obvious they were.

It didn't prove that they had always been noticed by the Russians, but it certainly proved that they could have been. It showed just how easy it was to detect that someone was following you if you wanted to. The conclusion was that it was very likely that all the cases involving double agents had been blown, since they always involved Watchers.

**Who's who at the embassy?** Let us suppose that we discover from our taps on the switchboard telephone lines that there is a person called Mr Ivanov who is an agent; see *Intelligence Officer, how to identify*. However, there is no Mr Ivanov on the embassy's staff register. Who is the mystery voice on the phone?

The answer is that we collect information on the movement of all Russians connected with the embassy. Our static observers in the house across the road from the embassy watch them coming and going through the embassy gates, and compile a complete log. By comparing this log with the times at which Mr Ivanov comes to the phone, the members of staff are one by one eliminated, until only one is left: Mr Ivanov.

The beauty of this technique was that the Russians couldn't defeat it. They had to go out to meet their agents, and we identified the whole lot. This was confirmed in 1967 when one of their people, Oleg Lyalin, defected, and gave us a list of the agents he knew within the embassy. We knew the lot; in fact, we knew more than he did – he was unsure about one or two of them.

**Wireless in the home** One of the problems with having a powerful interest in wireless was that wirelesses in those days had so many wires. In our house there were wires everywhere.

One of them was an aerial wire which hung down over our marital bed. I am told that one night I must have been dreaming of sailing (which is perfectly possible, as I loved sailing) because I woke Lois up by sitting bolt upright in bed hanging on to the aerial wire and shouting 'Get that sheet in'.

**Wives**   If a person has signed the Official Secrets Act and you want to send him to gaol, all you have to do is to ask his wife whether she knows where he works. If she says 'Yes', he has told her an Official Secret. There are no exceptions for wives.

In practice, however, MI5 expected the wives to help when help was needed. They liked using the wives because they didn't expect to be paid. Or, to be precise, if any of them did expect to be paid, they were wrong. We used a lot of wives in crowd scenes in the operation to bug the CPGB; see *Bugging the* CPGB.

When my wife Lois married me, she thought she was marrying a farmer. This was not because I misled her, but because at the time it was true. At least, I was at Oxford reading Agricultural Science, and had already worked on farms for three years, so it was a fair enough guess that farming was what I would do.

Being married to an Intelligence Officer is the exact opposite of being married to a farmer. A farmer's wife shares everything, whereas an Intelligence Officer's wife (in theory, at least) shares nothing except the crowd scenes.

In my case, it was a bit better. When I lost my driving licence (see *Toad, Ingenious Mr*) Lois started to drive me around. This was very good, as it turned some of my business trips into family outings. Lois would drive me to my meeting in Oxford or Cheltenham or wherever it was, and the children would pile into the back, and while I was at the meeting they would have a picnic.

Nevertheless, wives and children should not normally be taken on intelligence operations; see *Children*.

**Women**   There were two sorts of women who got involved in the Service, chorus girls and nuns. The former flitted round the edge never really becoming involved at all, while the latter dedicated their lives to it in a way few men would do. They tell me it is much the same in business.

In my day at MI5, the first group was best seen in the Registry, which was manned (as we were then allowed to say) by a bevy of debutantes, known as the Registry Queens. For some notes on them, see *Class*.

The other ones were the nuns. You know how nuns shut themselves away and devote their whole lives to their belief in God. Well, Evelyn McBarnet was like that except that she believed in MI5 rather than God. Maybe she went home at night, but it was hard to imagine her out of the office.

She was a research officer, and she was very good indeed. It was not just that she was efficient and intelligent, she also had a very perceptive nose for rotten apples. If I wanted an opinion on the integrity of someone in the Service I didn't know too well, I would go to Evelyn. She worked very closely with Anne Last, who was also very good at assessing people.

These two were among the very few people who saw through Blunt and Philby right at the start, and stuck to their guns until they were finally proved right.

Evelyn McBarnet had a notebook which Anne had given her before she left in 1953. In it was a list of people who she thought were almost certainly spies, and Evelyn said she agreed with every one. Two of the names were of MI5 men: Roger Hollis and Graham Mitchell; see *Mitchell, Graham*.

This list was written in 1953, which was before Hollis became Director General, long before I arrived, and at a time when Arthur Martin was off in Malaya. If it shows nothing else, it shows that some very perceptive people were worried about Hollis and Mitchell a long time before Arthur and I took up the running. Patrick Stewart and Hugh Winterborn were two others.

I'm glad we had Evelyn on our side.

Not quite like nuns but pretty near it were the women

who supplied the transcription service. The main difference between them and Evelyn McBarnet was that while she was dedicated to MI5, they were dedicated to accurate transcription. They were very, very good at it.

**Wright, G.M.** (my father)   I got on very well with my father. We shared a great deal: an interest in wireless and new technology, an interest in doing things, not just talking about them, and a passion for security.

In the years before the First World War, these interests had got him a job as a research scientist with the Marconi company; see *Marconi, Guglielmo*. The company had from the start recognised the military value of wireless, and worked closely with the Admiralty. Put all these things together and it was not surprising that he was spending some of his time working out what could be learnt from the chatter emanating from the German High Seas Fleet based at Kiel. *WILHELMSHAVEN AND EMDEN, ON THE NORTH SEA.*

*DATE(S)? ?* What he came up with in the end was the essentials of Radio Direction Finding; see *RDF*. News of his discovery was transmitted to Reggie Hall in Room 40 at the Admiralty (see *GCHQ*), and Hall saw the importance of it immediately. He was so keen to get my father up to London without delay that he arranged for him to be shot up to London on the footplate of a railway engine.

During the First World War, 1914–18, he did more work on *RDF*, including going to Christiansa (now Oslo), where he set up an RDF station to monitor any movement of the German High Seas Fleet from their base in Kiel. *(Aaah...)*

After the war, he was involved in Marconi's move into broadcasting *PUBLIC*; see *Marconi, Guglielmo*. By the end of the 1920s he was Head of Research, and hence involved with the firm's pioneer work in short wave 'beam' radio. This was exciting stuff, enough to make all the newspapers publish major accounts of it, the disinformation prize going to the *News of the World* for its story about 'Space-eating Beams'.

However, the item which made the biggest story was his work on a facsimile machine capable of transmitting

*IN FACT, RDF WAS USED BY THE ARMY, IN 1915, FIRST, IN NORTHERN FRANCE — NOT "INVENTED" BY AUTHOR'S FATHER. (WHO MAY, HOWEVER, HAVE DEVISED SOME IMPROVEMENTS.)*

documents across the Atlantic. One paper carried the headline '$5,000,000 loan by radio' over a story that a Lloyd's Bank cheque had been faxed to New York. But the best was when Gertrude Lawrence, the most popular musical comedy star of the day and on her way to Hollywood to make what she called 'audible motion pictures', wrote a letter of goodwill to the readers of the *Daily Sketch* from a New York hotel and transmitted it to London using my father's machine. It was the top story of the day in the *Sketch*.

All this was, however, so far ahead of its time that it attracted little commercial support. It was by then the beginning of the Depression, and the research side of the firm was virtually closed down. My father lost his job and I had to be pulled out of school and find a way to support myself. My father started drowning his sorrows in whisky at a rate of three bottles a day.

At this point my mother came into her own. She went straight to the top, writing to the Prince of Wales saying that it was a ridiculous waste for one of the country's best brains to be pickling itself in alcohol. One way or another it seemed to work, because my father was reinstated by Marconi, becoming their Engineer in Chief (which meant being overall head of the production and research divisions, with a seat on the board).

He was a great favourite with my children. This was partly because there were interesting things at his house, like the radio shed in the back garden with a huge aerial on it. It was also because they associated him with other exciting things like Guy Fawkes Night, when he always looked after the bonfire. But perhaps most of all it was because he lived with my mother, who grew into the perfect grandmother, with snow white hair, sparkling eyes and delicious cakes always ready in case grandchildren called. –

**Writing, secret** Secret writing is done with a large variety of chemicals, but the principle involved in the process is always the same.

Let us suppose that you are a Russian agent. You are given a book made of special paper impregnated with a particular chemical. When you want to write a secret letter, you first write a cover letter, saying 'Dear Aunt Mabel' or whatever, and then lay a page from the special book over it as if it were carbon paper. You write the real letter on this, generally writing at right angles to the cover letter so that the two images are not too confused. Thus an image of the secret letter, made up of infinitesimal traces of the impregnating chemical, is laid down on the sheet on which the cover letter was written.

You can get rid of any tell-tale indentation by writing with the paper on glass or some other very hard surface. If you are still worried, you can steam it over a kettle to remove all traces of indentation.

At the receiving end, the development process involves making the traces of chemicals change so that they become visible. This will generally be a chemical reaction.

The problem for counter-intelligence organisations is slightly different. They want to read the secret writing, but their first problem is that they do not know which of perhaps hundreds of letters has secret writing on it, and do not know which of thousands of different chemicals are being used. They would have to test every piece of paper for every chemical, which would be impossible.

That was the task we set the AWRE. What we needed was a procedure for scanning thousands of documents very quickly and seeing whether there was any secret writing on them, without knowing what chemical was being used. They came up with an answer; see *AWRE*.

**X-rays**  X-rays have two basic purposes: (a) to pick combination locks and (b) to find out what is in a tin can without opening it. (They also have certain medical and general uses.)

Development of these techniques was carried out for us by the Atomic Weapons Research Establishment.

The main problem with using X-rays to investigate the locks of safes was getting through the thick front plating. The AWRE people found a way round this by coming in from the side. You take several X-ray photographs of the lock from different angles, and from these you can build up a picture of the interior, showing all the moving parts. You can then see what positions the parts have to be got into in order to allow the door to open, and can work out the sequence of movements of the dial which will get them into this state.

Seeing inside tin cans without opening them presented a different problem. It was particularly useful for checking on dead letter boxes – small containers made to look like bolts or twigs, containing messages on microfilm or whatever.

There were two problems about opening them. The first was that they were sometimes booby trapped. If the Russians knew we were searching for a dead letter box, they would leave one around with a detonator in it which blew your hand off. The second was that they often left bits of undeveloped film in them, so if you opened it in daylight the film would be fogged, and they knew that you had been there. THE SWINE!

X-rays again came to the rescue. The AWRE developed so-called soft X-rays, whose wavelength and power was carefully controlled so that it would not fog light-sensitive film. This is the technology which was later developed for the baggage inspection units at airports.

ZIMMERMANN TELEGRAMM...